# ROMILLY'S VISITS TO WALES
## 1827-1854

Joseph Romilly in March 1836

# ROMILLY'S
# VISITS TO WALES
# 1827-1854

EXTRACTS FROM THE DIARIES
OF THE REV JOSEPH ROMILLY

Fellow of Trinity College, Cambridge
Registrary of the University
and Rector of Porthkerry, Glamorgan

edited, introduced and annotated
by
M.G.R. MORRIS

GOMER

First Impression—1998

ISBN 1 85902 454 8

Printed at
Gomer Press, Llandysul, Ceredigion, Wales

To Susan,
Rebecca, Christian and Ruth

# CONTENTS

# LIST OF ILLUSTRATIONS AND MAPS

## MAPS

# PREFACE

I first heard of Romilly's diaries in 1977, when the Rev (now Canon) William Price of St David's University College, Lampeter, passed on to me a letter from Mr P.J. Barnwell in Cambridge. Local history had become an absorbing hobby, so I was glad to learn of this colourful source—all the more when I found how closely Romilly had been connected with my parish. He had even come to morning prayer in what is now our dining room, dined in what is now the drawing room, and doubtless withdrawn after dinner to what is now our bedroom; so his shade dogs my footsteps. I hope he is not the well-attested Rectory ghost.

Mr Barnwell kindly sent me a list of Romilly's visits to Wales, not quite complete as it turned out, and put me in touch with Dr J.P.T. Bury, who had published selections from the diaries in 1967; they cover the years 1832-42, but relate mainly to Cambridge. A further selection has recently been published by Mrs M.E. Bury and Dr John Pickles to bring the story down to 1847. It was a pleasure to meet them both in Cambridge, and see their affection for Joseph Romilly. They told me a lot about him and answered my questions. Mrs Bury put me further in her debt by transcribing a long passage which I had overlooked, by drawing my attention to others and by clearing up many obscurities. Dr Pickles has also taken the trouble to check several points for me, and both of them read an early draft of my Introduction and suggested improvements. For all this help and encouragement I am grateful.

The idea of publishing those parts of the diaries that relate to Wales has long been in my mind. If Mr David Fanning of Hallmark Books, Penarth, had not invited me to write for him, in October 1989, this project might never have been started. He generously let me change publishers when difficulties arose. My hope that the work would appear in October 1991, two hundred years after Romilly's birth, proved unrealistic. The delay has meant, I am sure, a much better book—certainly a longer one.

I have many others to thank: first, the University Library, Cambridge, for giving me permission to publish these extracts. Cambridge is a long way from Pembrokeshire, so the staff supplied photocopies. Eventually I was able to go and read the original diaries. Miss Jayne Ringrose, Under-Librarian, guided me, and later checked some doubtful passages in my transcriptions.

When I came to annotate the text, I found the Library and the Record Office in Haverfordwest, as always, mines of information. Their staff cheerfully helped me dig. Mr Clive Hughes, then Archivist-in-Charge at the Record Office and now ordained, proved to be an expert on ships; his colleague, Mrs Corinne Streets, filled me in on the Eatons of Parc Glas. (Her death in 1993, aged thirty-four, was very sad.) Mr James Eaton-Evans of Haverfordwest, who is descended from Roger Eaton's sister Mary, added further particulars. Mrs Nona Rees let me use St Davids Cathedral Library while the books were withdrawn for cataloguing; I have since found further nuggets in that collection. Mr David Bleines of Tenby Museum, Mr E.W. Thomas of Anglesey Area Record Office, and Miss J.M. Wraight of the National Maritime Museum answered my queries; so did Miss Sue Berry of the Somerset Record Office, Mr S.D. Hobbs (Wiltshire County Archivist), and Mrs Avril Kear at the Gloucestershire Record Office. Many other problems were solved in Carmarthen Library, Cardiff Central Library and the National Library of Wales, where again the staff gave me every assistance.

Mrs Anne David, born an Allen of Cilrhiw and therefore related to Romilly, has lent me books and shown me family portraits; she has kindly allowed me to reproduce some of the portraits here. Mr and Mrs Thomas Lloyd of Freestone Hall have willingly helped me from their specialised knowledge. Mrs Lloyd is one of the Cresselly Allens (alas, I must say 'was'; she died tragically in 1996). She let me see many unpublished family documents; I am grateful for permission to print extracts. Her brother, Mr Hugh Harrison-Allen, inherited Cresselly in 1992, and has kindly supplied an early picture of it. Mr Lloyd is an authority on Welsh buildings; I have relied heavily on his expertise.

Canon William Price has put me right on many points from his extensive knowledge of Welsh (particularly ecclesiastical) history. Canon Richard Fenwick, now Dean of Monmouth, gave me material on Porthkerry and identified Canon Tate of St Paul's. Another friend, Fr John Barnes, ironed out a few last-minute creases. My brothers, Canon Peter Morris and Mr Gordon Morris, the latter living conveniently in Bristol, have answered my questions with their usual care. Whenever I have been stuck on a point of style or punctuation, Peter has never failed me.

Over two decades I have amassed a rich deposit of information on this area; some of it, from Mrs George Brownrigg, Mrs Fenner Clayton, Dr P.M.S. Jones, and the Owen family at Cold Blow, Narberth, proved useful for this book. Others have added to it, or solved points that puzzled me: Mlle Emmanuelle Chalbos (now Mme Cornet), the Rev D.B.G. Davies (Vicar of Laugharne), Mr Geoffrey Eatough, the Very Rev J. Wyn Evans (Dean of St Davids), Mrs Gillian Gammage, Mrs Kay Halliwell, Mrs Margaret Jones, Wing Commander K.D. McKay, Mrs Kathleen Malings, Col Andrew Man, Mrs Michelle Mathias, Mr Kenneth Richardson, Mr L.S. Thomas, Mr Roland Thorne, Mr W.R.P. Welch, and some informative members of the Dyfed Family History Society—I never discovered their names—to whom I gave a talk on Romilly.

In the hunt for illustrations I have been helped not only by some of those already mentioned but also by Mr John Davies and Miss Helen Palmer at Carmarthen Record Office; Mr Andy King at Bristol Industrial Museum; Mrs Patricia Moore, the Glamorgan Archivist (since retired), and her staff; Miss D. Dyer at Bristol Central Library; Mr Bryan Lawrence, Local History Librarian at Powys County Library, and Mr Richard Morgan, Powys County Archivist, both in Llandrindod Wells; the staff of Cardiff Central Library, which houses a collection of watercolours and drawings by Charles Norris; and the staff of the National Library of Wales, where the searcher for buried treasure so often finds himself like a prince of Serendip. Dr Pickles saw that I received a fine copy of Romilly's portrait, and Trinity College and the University Library supplied a print of the only known photograph of him. One of my parishioners, Mr Geoff Scott, has drawn Parc

Glas with the owner's kind permission. My thanks go to all these, and to those whose permission to reproduce pictures is listed on pages viii-ix. Not all the material I have found has been used, and some that I sought has not been forthcoming; in particular, and with regret, I have failed to find a portrait of Rosa Jones of Fonmon, and the early photograph apparently showing Porthkerry church thatched cannot be traced.

If I have forgotten to acknowledge anyone's help, I hope he or she will forgive me. Need I add that none of those whom I have remembered to thank should be blamed for what I have written.

Too many books lack an index. Baron Campbell was right: 'So essential did I consider an Index to be to every book, that I proposed to bring a Bill into parliament to deprive an author who published a book without an Index of the privilege of copyright; and, moreover, to subject him, for his offence, to a pecuniary penalty'. The art of compiling one that is useful, accurate, consistent and thorough is not to be acquired without much tearing of the hair. My attempt lacks such colourful entries as 'Bottoms, their *raison d'être*', which enlivens the index to Kilvert's diaries.

History and biography are provisional arts; one is always learning more. It is nonetheless disconcerting when a new source disagrees with an earlier one, and when each check through the typescript reveals another blunder or infelicity. Experience has taught me that it is well-nigh impossible to eliminate every mistake in a book, however short. One like this, which relies so much on secondary sources, is apt to inherit errors of fact, as well as contain some home-grown ones. I plead invincible ignorance. The very process of retyping, as draft succeeded draft (eventually onto a word processor, which I acquired a bit late in the day), must have given rise to more; for these I plead carelessness. At least I spotted two choice, though not I hope Freudian, mistakes: 'the lady [lad] seduced her' and 'Charles Darwin the naturalist was her sister'—a spell-checker has its limitations. In proof-reading, the price of accuracy is eternal vigilance.

My publishers deserve thanks for their patience with my almost obsessive attempts to improve my text, and for the skill with which they have turned the final version into such a handsome book. I have been reluctant to stop searching for material, and now the task is over I feel bereaved.

It gives me particular pleasure to acknowledge the generous financial support voted by the College Council of Trinity College, Cambridge, and by the Isla Johnston Trust.

One of my predecessors at Lampeter Velfrey, Dr Charles Symmons, who held the living from 1794, hardly if ever set his foot in the parish for the thirty-two years he was Rector, but spent much of his time in Chiswick, writing books. (He may have met Romilly there.) Whenever I feel guilty about the hours I have devoted to editing these diaries, I reflect that there is an honourable tradition of scholarship in country rectories, and that at least I have not been an absentee. Besides, everyone needs a hobby; there is more to life than one's job, even the duties of a clergyman. Like my father, I have found gardening a healthy contrast, for it is solitary, physical work. Grubbing in libraries is equally satisfying. The past is an escape from the pressures and worries of the present; it gives a sense of proportion, and, when research brings to light the forgotten history of one's own area, it makes those over-familiar surroundings sparkle with fresh interest. To no one is this more advantageous than the parish priest, who in the countryside still personifies the community's traditional identity.

My parishioners have given me so much during the twenty-five years I have lived here that I ought to inscribe this book to them. But I choose to dedicate it to my wife and children, who have given me even more—more than I can ever repay.

# LIST OF ABBREVIATIONS

| | |
|---|---|
| Allen Papers | Letters etc belonging to the Allen family |
| *Arch. Camb.* | *Archaeologia Cambrensis* |
| Burke | Burke's *Landed Gentry of Great Britain* (1914, unless another edition is cited) |
| Bury | J.P.T. Bury (ed), *Romilly's Cambridge Diary 1832-42* (Cambridge, 1967) |
| Bury & Pickles | M.E. Bury and J.D. Pickles, *Romilly's Cambridge Diary 1842-1847* (Cambridge, 1994) |
| C.U.L. | Cambridge University Library |
| *D.N.B.* | *The Dictionary of National Biography* |
| *D.W.B.* | *The Dictionary of Welsh Biography down to 1940* |
| *Enc. Brit.* | *Encyclopaedia Britannica* (Chicago, 1971, unless a later edition is cited) |
| Foster | J. Foster, *Alumni Oxonienses* (1715-1886) (London, 1888) |
| H.Ref.Lib. | Haverfordwest Reference Library |
| *J.H.S.C.W.* | *Journal of the Historical Society of the Church in Wales* |
| *J.P.H.S.* | *Journal of the Pembrokeshire Historical Society* |
| *J.P.L.H.S.* | *Journal of the Pembrokeshire Local History Society (The Pembrokeshire Historian)* |
| *J.W.E.H.* | *Journal of Welsh Ecclesiastical History* |
| *J.W.R.H.* | *Journal of Welsh Religious History* |
| N.L.W. | National Library of Wales |
| *N.L.W.J.* | *National Library of Wales Journal* |
| O.D.C.C. | F.L. Cross (ed), *The Oxford Dictionary of the Christian Church* (London, 1963) |
| Pembs R.O. | Pembrokeshire Record Office, Haverfordwest |
| R.C.A.H.M. | Royal Commission on The Ancient and Historical Monuments and Constructions in Wales and Monmouthshire, *An Inventory of the Ancient Monuments in Wales and Monmouthshire* vol V (London, 1917) |
| *Trans. Cymmr.* | *Transactions of the Honourable Society of Cymmrodorion* |
| Venn | J.A. Venn, *Alumni Cantabrigienses* part II (1752-1900) (Cambridge, 1951) |
| *W.W.H.R.* | *West Wales Historical Records (Historical Society of West Wales Transactions)* |

References to colleges etc are to Cambridge unless another place is specified

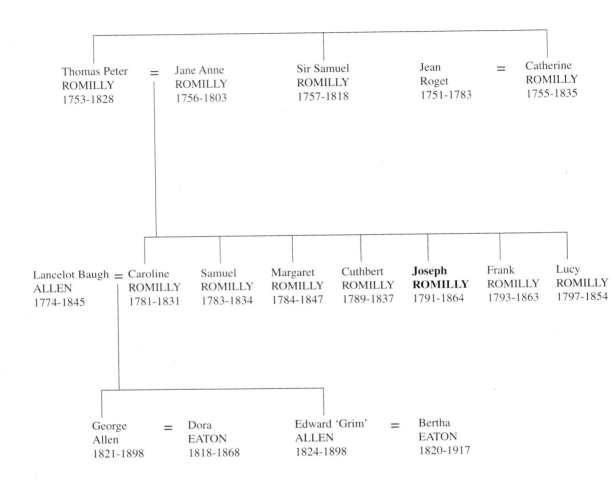

Joseph Romilly's Immediate Family.

# INTRODUCTION

## 1 ROMILLY AND HIS FAMILY

In the autumn of 1791, all eyes were on France. A radical constitution had been imposed, Church lands nationalised and sold, Louis XVI detained in the very act of fleeing the country. Two great forces, the old regime of absolute monarchy and the new ideals of reform and liberty, were colliding. The resultant sparks, soon to be fanned by a Corsican soldier named Buonaparte, would fire a trail of gunpowder across the continent for years to come.

Into this tense world, on 9 October, Joseph Romilly was born. French blood flowed strongly in his veins, though the family had quitted its homeland some ninety years before. Joseph's great-grandfather, Étienne Romilly, had lived at Montpellier, a Huguenot centre in southern France. He moved to England after Louis XIV revoked the Edict of Nantes, depriving French Protestants of their freedom of worship, and settled as a waxbleacher at Hoxton in Middlesex, where he married Judith de Monsallier, another refugee. Their son Peter, a jeweller's apprentice in the city, married Margaret Garnault and had nine children.[1]

Six of them died young. The surviving daughter, Catherine, also married into a Huguenot family, the Rogets. Her son, Peter Mark Roget, Fellow and Secretary of the Royal Society, was a polymath, with the inquiring mind and encyclopedic interests of a Wren or a Benjamin Franklin. One observation of his, published in 1824, was to lead to motion pictures. He is known today for his *Thesaurus of English Words and Phrases*, which has been the salvation of many an author.[2] Catherine's brother Sir Samuel Romilly held the post of Solicitor General in the 'ministry of all the talents'. He strove to reduce the number of crimes—over two hundred—which in those days were punishable by death, but he had little success. When his wife died, he cut his own throat in grief, leaving others to carry on his liberal ideals. Two of his sons played host to Joseph in Wales: Sir John (later Lord Romilly), who was Master of the Rolls, and his younger brother Edward, at one time M.P. for Ludlow.[3]

Thomas Peter Romilly, Joseph's father, was Samuel's elder brother. He married his first cousin, Jane Anne, daughter of Peter's brother, Isaac Romilly, another Fellow of the Royal Society. Again there were nine children, Joseph being the seventh.[4] The eldest was Caroline Jane, a 'gentle, good creature'[5] ten years Joseph's senior; she married Lancelot Baugh Allen, known as Baugh (as in 'law'). Next came Samuel, who entered the army and became a lieutenant colonel. His boy, George, later Director of the French Hospital, appears in these pages as Joseph's young nephew.[6] After the sixth child, Cuthbert, died of influenza in 1837, the two other sisters, Margaret and Lucy, went to live with Joseph at a house in Cambridge.[7] They appear in the diaries as 'the women', with whom Joseph corresponded on his travels. The only other child of Thomas Romilly that needs mentioning is Francis (Frank). He (and possibly his younger daughter, Sophie) is also referred to in these extracts.

The family had moved west from Hoxton to Soho, about a mile inside the edge of London. This was another area where Huguenots had congregated, having found the city itself less than welcoming to their competitive skills. Here, in Frith Street, Joseph was born. He was christened close by in St Anne's church, one of Wren's less inspired designs, the burial place of the ill-starred Baron von Neuhof (King Theodore of Corsica) and later, in 1830, of William Hazlitt.[8]

In 1808 Joseph entered Trinity College, intellectually the most splendid in Cambridge (its members have been known to point out that God himself is a Trinity man). He graduated fourth wrangler,[9] that is, placed fourth in the list of those with first class honours in mathematics. He was elected Fellow of Trinity in 1815, serving briefly as Junior and Senior Dean. Then, in 1832, came the turning point in his life, when the University chose him as its Registrary. This important office, dating back to 1506, combined secretarial and public duties with custody of the University's records.[10] Eight years later he became a Senior Fellow, one of the nine men, including the Master, who until 1882 governed the College. He enjoyed a ground-floor set of rooms immediately to the south of the Great Gate, looking over the vast expanse of Great Court.[11]

In those days—it was changed after Joseph's death—Fellows were obliged to refrain from marriage, and to take holy orders within seven years of their election.[12] Five years passed before Joseph was made deacon, on 11 June 1820, by the Bishop of Norwich, standing in for the Bishop of Bristol, Lort Mansel, who happened to be Master of Trinity. His fellowship sufficed as the 'title' needed for ordination. He was priested in 1821.[13] There is little evidence that he carried out specifically priestly duties, but the step was required by law if he was ever to hold a benefice. It seems unlikely that he contemplated leaving the College; he could, however, accept a living as a non-resident parson—calls to reform that widespread abuse were only just beginning.

Thanks to his family, a suitable benefice lay in Wales. Uncle Samuel had invested his savings in 1812 by buying the Porthkerry and Barry estate on the Glamorgan coast, almost two thousand acres; and this, including the advowson or right of presentation to the parish church, passed to his children. For some reason they preferred another priest when the living fell vacant in 1823. When the chance came again, in 1830, they presented Joseph.[14] He held the rectory for seven years. Like many incumbents in those days, he relied on a curate to look after the parish, and contented himself with four brief visits.[15] To be fair to Joseph, his duties in Cambridge kept him busy, at least in term-time; amongst other things he was cataloguing the University's papers.[16] Nor was his parish demanding. Barry itself hardly existed. Only after 1850, when it had perhaps thirteen households, did the Romillys begin expanding it as a model village,[17] and by 1881 its population was still only eighty-five. Then the docks were built, and by 1901 there was a town of twenty-seven thousand people. Today, Porthkerry retains its rural character, though its peacefulness is not a little reduced by the nearness of Cardiff Airport.

Discount the aeroplanes, the railway viaduct and the distant glimpse of modern Barry, and the Porthkerry of Joseph's day is not hard to picture.

This was not his only ecclesiastical post. In 1837 he accepted a chaplaincy from his friend Thomas Musgrave, who had just relinquished the job of Senior Bursar at Trinity, responsible for the College's valuable estates, and become (after a few months as Dean of Bristol) Bishop of Hereford. Ten years later, when Archbishop Vernon Harcourt, aged ninety-one, expired after falling in a pond, Musgrave was promoted to York.[18]

During the Cambridge vacations Joseph liked to travel. His first visits to Wales, apart from coming to Clyro in 1820[19] to marry his cousin, were in 1827: a day trip to Gwynedd from Liverpool, and his passage home from a tour of Ireland. Four times, in 1830, 1831, 1834 and 1836, he visited Porthkerry, and saw some of the south-east corner of Wales. Pembrokeshire had seemed to him frightful, but his brother-in-law drew him there in 1837. This was his most extended tour: after nearly three weeks based near Narberth, he travelled into Cardiganshire and across mid Wales to Liverpool. Evidently he enjoyed himself, for he returned to Pembrokeshire the following year for a fortnight, looking in at Porthkerry, of which he was no longer Rector, on the way home. The 1840 visit also lasted about a fortnight; this time he came into Wales from Herefordshire. For some reason he neglected his Welsh relations after that (though he saw some of them in England) till 1854, when he divided his stay between cousins near the English border and nephews near Narberth.

To appreciate the later visits to Wales, we need to know more about his brother-in-law, Baugh Allen, and his numerous relatives. A good bit older than Joseph, having been born in 1774, Baugh came from a prolific Pembrokeshire family: he himself was one of twelve (some say thirteen),[20] all but two of them girls. The Allens were middling gentry, landed but not titled. They furnished the usual quota of country clergy, army officers and lawyers. What makes them of particular interest is that they married into families that are household names. Elizabeth, Baugh's eldest sister and ten years his senior, married Josiah Wedgwood, son of the famous potter. She was an auburn-haired

Baugh Allen in about 1810

beauty, painted by Romney. Their romance began when Josiah stayed at Cresselly, the Allens' home, for the Haverfordwest summer races of 1792.[21] Josiah's elder brother John, a banker, married Elizabeth's sister Jane, another beauty.[22] These two marriages produced sixteen more Wedgwoods. Josiah and John's sister Susannah became the mother of Charles Darwin. He married his first cousin Emma Wedgwood, daughter of Josiah and Elizabeth, and had an extraordinarily talented and intellectually well-connected family.[23] Many of them appear in *Period Piece*, an enchanting account of her childhood by Gwen Raverat, Charles Darwin's artistic granddaughter.

The degree of intermarrying among these people is remarkable. Two of Baugh's sisters married two brothers, just as his two sons were to marry two sisters. Three sets of first cousins in one generation married: John Wedgwood's daughter to Josiah's son, and two of Josiah's other children to children of his sister, Susannah Darwin. Another interesting alliance was forged by John Wedgwood's son Thomas, a lieutenant colonel in the Scots Fusilier Guards. He married his second cousin Anne Tyler, eldest daughter of Admiral Sir Charles Tyler, who commanded the 80-gun *Tonnant* at Trafalgar.[24] Both Col Wedgwood and his wife appear in these extracts, as do the Tylers, who lived not far from Porthkerry.

Another of Baugh's sisters, Catherine, second in the family, married the widowed James Mackintosh in 1798. They met at Cote House, Bristol, home of John and Jane Wedgwood. Mackintosh had made a name for himself with a political pamphlet on the French Revolution. This led to a legal career, where his forensic eloquence was praised by no less an orator than Thomas Erskine. 'The king of all the talents', Coleridge called him, though he disliked and lampooned him. Appointed Recorder of Bombay and knighted in 1803, he came down to Cresselly with his wife and daughters (one of whom married a son of Josiah and Elizabeth Wedgwood) before sailing for India the following February. On his return in 1813 he entered Parliament as a Whig and took up Sir Samuel Romilly's crusade for penal reform. He wrote some original historical books; a phrase from that early pamphlet, 'masterly inactivity', is still quoted. Lady Mackintosh died while visiting her sister Jessie near Geneva in 1830. Two years later Sir James died too, as an indirect result of swallowing a chicken bone.[25]

Jessie, another striking young lady, with large grey eyes, dark and vivacious, married brains rather than beauty. Jean Charles Léonard de Sismondi was short, ugly but clever: he published a history of the Italian republic in sixteen volumes and a French history in thirty-one. He was friendly with Florence Nightingale's father, thanks to the Allens, whom her mother had known since childhood. Young Florence stayed with Sismondi at Geneva, charmed by him and his intellectual circle of Italian exiles.[26]

The only Allen sister to make a marriage she regretted was the gentle Harriet, who came between Baugh and Jessie in age. Matthew Surtees, a well-connected parson (his sister married Lord Chancellor Eldon), had an 'odious disposition, jealous, ill-tempered, and narrow'; however, a kindly providence gave her eighteen years as his widow.[27] An even longer widowhood fell to the lot of Caroline, the fourth daughter. The Reverend Edward Drewe, her husband, died seventeen years after their wedding, leaving her with a large but consumptive family. One child, Harriet Maria, married Robert Gifford, who as Attorney General in 1820 prosecuted the Cato Street conspirators for plotting to blow up the Cabinet, and led the attempt in Parliament to divorce Queen Caroline and deprive her of her title. Harriet's sister Georgina married an Exchequer judge, Edward Alderson; their daughter (also Georgina) married the 3rd Marquess of Salisbury, later Prime Minister, in 1857.[28] Again the Allens had become allied to distinguished men in the public eye.

Baugh also came to earn his living from the law. Through the influence of his elder brother, John Hensleigh, M.P. for the Pembroke boroughs, he obtained a clerkship in the Petty Bag Office of the Court of Chancery,[29] having been called to the bar many years earlier. He rose to become one of the Six Clerks, who dealt with that Court's proceedings and who found the paperwork a rich source of fees. (The post was abolished in 1843, two years before his death.)[30] Previously, from 1805, he had held the office of Warden of Dulwich College, exchanging it for that of Master in 1811. At that time it was a modest establishment comprising a small school and almshouses for a dozen poor people; Soane would shortly add the famous picture gallery. Baugh once let his room for a breakfast party that included the Scottish poet Thomas Campbell and the French emigrée and woman of letters Mme de Staël.[31]

Having resigned as Master in 1819, Baugh was free to marry Romilly's sister Caroline.[32] Though already approaching forty, she gave him two sons. They were close to their uncle Joseph and often appear in his diaries.

Both went up to Trinity. The elder, George, 'is a prodigy of a child' (wrote Aunt Jessie when he was six) 'and will be a very clever man if well managed'. He fulfilled her expectations by becoming a special pleader—a barrister whose work was confined to chambers. Edward, as befitted the younger son, took holy orders. He held the family living of Porthkerry, where the east window in the church is his memorial, and a prebend (Fairwell) in Llandaff Cathedral. His schooldays were unhappy: at fourteen he ran away from Westminster, causing his father protracted anxiety. Jessie felt 'there was something to be feared in the mind of the child'. She recommended a *pension* she knew in Switzerland, where instead of 'hammering on at the Greek and Latin', which was all the boys

Caroline Romilly, Mrs Baugh Allen

were taught at that 'horrid Westminster', he would learn modern languages and the natural sciences; 'it is a shame for a man to walk the world and know no more of it than the babe unborn—here they suck it in with the air they breathe'. This enlightened scheme came to nothing. The fact that Edward had earned the nickname 'Grim' suggests

George Allen                                    Edward Allen ('Grim') as a boy

a sullen or melancholic personality. Jessie wrote of him, 'I believe that slow and cold exterior hides a secret and precious fire'.[33]

The brothers married sisters. George chose Dorothea (Dora) Eaton in 1846, and Edward her younger sister, Bertha, two years later. The Eatons lived at Parc Glas, a medium-sized stuccoed mansion at Crinow, just outside Narberth, distinguished by a classical porch (too small to be rated a portico), some elegant plasterwork and a pair of Ionic columns in the drawing room. James Eaton, a local mercer, seems to have built an earlier house on the site.[34] When he died in 1807, his son Roger inherited it; he married Dorothea Wilmot and had five children. The only boy, James, lived but briefly. The eldest girl, Mary, married someone with the unlikely name of Xavier de Castanos Royds Peel; Romilly refers to her accordingly as Aunt Peel. Xavier, elder son of Jonathan Haworth Peel of Cottsmore (first cousin of Sir Robert Peel, the Prime Minister) and Ellen Royds, was named in honour of the Spanish general Francesco Xavier de Castaños, to whom a Napoleonic army had surrendered, at Bailén, nine days after Xavier was born.[35] Anna Maria's husband was Charles Delabere Pritchett Jones, son of the Rector of Crinow whose preaching Romilly criticises. She died in 1842 after giving birth to a daughter. (Anna has left a delightful fragment of diary, covering part of 1838 and 1839.[36] She was on the continent when Romilly called at Parc Glas and does not mention him.) Dora and Bertha were the youngest children.

How did these families meet? Baugh's father, John Bartlett Allen of Cresselly, bought part of the former Whitland Abbey sheep grange in the parish of Lampeter Velfrey from

William Knox of Slebech. On his death in 1803 he left it to Baugh, who let the land to tenants. By 1826 he had built a new house there; it took its name from the nearby farm, Cilrhiw. At first he rented it to Capt William Twyning of the Royal Artillery (Dulwich remained his real home). A modest, whitewashed dwelling, Cilrhiw was extended over the years, but it has never reached the size or formality of Parc Glas.[37] Since the houses were hardly two miles apart, the Allens and Eatons struck up an acquaintanceship, which ripened over the years into a double romance.

Neither ran smoothly. Baugh strongly opposed his elder son's engagement. He may have felt that the Eatons were not good enough for the Allens because their money had come recently from trade, whereas the Allens had long held land (with coal mines—and Cresselly had been acquired by marriage); moreover the Eatons had had to *apply* for a coat of arms. Certainly he wrote to Romilly, 'he would rather see G. hanged than living at Mrs Eaton's'. Romilly himself counselled George to postpone a wedding till he was sure of at least £500 a year and an increasing income from the bar. He found Dora irritating: 'she talks so countrified that I thought it quite ludicrous'—worse, she had no idea how to play whist. Once Baugh was dead, however, the romance could take off. After just six months' mourning, George and Dora were married.[38]

Bertha and Edward's courtship also led to storms, but for a different reason; here, the opposition came from the bride's family. Mrs Eaton sent a violent letter to Edward because he refused to settle on her daughter all her fortune. She tried to get Romilly to interfere. He declined, but stigmatised his nephew's conduct as obstinate, selfish and unjustifiable. The very next day came a wild letter from Edward asking him to marry him almost immediately, without beadle, bridesmaid or wedding breakfast. Soon afterwards Edward gave way over Bertha's settlement, and his uncle went down to Bristol to conduct the ceremony; it was in Clifton church, where Mrs Eaton had herself been married. The event, on 2 February 1848, brought out the best from Romilly's pen, though a censorious hand has unfortunately crossed out a total of seven lines.

The proceedings opened awkwardly. Edward told the clerk, who was filling in the registers, that Mr Eaton had been a farmer. 'Oh no,' said Romilly, 'he kept his carriage and had a park round his house—he was a gentleman'. Mrs Eaton arrived on foot with the bridesmaid (her niece, Miss Hardy,[39] pleasing but very plain). She was much vexed at Edward's oddity, and asked Romilly to remonstrate with him. He again refused to meddle, but confided to his diary the comment that Edward was 'certainly vexatiously strange and vastly self-willed'. Half an hour late, at half past eight, the bride appeared in a fly, escorted by a Col Hawkshaw,[40] lame from a cannonball wound. He was to give her away. Mrs Eaton had offered fifty guineas for Bertha's wedding clothes, the same as Dora's, but it had been refused. Bertha wore a brown russet stuff gown, very ordinary walking bonnet and shawl, cotton stockings and brown gloves, and looked jaded and harrassed. The groom had on a shabby sort of chesterfield (a long overcoat) and black gloves. 'I never saw such a marriage in my life,' Romilly wrote. Not the least oddity was the wedding breakfast. It should have been held before the service, at the Great Western Hotel, but nothing was ready; and afterwards the party divided, Edward, Bertha and the best man returning to the hotel, and the bridesmaid, Mrs Eaton, the colonel and Romilly going to Mrs Eaton's lodging, where Romilly boiled eggs in a saucepan.[41]

George and Edward had acquired a stepmother. The announcement in June 1841, after ten years' widowhood, that Baugh was to wed Miss Georgiana Bayly, aged thirty-six (Baugh was sixty-seven), rated six exclamation marks in Romilly's diary.[42] She was a Wiltshire lady, of better stock than the Eatons, being the granddaughter of the 4th Earl of Jersey: 'very fair, fat and good humoured' according to Romilly, who met her on his last visit to Wales. She had wasted no time in giving Baugh another son, Charles, then two more children. The second boy followed a family habit by marrying a Wedgwood; from them descended another line of the Allens, which occupied Cilrhiw after the death of George and Dora's youngest child, Rachel, in 1949.

Today, Cilrhiw mansion and Parc Glas are no longer in the family, and Joseph's diaries, which Rachel inherited, have gone back to Cambridge. But though he himself left no children, there are still a few Welsh people who, thanks to his sister's marriage with Baugh Allen, share some of the French Romilly blood.


## 2   THE DIARIST AND HIS TIMES

Romilly's diaries do not stand in their own right as literature, like Kilvert's polished drafts. No angel satyr walks these hills. The appeal is narrower—which is not to say that Romilly was a dull writer. These extracts give us some glimpses of Wales, and a few of England, from the closing years of George IV to the first seventeen of Queen Victoria, through the eyes of a cultured outsider.

It was a time of momentous change: reform of the voting system; slavery abolished in the empire; Chartists and Rebecca rioters at home; revolution on the continent of Europe; the start of the Crimean War. Romilly, a keen Whig, favoured reforming both Parliament and University; but issues like these are not prominent in his diaries. The riots at Merthyr Tydfil and the Chartist uprising at Newport receive only a passing mention.

The reader is hardly made aware of the Welshness of Wales, apart from the Eisteddfod and a few characteristic sights like coracles. As an English priest of the Established Church, consorting mainly with those of his own class, Romilly did not meet many of the Welsh-speaking Nonconformists, whose numbers and influence were increasing fast. He heard a little Welsh in church, but English appears, misleadingly, as the dominant tongue. When his cousin at Porthkerry claimed that 'almost all the parishioners speak English' (26 August 1838), no doubt he meant that they were bilingual—a patronising argument for appointing an English-monoglot Rector. Romilly himself, to his great credit, had taken the trouble to learn some Welsh for Porthkerry. Early in 1831 he was reading the Welsh Bible, and a good deal of Welsh grammar; and he kept up the Bible at least till the autumn of '33. When his nephew Edward Allen fancied the living of Lampeter Velfrey in 1850 he noted that 'Edward knows little or no Welsh, and the

Bishop will certainly require proficiency in Welsh in the next incumbent'. The Bishop did—it became a cause célèbre.[43]

What does stand out in the diaries, by contrast with our own times, is the social habits, the changing modes of travel, and the size and appearance of towns and villages.

The gentry pay their calls, but only on the socially acceptable; cohabiting with one's cook means ostracism. Governesses look after their children. Backward schoolboys are given holiday tasks and coached in trigonometry. While the lower classes talk indelicately of serving cows, and assume that two male guests (one a cleric) will sleep in the same bed, their betters dress for dinner at three or five, and while away the evening with music, reading aloud or rubbers of whist. Servants are summoned for family prayers. We have to imagine the hot candlelight and the ladies in their long, fuller gowns, and remember that only the favoured few lived so graciously.

For both rich and poor the pace of life was leisurely, not because travel was rare (far from it), but because it was so slow. Thomas Jenkins of Llandeilo thought nothing of walking seventy-five miles, from Carmarthen to Tenby and Pembroke and then from Milford to Cardigan, the latter stage (over thirty miles) taking him fourteen hours, half of them in darkness.[44] Time did not matter when everyone had to walk or ride—or go by boat. Romilly spent eleven hours in a paddle steamer chugging from Bristol to Tenby, and, in a storm, Fanny Allen and the Sismondis took sixteen.[45] This world was already changing. Sail first bowed to paddle-wheels before Romilly was born; the propellor followed in the 1830s. But the best hope for speed—apart from balloons, which had limitations—lay with the trains. They made journeys fully three times faster than mail coaches; not faster perhaps than man had ever moved before, but certainly so over long distances on land. That Romilly saw the train's potential for speed is shown as early as 1838, when he called an average of twenty-one miles an hour not very fast, whereas the previous year an average of ten miles an hour by coach seemed a prodigious rate, as indeed it was. By 1854 the train from Pembrokeshire to Paddington was averaging thirty miles an hour; but at nearly £2 a ticket it was beyond the reach of ordinary folk.

As for buildings and places, we have to think ourselves back to the days when Cardiff's population was growing from six thousand to eighteen (it was smaller than Carmarthen in 1831)[46]—when the great houses like Fonmon and even Cresselly contrasted with the hovels that most people called home. Few buildings survive as Romilly saw them; all too many country mansions do not survive at all. The loss of a unifying vernacular in design and materials has been calamitous. That apart, villages have taken on a new dignity. To one born in Lampeter and familiar with that good-looking market town, it comes as a jolt to find it described as 'a poor miserable place of very few houses'; nor is modern St David's ('the city' long before its royal dubbing) 'a collection of a few miserable hovels'. True, Romilly's yardstick was Cambridge, so his architectural standards were high. He was ready to commend Pembroke Dock with its handsome stone buildings on a grand scale, or the striking, spacious interior of Tenby church, even if the surrounding houses were dismissed for their tasteless disorder. Nature's handiwork he admired, though not uncritically. By contrast, the expanding heavy industries at Merthyr and Swansea drew his interest; so the diaries conjure up miasmal smokestacks as well as unspoiled countryside.

We discover many curiosities. I had not realised that Bristol Zoo was already open in 1837, or that clipped poodles were then in fashion, or that George IV had been represented, by a careless artist at Milford, with two right feet. We meet the colonel known as the Legacy, the doctor who claimed to be the thirty-third of thirty-six children (all by the same mother), and the little boy who could read four languages upside down. We eat a prodigious dinner with seven vegetables, only three shillings a head, and are offered a nine-pound fresh salmon for four shillings. We hear of sack races at Aberdyfi and of the early struggles of the College at Lampeter. We are introduced to the Archdeacon who stayed in bed for months on end or walked ten miles a day before breakfast. He held the archdeaconry for over fifty years, and employed a servant rescued at sea near Java; Romilly hints that he may have been a Maori. (According to Kilvert, the Archdeacon used to swim out to the dangerous rocks called the Bishop and his Clerks. One day he challenged the then Bishop of St Davids, with whom he was walking along the shore, to swim to them with him for a wager.)[47]

With his cheery disposition, well-placed relations and wide circle of acquaintances (he met both nobility and royalty through his University office), it is no surprise that Romilly had the entrée to so many houses. The lordly Hafod would not open to him, but a High Sheriff and his wife got out of bed to give him breakfast and do the honours of their estate. This surely went beyond the convention whereby the Gardiners could see over Pemberley, or the Duke of Wellington encouraged visitors to Stratfield Saye to ring and ask to see inside, rather than peer in through the windows.

Not that Romilly was a snob. He called on cottages as well as mansions. People interested him, whatever their class. The ramblings of a Marquess, the chatter of travelling companions, a remark by the coachman: all appealed to him. A life-long bachelor, he had an eye for a pretty girl, and approved of her if she talked sensibly. Miss Jones of Fonmon, with her light fairy figure, laughing eyes and auburn ringlets, caught his fancy; her spirited, informed conversation added to her charms. He delighted in younger children too. Fat ones appealed to him, bright ones even more. There is no hint of the hidden passions of Frank Kilvert, with his nine-year-old Gipsy Lizzie—what has been called his Lolita complex, a penchant for nubile brunettes.[48] Romilly comes over as a plainer character, less poetic, or perhaps less given to confiding his inner moods and feelings to paper.

Occasionally he made a comment worthy of Jane Austen. 'After tea Miss Isobel gave us some music, to which we attended as little as people usually do to pianoforte playing'. He was quick to note anything comic. In pouring rain, a landowner insisted on showing off the best views he had contrived from his garden. 'We had however to draw a good deal on our imagination as the mist was heavy in the back ground'. Dull or eccentric preachers are paraded before us with their mannerisms and mispronunciations. Welsh *penillion*, the art of singing poetry in counterpoint to a traditional tune on the harp, seemed to him 'awful howling', 'irresistibly absurd'; no better than the 'untunable bellow' which he heard in my own parish church. It was his nature to see the funny side of life. Like Elizabeth Bennet, he laughed at follies and nonsense, whims and inconsistencies. His friend Adam Sedgwick—the geologist who coined the term 'Cambrian' for the ancient rocks of Wales—called him ' a merry, genial man', attributing it (with unscientific logic) to his French blood.[49]

To such gifts, Sedgwick went on, he had added a vast store of literature.[50] Romilly often referred to his holiday reading. Mathematics may have been his subject (until 1824[51] it was the only tripos, or honours examination, at Cambridge), but the classics and English literature were well to the fore at Trinity. Part of Romilly's duties as Registrary was to translate documents into Latin. He became fluent in several languages, both living and dead. He could afford to buy books, for he had private means to supplement his dividends as Fellow and fees as Registrary. Uncle Samuel left him money, and his father had set up a fund from which he benefited increasingly as his brothers and sisters died and their share passed to him.[52] And for seven years he had his stipend as Rector of Porthkerry. By nature he was a generous but frugal man, kind to others but remarkably self-denying. He kept no horse or carriage, and studied economy on his travels.

All in all, he comes over as a man of great consistency. The Romilly of the earlier diaries is the same as the Romilly of 1854. He does not age, though he mellows in judgement. So far as his personality can be truly gauged from his journals—and he wrote for his own eyes only—he appears sociable, observant, critical and amused: someone it must have been stimulating to know. The Duke of Sussex called him a 'devilish good fellow'.[53] His character is as attractive as the record of his days is interesting; these extracts can be enjoyed, I came to realise, for either quality. For I began the task of editing merely to share with others Romilly's account of Wales. I ended it warming to the man himself.

## 3   THE DIARIES AND THIS EDITION

Romilly's great-niece Rachel Allen inherited the diaries from her father, and gave them to the University Library at Cambridge. All but three of the forty-one notebooks were handed over in 1934, and the remainder four years later.[54]

The volumes are not uniform. The one that covers October 1827 is like a policeman's notebook, six and a half inches by four. Three years later Romilly made use of the pre-printed *Gentleman's Pocket Book*, three inches by about four and a half. It allowed only brief entries. By 1834 he had changed to a blank notebook four inches by six and a third, which gave him room to write as much as he liked each day. The diary for 1836 reverted to the format of 1827. In 1854 he was using a book seven and a quarter inches by four and a half, and fully an inch thick, again with unruled pages but written this time across the longer dimension like a cheque-book. The handwriting, except in this latest diary, is very small, but always neat and clear. Apparently he used a quill pen, even after

A page from the diaries

improved steel-nibbed pens became readily available.[55] He must have carried an inkwell, for we find him on one occasion writing his journal sitting on a stone by the roadside.

How accurate are the diaries? So far as I have been able to check them, they seem to be reasonably trustworthy. Thomas Jenkins, for example, confirmed in his own diary the story about the deaths on Llandeilo bridge (though Romilly's 'very lately' was in fact twenty-one weeks earlier). Impressions of people and places will always be subjective. It is not easy to find corroboration of Romilly's opinions, but when one does turn up, as with Lady Charlotte Guest's reaction to Lord Bute's speech, his view is upheld. Like most of us he sometimes misheard a name: Capt 'Crombie' at Pembroke Dock was in fact called Cumby, and Mrs 'Barry Cornwall Wilson' at the Cardiff Eisteddfod was Mrs Cornwell Baron Wilson. Instances could be multiplied. Romilly's spelling of Welsh names was surprisingly good: he used the correct Welsh 'Solfach' for 'Solva', and his 'Llahuaddin' is closer to 'Llanhuadain' than our anglicised 'Llawhaden'. His etymologies could be mistaken or even perverse. Blaenpant could not be named 'Black Grove' after its avenue of dark firs, since Blaenpant means the top of a valley; and St Govan certainly did not derive from King Arthur's Italian brother-in-law, Giovanni, but perhaps from Gobhan, St Ailbe's Irish cook.[56]

Transcribing the diaries has posed few difficulties; editing them has been less easy. I have kept Romilly's peculiar spelling ('birth' for 'berth'; 'cieling' for 'ceiling'; 'plaid' for 'played') and his use of figures ('6½' for '6.30'). They are part of the flavour of his style and period, and it would be a pity to lose them. Besides being old fashioned, his spelling sometimes has an American ring: to take four examples from August 1840, we have 'center', 'honors', 'favorites' and 'labor'. He used abbreviations like '&', 'wch', 'tho', 'mor$^g$', '=ly', 'N$^{ds}$'; I have written these out in full: 'and', 'which', 'though', 'morning', 'equally', 'Northumberland's'. I have also changed '∴' to 'therefore' and (with regret) '>$^{st}$' and '☾ light' to 'greatest' and 'moonlight'. That avoids either obscurity or a rash of square brackets. The latter I have kept for rare insertions of my own, to explain a point that might trip the reader up, such as whether a time is a.m. or p.m. More difficult were the abbreviations for people's names, such as 'G.A & G.R.': the sensible solution, I decided, was to spell them out in full ('George Allen and George Romilly'), hoping I had guessed their identity correctly. 'G[eorge] A[llen] and G[eorge] R[omilly]' would look irritatingly pedantic. I have not thought it necessary to spell out every initial (such as 'O. Cromwell'), only those that might puzzle the reader.

Romilly had his own ideas on capital letters and punctuation. After much vacillation and soul-searching, I decided to modernise both, even though it seemed to contradict my policy on spelling—why not modernise or correct that too? But his use of colons and dashes is too fussy and his capitals are too inconsistent: 'welsh Curate' becomes 'Welsh Curate' a few lines further on; better to write 'Welsh curate' and have done with it. In the same way I have dealt with the few slips and gaps in the original manuscript, correcting them generally without comment. As for paragraphs, Romilly hardly ever needed them, since most daily entries were short. I have introduced them sparingly. For clarity, following Dr Bury's example, I have adopted a consistent form of day and date to head each entry. Romilly himself used several forms, and took to writing the heading in gothic script.

My aim has been to present an easily readable text, rather than an exact transcription peppered with square brackets and explanatory footnotes.

I have tried to identify the people Romilly mentioned. The nearer they lived to my own area, or the more likely they were to feature in reference books, the greater my success. Some still remain obscure. I have also tried to throw light on the places, objects and events that Romilly referred to, but again the results have been uneven.

Some readers will find more information than they judge necessary. That will be a matter of opinion. Rather than just explain obscurities, I wanted to supply enough material to enrich the reader's background knowledge and hence his appreciation of Romilly's own experiences. To the criticism that some of the latter hardly merit inclusion, I reply that not everyone will agree on what is interesting. Romilly's trivia may supply a reader with the very material he seeks, and unless the editor includes it, how is he to know what is missing? To keep only the best bits in the brief account of Romilly's early visits would be like removing the connecting string from a necklace: it would fall to pieces. Only in the 1854 visit, which Romilly recorded in detail, have I felt able to make a few cuts or substitute summaries, and these are confined to Romilly's days on the Welsh border.

Footnotes are expensive, explanations inserted into the text are distracting, and notes grouped at the end of a book are awkward to consult. I have chosen to put the notes after each visit. A mark in Romilly's text (*) tells the reader that a note is provided. Sources are listed after the notes and identified by numbers in the usual way. The reader can always skip these. I find myself that notes and references add interest to a text and send me off at many an interesting tangent. For the researcher they are indispensable.

Readers who are too young to remember imperial measurements and pre-decimal coinage will have to convert the old units. Twelve inches make one foot, and three feet make a yard (about eight and a half centimetres shorter than a metre). The pound sterling used to be divided into twenty shillings (s), each of twelve pence (d). Each penny could be divided into two halfpennies or four farthings. However, a shilling in the diaries should not be thought of as a modern 5p coin; it was immensely more valuable—a day's wage for a farm labourer. That puts into perspective Romilly's three-shilling dinner. His stipend as Rector of Porthkerry was nearly £16 a month; by comparison, Lord Bute's Cardiff estate yielded monthly rents of over £1,000.[57]

The call numbers for the entries transcribed in this book (not necessarily for the whole of the given year) are: 1827: Add 6808; 1830: Add 6811; 1831: Add 6813; 1834: Add 6817; 1836: Add 6818; 1837-8: Add 6819; 1840: Add 6820; and 1854: Add 6833.

## NOTES AND SOURCES

1 Venn, IV, 351; Burke's *Peerage* (1970 ed), 2287; P. Medd, *Romilly* (London, 1968) [hereafter Medd, *Romilly*], 20 (this is a life of Sir Samuel, not Joseph). Étienne died in poverty.

2 M. Lloyd (ed), *Roget's Thesaurus of English Words and Phrases* (Harlow, 1982), xiii-iv; *Enc. Brit.*, vol 15, 898, and vol 19, 442-3; *D.N.B.*, XLIX, 149-151. Roget invented a traveller's chess set: Bury & Pickles, 166.

3 *Enc. Brit.*, vol 19, 587; *D.N.B.*, XLIX, 191. Edward was M.P. 1832-5; Mrs Bury quotes Romilly (11 January 1835): 'Edward has lost his election by 5 votes', ascribing the result to his opponent's bribery.

4 Burke, 1624; Bury & Pickles, 242-3.

5 H.E. Litchfield, *Emma Darwin* vol I (Cambridge, 1904) [hereafter Litchfield, *Darwin*], 54. By 1825 Caroline had 'grown into a woman mountain': letter to Jessie Sismondi in Allen Papers.

6 Bury, 251.

7 Bury, xii, 111, 115. The house was in Hills Road. Romilly's family home, 1810-37, was in Dulwich: Bury & Pickles, xiii.

8 Bury, viii; Bury & Pickles, xiii; W.G. Morris, *The Homeland Guide to London* 7th ed (London, no date), 105-6; J. Summerson, *Architecture in Britain 1530-1830* (Harmondsworth, 1970), 560, 566; *Enc. Brit.*, vol 20, 831. St Anne's was blitzed and has been demolished. Frith Street is now crossed by Romilly Street.

9 For an interesting discussion on the Cambridge wranglers and the gaps between their marks, see F. Galton, *Hereditary Genius* (London, 1962), 58-64. Sir Francis Galton was Charles Darwin's cousin, and so connected with Romilly.

10 Bury, ix; *D.N.B.*, XLIX, 187; H.P. Stokes, *Ceremonies of the University of Cambridge* (Cambridge, 1927), 11; F. Stubbings, *Bedders, Bulldogs and Bedells* (Cambridge, 1991) [hereafter Stubbings, *Bedders*], 50. 'Registrary' for 'Registrar' seems to be unique to Cambridge.

11 Bury, ix, 3. On the 'Seniority', see G.M. Trevelyan, *Trinity College* (Cambridge, 1946) [hereafter Trevelyan, *Trinity*], 17, 103.

12 According to Mrs Bury. Trevelyan, *Trinity*, 107, referring to the statutes of 1860-1, says ordination was required within seven years of graduating M.A. unless the Fellow held certain (unspecified) offices.

13 Information from Mrs Bury and Mrs Margaret Jones (Secretary to the Bishop of Hereford), Mrs Jones quoting *Crockford's Clerical Directory* (1860) for Romilly's priesting. Dr Pickles pointed out that the Bishop of Bristol was also Master of Trinity; he died on 27 June 1820.

14 D. Moore (ed), *Barry The Centenary Book* (Barry, 1985) [hereafter Moore, *Barry*], 169; N.L.W., LL/P/1897. *D.N.B.*, XLIX, 187, omits this preferment.

15 N.L.W., LL/NR, does not list any papers relating to Romilly's non-residence. Bury & Pickles, xi, curiously says he was non-resident 'but he never had a parish'.

16 *D.N.B.*, XLIX, 187.

17 Moore, *Barry*, 169, 195.

18 Bury, ix; J. Haydn (with H. Ockerby), *The Book of Dignities* (London, 1894, reprinted Bath, 1969), 440; *D.N.B.*, XLIX, 187; O. Chadwick, *The Victorian Church* part I (London, 1966), 237. Vernon Harcourt died in office nine years after preaching his farewell sermon in the Minster: C. Smyth, *Cyril Forster Garbett Archbishop of York* (London, 1959), 513.

19 Bury, xi. The diaries begin in 1818, a daily chronicle on 7 February 1829; there is no account of the 1820 visit. Other early visits to Wales may have occurred.

20 The third, Mary Ann, died young, and the tenth (eighth girl), Octavia (1779-1800), had tuberculosis: family tree, 1904, in Allen Papers; B. and H. Wedgwood, *The Wedgwood Circle 1730-1897* (Ontario, 1980) [hereafter Wedgwood, *Wedgwood Circle*], 107. R.M. Grier, *John Allen, Vicar of Prees and Archdeacon of Salop. A Memoir* (London, 1889), 4, made it eleven daughters; this is confirmed by an older MS family tree in Allen Papers, which gives Joan as the sixth child, dying at 22 months. Octavia would not then have been the eighth girl. Was Joan forgotten by the family—if so, why? Was she handicapped in some way?

21 Litchfield, *Darwin*, 3; E. Inglis-Jones, 'A Pembrokeshire Family in the Eighteenth Century', *N.L.W.J.*, vol XVII (1971-2) [hereafter Inglis-Jones, 'Pembrokeshire Family'], part I, 137.

22  Litchfield, *Darwin*, 5; Burke's *Peerage* (1970 ed), 2776.

23  Burke, 498; *D.N.B.*, LX, 140-7; Burke's *Peerage* (1970 ed), 2776.

24  Burke, 1914. Tom Wedgwood fought at Waterloo. A journal of his service in Portugal survives in private hands.

25  Litchfield, *Darwin*, 5, 27; *D.N.B.*, XXXV, 174-7.

26  Litchfield, *Darwin*, 8; Inglis-Jones, 'Pembrokeshire Family', part II, 224-5; *Enc. Brit.*, vol 20, 576-7; C. Woodham-Smith, *Florence Nightingale* (London, 1952), 19. Florence's sister Parthenope corresponded with the Allens, many of her letters surviving.

27  Burke, 1815; Litchfield, *Darwin*, 7, 34. Harriet, nicknamed 'Sad', had no children.

28  Litchfield, *Darwin*, 5; *D.N.B.*, XXI, 306; Wedgwood, *Wedgwood Circle*, 375; *Enc. Brit.*, vol 19, 946.

29  D.G. Evans, *A History of Wales 1815-1906* (Cardiff, 1989), 157.

30  N. Underhill, *The Lord Chancellor* (Lavenham, 1978), 36, 87, 117, 176. The date of the Six Clerks' abolition is sometimes given as 1842. Medd, *Romilly*, 28-9, says their office was virtually a sinecure, solicitors doing nearly all the work. Baugh would have had compensation, based on his age and earnings; a colleague had £44,647. However, a letter (8 June 1844, in Allen Papers) from Baugh to his new father-in-law, Mr Bayly, says that Georgiana's income would be 'very narrow' if he died.

31  Inglis-Jones, 'Pembrokeshire Family', part II, 221. Sir James Mackintosh organised the party, which was too big for his own room: A.O. Allen, *John Allen and His Friends* (London, no date, c1901?), 190. Baugh was elected Warden by lots drawn from a shortlist of two; he agreed to pay the loser 100 guineas, then had to spend £40 dining the six unsuccessful candidates: E. Meteyard, *A Group of Englishmen (1795 to 1815) being Records of the Younger Wedgwoods and their Friends* (London, 1871), 308; T.M. Rees, *Notable Welshmen 1700-1900* (Carnarvon, 1908), 213.

32  The date is disputed. Litchfield, *Darwin*, 53, referring to a letter of 22 November 1813, says that Dr John Allen, Warden of Dulwich, failed to get permission for Baugh to marry and stay on as Master (in 1811, according to *D.W.B.*, 5). (Edward Alleyn, founder of Dulwich College, had willed that the Master and Warden were to be unmarried—and always named Alleyn or Allen!) Burke (1906 ed), 15, gives 13 May 1813 for the wedding; F.S. Allen, *Family Records of The Allens of Cresselly, and Some Family Letters, &c* (London, 1905), 20, gives 1820, confirmed by MS notes in Allen Papers; Venn, vol I, 38, agrees. Wedgwood, *Wedgwood Circle*, 182, 184-5, says that Baugh married, on resigning the Mastership, two months after Jessie Allen and Sismondi, who were wed on 19 April 1819. A letter from John Hensleigh Allen dated 16 June (Allen Papers) calls Baugh's 'bien-aimée' his 'intended'; the postmark ends in an '0', so that supports 1820. Bury & Pickles, 242, opts for 1813.

33  Burke (1906 ed), 19; Bury, 157, 236; letters from Jessie Sismondi, October 1827, November 1838 and October 1841, in Allen Papers. Public schools were not quite so narrow-minded: see M. McCrum, *Thomas Arnold Head Master* (Oxford, 1989), 60-5, 124-8.

34  According to Cadw, a farmhouse (built in the mid-eighteenth century, presumably by James Eaton) was extended c1800 with a cross-wing; but if we can trust a drawing by M.P. (Mary Peel?), apparently made in 1862 and showing the house fifty years before, the extension was added by Roger Eaton after 1812. The drawing room was originally the dining room. I am grateful to the present owner, Mr W.R.P. Welch, for allowing me to see inside again, to Mrs Michelle Mathias for the Cadw report, and to Mr Thomas Lloyd for the drawing.

35  Burke (1906 ed), 1310-2, 1452; J.B. Payne (ed), *Haydn's Universal Index of Biography from the Creation* [sic] *to the Present Time* (London, 1870), 87; C. Barnett, *Bonaparte* (London, 1978), 146-7. Xavier's younger brother was christened Wellington; their sister escaped with the name Helen.

36  Pembs R.O., DX/4/35: 'nearly ten months of my life are here recorded [15 July 1838—1 May 1839]—if it is all castle building & inflated nonsense I am sorry'. Several sheets are missing. Between 19 July and 25 September she was in France or Belgium. I have quoted the diary in the note on 7 September 1854.

37  Pembs R.O., uncatalogued deeds, with conveyance dated 7 July 1797; M.G.R. Morris, *Princes Gate*, (Lampeter Velfrey, 1987) [hereafter Morris, *Princes Gate*], 24-8, with illustration.

38  Bury & Pickles, 109-10, 182; Morris, *Princes Gate*, 27 (the Allens *inherited* their coat of arms!).

Romilly's criticism of Dora came after the wedding; by 1854 all was harmonious, and he was coaching her at whist (5 September).

39 Mrs Eaton's sister Anna Maria Wilmot married the Rev John Hardy of Calstone, Wiltshire, in 1819, so Miss Hardy was probably no spring chicken. Wedding in Crinow church register.

40 It may be no coincidence that there are Hawkshaws in the Wedgwood family tree. Sir John Hawkshaw of Hollycombe had a son named Clarke, who married Cecily Wedgwood (1837-1917), granddaughter of Josiah and of Elizabeth Allen: Wedgwood, *Wedgwood Circle*, 270, 312, 379. Sir John (1811-1891) was a distinguished engineer, responsible for the Severn Tunnel: *Enc. Brit.*, vol 11, 186; M. Magnusson (ed), *Chamber's Biographical Dictionary* (Edinburgh, 1990), 680.

41 C.U.L., Add 6825 (Mrs Bury drew my attention to this passage). The hotel was at the foot of Brandon Hill, which, Romilly said, Elizabeth I had given for the women of Bristol to dry their shifts.

42 Bury, 217. Lord Jersey was a leading macaroni.

43 Information from Mrs Bury, quoting Romilly, 4 January 1850. The dying Rector, Seaton, was notorious for his lack of Welsh: see 19 August 1838 and 6 September 1854 and notes. For the fuss that attended the choice of Richard Lewis to succeed him, see M.G.R. Morris, 'Bishop Richard Lewis: His Life Before Llandaff', *J.W.E.H.*, vol 4 (1987), 68-9. Mrs Sismondi wrote to Baugh, 6 October 1841, referring to his new wife, Georgiana, 'I wish I was at hand to learn Welsh from her, but I guess she would leave me far behind'; letter in Allen Papers.

44 D.C. Jenkins (ed), *The Diary of Thomas Jenkins of Llandeilo 1826-1870* (Bala, 1976), 45.

45 Inglis-Jones, 'Pembrokeshire Family', part III, 341.

46 J. Williams, *Digest of Welsh Historical Statistics* vol I (Aberystwyth, 1985), 62-3.

47 W. Plomer (ed), *Kilvert's Diary* vol 2 (London, 1939), 65. Canon William Price confirms that it was this Davies and not his successor, Richard William Payne Davies. Which Bishop was Kilvert referring to? The Archdeacon served under three: Burgess, Jenkinson and Thirlwall. Canon Price argues that if Kilvert had meant Thirlwall he would have written 'the bishop', not 'the then bishop'; he also suggests that Davies may have issued the challenge before he became Archdeacon. That effectively adds three more candidates. Samuel Horsley's main relaxation was rowing (boats, not arguing), and Lord George Murray had been in charge of the Admiralty's semaphore telegraph. Davies was only about sixteen when Horsley was translated to Rochester. After him came William Stuart, who went on to be Archbishop of Armagh. Canon Price favours Burgess or Jenkinson. No one in his right mind would swim to those rocks.

48 B. Colloms, *Victorian Country Parsons* (London, 1977), 171-2, 178. Dafydd Ifans, however, protests at cruel misinterpretations of Kilvert's essential innocence. Thoresby Jones (or his revisers) put it delicately: 'he was especially attracted by the fresh unfolding loveliness of adolescence'; though one wonders at his references to bare bottoms and his offer to whip a girl or watch while her mother flogged her. Colloms gives Gipsy Lizzie's age as eight (hardly nubile!); Ifans, relying on the 1871 census, puts her at nine, and identifies her with Elizabeth S. Jones, born in Pontypool but brought up with her grandfather near Clyro. Is anything known of her later life? D. Ifans (ed), *The Diary of Francis Kilvert June-July 1870* (Aberystwyth, 1989), x, xx, 108; P.T. Jones, *Welsh Border Country* (London, 1949), 40.

49 *D.N.B.*, XLIX, 187.

50 For information on Romilly's books, many of which are now in the University Library, see Bury & Pickles, 141. His literary judgement was sometimes severe. *Jane Eyre* (published in October 1847) he found 'coarse and unnatural and dull', and having read out loud *The Tenant of Wildfell Hall* (published the following June) he thought that Currer Bell—meaning Acton Bell, the pen name of Anne Brontë—must be a 'coarse violent man'. 13 April and 28 November 1848; entries supplied by Mrs Bury.

51 Bury, ix, says 1822. Trevelyan, *Trinity*, 93, agrees that demand for a classical tripos attained success in 1822, but on page 89 he says that there was no other tripos but mathematics till 1824. Mrs Bury, quoting Cooper, *Annals of Cambridge*, vol IV, says that a grace passed the Senate in 1822 'for establishing an annual voluntary classical examination of those persons who obtain mathematical honours for the degree of B.A.'; she presumes it took till 1824 to get the examination organised. Stubbings, *Bedders*, confirms 1824, and adds that 'tripos' comes from the three-legged stool on which early Cambridge examiners sat. See also Bury & Pickles, 234.

52 Information from Dr Pickles. For example, on 18 May 1854 Romilly received £538 4s 2d in dividends: C.U.L., Add 6833 (inside front cover).

53 Bury, 55. The Duke's brother of Gloucester was then (1834) University Chancellor.

54 Bury, ix; Bury & Pickles, 141.

55 According to Mrs Bury and Dr Pickles.

56 S. Baring-Gould and J. Fisher, *The Lives of the British Saints* vol III (London, 1908), 143-7. See also B.G. Charles, *The Place-Names of Pembrokeshire* (Aberystwyth, 1992), 677.

57 J. Davies, *Cardiff and the Marquesses of Bute* (Cardiff, 1981), 167.

# 1  THE MENAI BRIDGE

## 12—13 September 1827

Romilly's first visit to Wales of which he has left a record was part of a round tour of the British Isles with his brother Cuthbert. They reached Liverpool on 10 September, went to the Golden Lion (where they were 'waited on by a black'), and whiled away the evening at the Playhouse watching *Robinson Crusoe*. Next day they heard music and singing at the Blind School, looked at the Botanical Garden and the New Market, and sat through a performance of *The Tempest*, despite having to make an early start in the morning.

Their excursion to Wales on the 12th was to see the magnificent suspension bridge over the Menai Straits, opened the year before, and for size and strength a wonder of its age. Telford designed it to carry the Irish mails across to Anglesey, as the final link in his road to Holyhead. The Admiralty had imposed tough conditions to keep the Straits open to shipping, but Telford met them with a triumph of iron technology.

The Romillys chose to travel by sea, courageously entrusting their lives to a primitive paddle-boat. The voyage out proved exceedingly uncomfortable for them, packed into a stuffy cabin for eleven hours with vomiting passengers while the steamer butted into a head wind at about five knots.

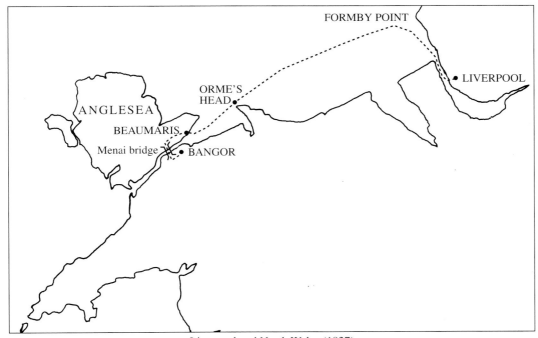

Liverpool and North Wales (1827)

**Wednesday 12 September** Rose at 6. (N.B. It takes us 2 hours to get up and breakfast.) Aboard the Bangor steamer* *Ormrod* at 8: waited till ½ past. Disgusting day; wind in our teeth, tide against us, heavy rain. Obliged to go through Formby Channel (18 miles round).* Economical, went in steerage, which was half price. There found 4 gentleman-like young Irish men and 3 Welsh women with their nasty black men's hats. The English ladies with us and 2 of the Welsh vastly sick. The English ladies were no ladies at all, but ugly illmannered women, saving one who was prettyish and had a pretty brother. All obliged to cram into the hot stinking fore cabin with Cuthbert, properly called the Black Hole—suffered with heat; people sick right and left.

At nearing Orme's Head the rain ceased and the sun showed his face—very glad to see him. The coast bold and rocky and in parts highly cultivated; exceedingly picturesque. Occasional showers with ornamental rainbows. Bothered with the sea which washed over the ship. When we reached Beaumaris* [the] sun was just set. Could not see the bridge very well, for light was very scarce. Arrived at 7½ at Menai Hotel. Abominable stupid hostess who wasted half an hour before she began preparing dinner. The 4 Irishmen (careless dogs, just like them) had been late in enquiring for beds (we did it instantly); they were sent back to Bangor to sleep and dine.

At 8 Cuthbert and I went to see the bridge*—nasty walking on rough slippery ground by star light for 2 blind blunderers like us. Got under the lowest arch—charmed with its great height (100 feet). Thought the stretching out of the long black line of the bridge from pier to pier very fine. No light but stars and occasional phosphorescence from sea-weed. Over the bridge; much delighted with its huge chains.

The Menai Bridge

Back to hotel at 9¼; they (our 5 companions) had waited a little for us. Capital supper, salmon, mutton and ale of the country—all excellent. After supper had brandy &c. We were first to rise from table. The company sensible tradespeople: one (who said Grace) told us "that he had not mentioned his country to us", at which we all laughed, for he spoke the broadest Irish conceivable. To bed a little after 11. We had expected to make this voyage in 6 hours and were out 11 and famished with hunger.

**Thursday 13 September** Rose at 5½. Posted away to Menai bridge—beautiful morning. Bridge prettily lighted up. No notion of its magnitude till one gets under it— from water can't judge at all. Not lucky enough to see a vessel go under or carriage drive over—nothing but men and horses. Walked a little in Anglesea: there "dym sassen".* Got a little way into a low dark damp cave which led to where chains are fastened on Anglesea side.

After breakfast walked with one of our fellow travellers to Bangor (not 2 miles); beautiful views all the way of the bridge. The Cathedral* very indifferent, Perpendicular [?]* Gothic with wretched tower. Walk down from Cathedral to water edge very parkish. Bangor prettily situated. Bought 2 inkstands, one of the Bangor slate and one of the neighbouring marble. Here embarked; views very fine. Beaumaris apparently an ugly town. Wind and tide in our favor; good sunshine; charming passage. Reached Liverpool at 3.

### NOTES

**12 September** The steam packet service between Liverpool and the Menai Straits—Beaumaris and Bangor—dated from the early 1820s, and developed by 1828 into a daily sailing (except for Sundays) during the summer and three sailings a week each way in winter. The boats left Liverpool from George's Dock, Pier Head. A rival company also ran a service. The voyage took five or six hours if conditions were favourable, but the Romillys (as Joseph noted) were unlucky. The fare was five shillings second class, and double that for first. The Romillys were not to know that four years later another steamer from Liverpool, the *Rothesay Castle*, would go aground as it approached Beaumaris, with heavy loss of life. Her captain, Lieut Atkinson, who was said to have been drunk and abusive, may have commanded the Romillys' packet in 1827.[1]

The steamer was forced to take the narrow channel past Formby Point, at the north end of Liverpool Bay.

Beaumaris was described in 1821 as the largest and best-built town in Anglesey, one 'rather calculated for great retirement, than for active bustle; but being the county town, it is now and then enlivened by the gaieties attendant upon assizes, elections, and other public meetings'. The best inn was said to be the Bull's Head.[2]

The Menai bridge, opened in January 1826, was Thomas Telford's masterpiece: 579 feet in span, with 100 feet of headroom for shipping, and approached by viaducts with three arches (four on the Anglesey side) over fifty-two feet wide. Sixteen chains made of wrought iron bars supported the deck, which provided two carriageways, each twelve feet wide and separated by a six-foot-wide footpath.[3]

**13 September** 'dym sassen': not an Englishman (dim Saeson). Already Romilly was showing an interest in the Welsh language.

Bangor in those days consisted of little more than 'one long, neat, respectable street, not straight, but serpentine, broken by frequent openings, and by green trees', with the Cathedral in the middle.[4]

Bangor Cathedral claims to be the oldest of the Cathedral foundations in Wales, going back to St Deiniol in the first half of the sixth century. It is a low, cruciform building about 230 feet long, with a western tower, not much over sixty feet high. The present suggestion of a central tower dates (apart from the pyramidal roof and battlements of 1966-7) from Gilbert Scott's extensive rebuilding after 1868; it was intended to be much higher. The interior had been reordered in 1824, when the crossing lost its medieval piers.

Romilly wrote '⊥ Gothic'; Mrs Bury thinks the symbol meant Perpendicular, a style more evident in the Cathedral before Scott rebuilt the transepts.

SOURCES

1   M. Elis-Williams, *Bangor Port of Beaumaris* (Caernarfon, 1988) [hereafter Elis-Williams, *Bangor*], 52; E.A. Williams (G.W. Griffith, trans), *The Day Before Yesterday* (Beaumaris, 1988; originally in Welsh, 1927) [hereafter Williams, *The Day*], 78, 143-4, where it gives '*Osmond*', perhaps a misreading for Elis-Williams's '*Ormerod*'; A. Pearson, *A Spinster's Tour Through North Wale*s (Llandysul, 1988), 14, 36. Mr E.W. Thomas of Anglesey Area Record Office drew my attention to this disaster.

2   *The Cambrian Tourist, or, Post-Chaise Companion* 5th ed (London, 1821), 294-5 and endpaper.

3   J.P.M. Pannell, *Man the Builder* (London, 1977), 228, 233; Williams, *The Day*, 59-61, with sketch of the bridge by Felix Mendelssohn, August 1829. G.J. Freeman, *Sketches in Wales* (London, 1826) [hereafter Freeman, *Sketches*], 172-4, describes the partly-built bridge, visited on 27th June 1825.

4   Freeman, *Sketches*, 158; Elis-Williams, *Bangor*, Ordnance Survey map of 1831 facing page 16.

5   J.W. J[ames?] and J.T Davies, *The Story of Bangor Cathedral* 3rd ed (Gloucester, no date); P.H. Ditchfield, *The Cathedrals of Great Britain, Their History and Architecture* (London, 1916), 466-8; A.S.B. New, *A guide to the Cathedrals of Britain* (London, 1980), 24-6; A. Lockhart (ed), *The Cathedral Church of St Deiniol Bangor* (Andover, 1994).

# 2 MILFORD TO HEREFORD

## 16—18 October 1827

After this excursion, the brothers resumed their journey into Scotland. They climbed Ben Lomond and stayed at Dalquharran Castle, south of Ayr. On 28 September they sailed from Portpatrick, near Stranraer, in the 40-horsepower *Dasher*, and landed at Donaghadee, near the entrance to Belfast Lough in Ireland. They went north to see Coleraine and the Giant's Causeway, before working their way eastwards round the coast back to Belfast. Thence they travelled south to Dublin, visiting several places of interest like Powerscourt and Ferns Castle as they continued down to Waterford, calling on their elder brother, Samuel, at Duncannon Fort. At one point they complained about the length of the Irish miles. Their guide explained that 'they were measured by a mad dog with a piece of worsted tied to his tail'. (In fact the Irish mile was 2,240 yards, 480 yards longer than the English.)

On 16 October they sailed from Dunmore, near Waterford, for Milford Haven, about a hundred miles as the crow flies. The average length of the crossing the year before was three minutes under twelve hours, so, considering the weather, they made good time.[1]

The packet service to Ireland had been running since 1785, from a landing at Hubberston Hakin. Milford itself was founded six years later (the year of Joseph's birth) as a base for whaling; it was designed by a French émigré, Jean-Louis Barrallier. Since Telford's improvements to the Holyhead road, traffic on the south Wales route had fallen off. In 1814 the naval base was moved across to Pater. Six months before the Romillys arrived, a committee had published plans that led to the building of a new road from near St Clears to the south side of the Haven at Hobbs Point, which Telford had recommended as the base for the Irish packets. This road was completed by 1839; two years earlier the packets moved to Hobbs Point—another blow to Milford's prosperity.[2]

The brothers took the mail coach along the Tavernspite Trust's turnpike, which branched off at Robeston Wathen through Narberth and Cold Blow to Tavernspite; the Main Trust's road led on to Llanddowror and St Clears and thence to Carmarthen. The fare was generally fivepence a mile, or a penny less for those travelling outside; the mail was exempt from tolls. This stage to Carmarthen was apparently performed by a unicorn or three-horse team, changed every seven or eight miles.[3]

At this first sight of south-west Wales, the works of nature met with Romilly's favour, those of man mostly with criticism. Inns varied from very good to wretched, villages mostly seemed miserable or beggarly, and even the fine new road beyond Llandovery was ill surfaced, so that the coach needed extra horses. His greatest scorn, however, was reserved for the Picton monument in Carmarthen.

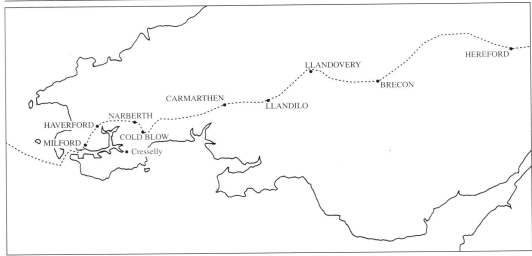

Milford to Hereford (1827)

**Tuesday 16 October** Violent wind and much rain; didn't leave our births till ¼ to 6 [p.m.] when we arrived in Milford, having left Dunmore at 4 [a.m.]. The passage is sometimes made in 8 hours and sometimes takes 36. Very squeamish both of us though not absolutely sick; no passengers but ourselves. The Haven is 9 miles long, and the sea very rough inside. Quite dark and misty when we arrived. Landed in a little boat;* our steamer the *Crocodile* (80 horse). The steward very civil. 4 steamers* on this station, one only 60 horse power, rest 80. The inn* a very good one; gave us a good dinner at 7½. After tea we plaid 3 rubbers of backgammon. Bed at 11.

**Wednesday 17 October** Left by mail at 9 o'clock. Pembrokeshire is frightful in my opinion. I was amused by their fashion of whitewashing* the houses, roofs and all, so that they looked as if they had been caught in a snow storm. At Haverford there is a large old ruined castle, which from the beggarly drawbridge* over the river looks well enough. Through Narberth and Cold Blow: most miserable places they are; Cold Blow a single public house.* If the country at Cresselly is not better John Allen's place* must be frightful. At Carmarthen is a column to Sir T. Picton:* it is by Nash and unlike any thing one ever saw. A hideous disproportioned Tuscan pillar, and from the balustrade rises a cylinder on top of which stands Picton. The cylinder is surrounded with halbards and pouches; military trophies at 4 corners. The only tolerable things about it are 2 bassos of a storming party.* At Carmarthen Cuthbert bought books for George and walked on; I caught him in a chaise* for we posted from Carmarthen to Llandilo, coach stopping at Carmarthen and leaving at 4½ [in the] morning. Road from Carmarthen very picturesque along the great Welsh river Towey. A good inn at Llandilo; arrived at 6½. Only one man in the room, who talked well for ½ hour and then went to bed. Horrid popping;* it was in compliment to a new married couple. They fired about every 5 minutes and had done so for 9 nights; how pleasant. An amiable lady boots. To bed at 10.

Haverfordwest, 12 November 1822,
showing the drawbridge and (right)
the old bridge

The original Picton Monument in
Carmarthen, designed by John Nash and
completed in 1827

**Thursday 18 October** Wretches never called us. My bustling of some use. I had to open the door and windows. Off at 6½, being only just in time. Scenery very pleasing: with water. Breakfast at Llandovery (15 miles), the inn wretched and the breakfast only so so; Llandovery a beggarly place* but finely situated. From Llandovery to Brecon is 21 miles, all performed in 1 stage. They have cut a superb new road, for 3 or 4 miles going out of Llandovery. Obliged to have 6 horses. The road is in an imperfect state of macadamising.* A sensible Welsh curate, who talked well about preaching and about Latin. A wiseacre on the coach tried to talk about classics with him and said he thought the *Pollio** 'rather pretty'. The situation of Brecon is very fine indeed: it is surrounded by the highest south Welsh mountains called the Beacons and has plenty of inequality of ground with wood and water. Our Welsh curate was ordained here. The scenery of Carmarthen and Brecknock very fine. Dined at Hereford sufficiently indifferently.

From Hereford Romilly wended his way back to London through Worcester, Broadway, Moreton and Oxford—where he observed that 'All Souls looks too white'— to Hyde Park Corner, whence he took a hackney coach to Dulwich.

NOTES

**16 October** One of the drawbacks of Milford was the lack of a pier, so that the packets had to lie out in the stream about three-quarters of a mile from shore. Passengers, luggage, mails and coal had to be ferried across—and, as Romilly observed, the Haven could be rough. After advice from Telford, a pier was built on the south side at Hobbs Point.[4]

The *Crocodile* was the largest of the mail packets, 237 tons and 118 feet long, with a complement of fifteen commanded by Capt C. Nuttall. The others were the *Sovereign* and *Vixen* and the 60-horsepower *Meteor*.[5]

The inn was probably the Lord Nelson, opened in 1800 by Peter Cross and named in honour of the Vice Admiral's visit two years later; but it may have been 'another respectable inn, much frequented by travellers', in the same street.[6]

**17 October** The whitewashed roofs were often remarked on by English visitors. A Norfolk woman travelling near Cardiff in 1827 noted, 'Lime is so plentiful here that the cottages are whitened all over even the roofs'; and Kilvert recorded in his diary, when he went to St David's in 1871, 'Like most of the houses in these parts the village roofs were all whitewashed and I kept fancying that snow had fallen and whitened the roofs'; he called it 'the weird ghostly-looking city'. Thomas Cullum, touring south Wales in 1811, noticed that even the bars of his bedroom grate were whitened.[7]

The drawbridge stood, somewhat precariously, on the site of the present new bridge (1837) and was kept in the early nineteenth century by an old man, Robin Rees. Fenton paid a halfpenny toll here. At about the same time, around 1810, a mob of women and children, taking a short cut to see off the militia (who were marching over the old bridge upstream), refused to pay, overpowered Mr Rees, and brought the whole rickety structure down. A warren of rat-infested lanes and dilapidated houses stood between the bridge and High Street until improvements just before or after Romilly's visit.[8]

Cold Blow's inn was the Windsor Castle, apparently on the site of what is now Big House.[9]

John Hensleigh Allen, Baugh's elder brother, lived at Cresselly, about eight miles off the Romillys' route to Narberth.

Lieutenant General Sir Thomas Picton (1758-1815) was a Pembrokeshire man. Wellington called him a foul-mouthed devil. While Governor of Trinidad he had approved an application to torture a young Creole girl, Luisa Calderón, suspected of being involved in robbing her Spanish lover. With her right hand and foot lashed together, she was hauled up by the left hand so that her weight pressed her left big toe onto a sharp stake. The first stretch on the picket lasted for forty-five minutes, the second for twenty-two. Then for eight months she was held in irons, unable to stand upright. Picton was accused of acting illegally, but after a retrial he was fortunate to be found guilty of nothing worse than carelessness. His conduct in the Peninsular War more than atoned for this lapse; the happy chance of his death at Waterloo made him a hero.[10]

John Nash's memorial to Picton had just been completed. Begun on 16 August 1825, it was seventy-five feet high and cost £3,000. The basso-rilievo on the east side of the pedestal showed Picton's death at Waterloo, that on the east, the siege of Badajoz. The other two sides bore long inscriptions in English and Welsh. A staircase wound up inside the column to a gallery with small cannon at the corners, beneath the General's statue, nine and a half feet high. By 1846 this inept composition had crumbled into ruin; a simple obelisk has been put up instead.[11]

A post chaise carried two passengers and was drawn by four horses ridden by postilions, unlike the larger mail-coach, which was driven by a coachman on the box. It was designed for fast, less uncomfortable, long-distance travel, requiring frequent changes of horses at posts along the route, and therefore expensive. The Romillys preferred to spend than wait for the mail.[12]

The firing of guns at a wedding was not an exclusively Welsh custom—nor confined to this period: after a reception at Coed-y-Ffynnon, Lampeter Velfrey, in 1904 the bride and groom left 'amidst deafening cheers and the firing of guns, &c'.[13]

**18 October** Llandovery had apparently not improved since Malkin's visit in 1803: 'Its buildings are mean, irregular, and unconnected, its streets filthy and disgusting'.[14]

John Loudon McAdam (1756-1836) was appointed Surveyor General of Roads in 1827. He believed that if the soil beneath a road could be kept dry it would support the traffic; so he paid great attention to drainage and to making the top surface waterproof. He laid three layers of two-inch stones, smaller than Telford used, and without Telford's gravel top. McAdam's method was cheaper but did not last so well. Tarmac dates from the 1830s, and came into its own when rubber tyres appeared; they tended to suck out the watertight stone surface which ironbound wheels had ground and rolled in.[15]

The *Pollio* is Virgil's fourth *Eclogue*, which in lines eleven and twelve refers to the consulship of Gaius Asinius Pollio in 40 B.C. The messianic theme of this poem has led to speculation that Virgil was prophesying the birth of Christ. It depends on one's definition of prophecy.[16]

## SOURCES

1 Pembs R.O., HDX/806/3, Report from the Select Committee on the Milford Haven Communication, 11 April 1827, 80, 93; it includes a map of proposed new roads, including one (fortunately not built) through the Marlais valley between Whitland and Narberth.

2 R. Thorne, 'Pembrokeshire in Wartime 1793-1815 1. Social and economic change' in B. Howells (ed), *Pembrokeshire County History* vol III *Early Modern Pembrokeshire, 1536-1815* (Haverfordwest, 1987) [hereafter Thorne, 'Pembrokeshire'], 371-7; D. Williams, *The Rebecca Riots* (Cardiff, 1955), 181-2, 186. Thorne says the Irish packet service dated from 1787.

3 H. Williams, *Stage Coaches in Wales* (Barry, 1977) [hereafter Williams, *Stage Coaches*], 21, 61, 63.

4 J.F. Rees, *The Story of Milford* (Cardiff, 1954) [hereafter Rees, *Milford*], 43.

5 Pembs R.O., HDX/806/3. In evidence, Henry Leach said the *Crocodile* was 370 tons. He thought her underpowered.

6 Thorne, 'Pembrokeshire', 373; Rees, *Milford*, 28, 122; *The Cambrian Tourist, or, Post-Chaise Companion* 5th ed (London, 1821), 115.

7 Williams, *Stage Coaches*, 94; W. Plomer (ed), *Kilvert's Diary* vol 2 (London, 1939), 64-5; N.L.W., MS 5446B, 87.

8 J. Brown, *Haverfordwest and Its Story* (Haverfordwest, 1882), 125-6; J. Brown (J.W. Phillips and F.J. Warren, rev), *The History of Haverfordwest* (Haverfordwest, 1914), 118-9 (quoting the earlier version, but with an illustration facing page 116); R. Fenton, *A Historical Tour Through Pembrokeshire* (Brecknock, 1903), 126. N.L.W., Haverfordwest Records, 1294, says a drawbridge existed in 1762: Richard Summers, a Haverfordwest merchant, had permission to repair it or erect a new bridge, affixing timbers in the quay to secure it.

9 Cary's *New Itinerary* (London, 1821), col 168; Leigh's *Guide to Wales and Monmouthshire* (London, 1935) [hereafter Leigh, *Guide*], 119; information from the Owen family of Big House, Cold Blow.

10 H.B. Robinson, *Memoirs of Lieutenant-General Sir Thomas Picton* (London, 1835), vol I, 156ff; S. Baring-Gould, *A Book of South Wales* (London, 1905), 199-201, Lord Birkett (ed), *The New Newgate Calendar* (London, 1960), 13-23; R. Havard, *Wellington's Welsh General A Life of Sir Thomas Picton* (London, 1996), 26, 42, 51-82, 89-92; the last two with prints of Luisa being picketed. If she was fourteen when they started torturing her it may have been legal. Baring-Gould says she was eleven; Havard proves she was over fifteen. F. Myatt, *Peninsular General Sir Thomas Picton 1758-1815* (Newton Abbot, 1980), 49-59, claims she was tortured for only a few minutes. E. Edwards, 'Some Unpublished Letters of Sir Thomas Picton', *W.W.H.R.*, XII, 134, goes further: Picton faced 'slanderous charges of cruelty brought forward by disreputable characters against his just and successful administration'.

11 P. Molloy, *Four Cheers for Carmarthen* (Llandysul, 1981), 13-8, with illustration; Leigh, *Guide*, 95; W. Spurrell, *Carmarthen and its Neighbourhood* (Carmarthen, 1879), 54. The relief panel showing Picton's death, made of stone with the word 'Waterloo' in metal—Mr Thomas Lloyd says the whole panel was painted to simulate metal—is preserved in Carmarthen Museum. R. Suggett, *John Nash Architect in Wales* (Aberystwyth, 1995), 116, says this was a replacement intended for the monument; see also pp 102-5, with a fine lithograph.

12 *Enc. Brit.*, vol 4, 963.

13 J.G. Jenkins, *Life and Tradition in Rural Wales* (London, 1976), 137; information from a family scrapbook lent to me by Mrs George Brownrigg.

14 B.H. Malkin, *The Scenery, Antiquities, and Biography, of South Wales* (London, 1804, reprinted 1970), 578.

15 J.P.M. Pannell, *Man the Builder* (London, 1977), 30-8; *Enc. Brit.*, vol 14, 490-1.

16 E.V. Rieu (trans), *Virgil, The Pastoral Poems* (Harmondsworth, 1954), 52-7, 136-43. Virgil said he was aiming at 'paulo maiora', a slightly loftier theme; 'rather pretty' hardly describes it. Pollio was himself a poet. His history of the fall of the Republic, like most of his writings, has been lost: *Enc. Brit.*, vol 18, 180.

# 3  THE RECTOR AT PORTHKERRY

## 9—16 July 1830

As the only Romilly in holy orders, Joseph was the obvious candidate for the family living of Porthkerry. He went up to London on 26 June to see the Bishop of Llandaff, Edward Copleston, who as Dean of St Paul's spent half the year in town (though, this being summer, he may have been attending the House of Lords). He dined with his cousin Dr Roget. George IV had died that day, and on the 28th, after the Bishop had instituted him to Porthkerry, Romilly spent a fruitless hour among the crowds, trying to see the processions for the new King's proclamation. On 8 July he went to town again by gig, visited Sion College (a clerical foundation and library, then in London Wall) with his brother Cuthbert, and then set off by the Bristol mail with a military lord, an invalid young man and a jailbird named Harry Pearce. The fare was £2 12s. Next day he took the mail coach to Cardiff—fare, twelve shillings—and laid out eight shillings on a guide to Wales and ten and sixpence on a map.

Porthkerry church stands on the coast where the land falls away through trees to the pebbled shore: a small, almost dumpy but delightful building, dominated by a squat, battlemented western tower. The nave, entered from a south porch, opens into a low chancel through a four-centred arch, which (with the surrounding wall) had to be entirely rebuilt in 1867 during Grim's incumbency. A northern transept was added at the same

Porthkerry church

time; it was enlarged in 1925 when the organ chamber was built, and serves as a vestry. Romilly would notice many other changes, particularly if it is true that in his day the roof was thatched.[1]

His first duty as the new Rector was to repeat his subscription to the Thirty-Nine Articles and read them to his congregation, like Mr Farebrother in *Middlemarch*. Who executed the Bishop's mandate to induct him into the temporalities of the benefice (institution being to the spiritualities) is unclear. Archdeacons—Llandaff had only one then—did not always induct a new parish priest themselves. The ceremony would have been brief: the Rector's hand laid on the key in the church door and tolling the bell sufficed to complete the legal process and announce his appointment to the parish.[2]

Whilst in the diocese, Romilly took the opportunity to visit Llandaff Cathedral. This was the 'Italian temple' erected in the ruins by John Wood of Bath in the 1730s. Bishop John Harris, once Rector of Lampeter Velfrey, who owed his mitre (it is said) to his book on fashion, subtitled *a Farewell to French Kicks*,[3] had planned to knock down the medieval west front, north-west tower and two bays of the nave, but luckily the money ran out. Romilly disliked Wood's classical style; yet the restoration was just as much of its age as Spence's at Coventry. Forerunners of a new and less elegant age were the ironworks at Merthyr, which Romilly also visited. Merthyr, with 30,000 people,[4] was by far the largest town in Wales, and the four ironworks were nearly the biggest in the world.

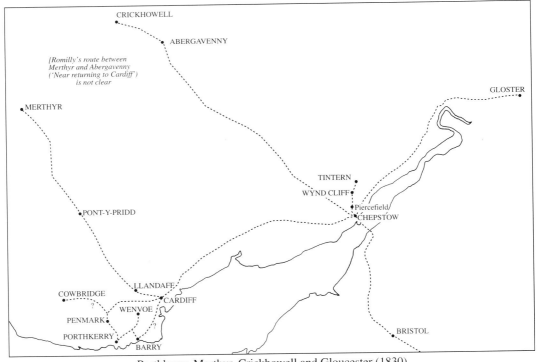

Porthkerry, Merthyr, Crickhowell and Gloucester (1830)

**Friday 9 July** Cardiff. There met Mrs Malkin and F. Taynton.* To Sir Charles Tyler's* at Cottrell,* where hospitality received. Miss Tyler* very agreeable; gave interesting account of Jumpers.*

**Saturday 10 July** Rode over with Mr Roper Tyler* to Penmark to see Dr Casberd,* as sour as a bear with &c; then to Porthkerry. I like much Mr and Mrs Churchwarden Evans—deformed young woman I took for a baby. Dined with the Tayntons, where met Dr and Mrs Malkin* and Major Taynton.* Slept at Bear at Cowbridge.

**Sunday 11 July** Gave breakfast to Taynton. By chaise with Taynton to read in at Porthkerry; dined between services with Churchwarden Evans. Then to Sir Charles Tyler's, where met Leach* and young Ackland.* Sir Charles fell into the fire* and frightened us. Dreadfully wet.

**Monday 12 July** Left Sir Charles on Curate; rode with Mr Whapham* to visit my glebe.* Called on all the farmers; fine view of sea from farmer Haynes's. Called on R. Tyler at Wenvoe;* visited Barry. Gave dinner to Whapham at Cardiff—dog-tired.

**Tuesday 13 July** Went to Llandaff. North and south doors are good Norman—west front and tower respectable transitional; modern Cathedral beastly. Met Tyler and Leach at Cardiff. To Merthyr through Vale of Taff; very fine indeed, passed the Pont-y-pridd*— saw little of it. Went all over the iron works; saw the casting.

Llandaff Cathedral in 1819: the 'Italian temple' behind the arcade

Cyfarthfa Ironworks, Merthyr Tydfil, in about 1825

**Wednesday 14 July** Near returning to Cardiff. Reached Abergavenny at 10. Called on Wedgwood's:* they lent me a horse (old Filkin) and I rode to Crickhowell. Dined with Mrs and Miss Wedgwood: only we 3. Enjoyed their sensible conversation.

**Thursday 15 July** Left (George) Abergavenny at 10½; reached Chepstow at 1. Visited Tintern, where I met Shepley* and sister and uncle Harrison* with his family. Up the Wynd Cliff; saw Chepstow Castle. After dinner dressed and hunted in vain for Aunt Roget,* who certainly lives at Ilfracombe.

**Friday 16 July** Met Mr Morgan at breakfast; he had done duty at Porthkerry on the 4th. Charmed at seeing me. To Piercefield* where met Shepley, and the Harrisons. All over the place with them; went to bathe. Left the George (Chepstow) at 5; again fell in with Harry Pearce.* Reached Gloster at 9; bought pins.* Mr Philpott* shook hands with me; he is canvassing for Gloster.

The next day, which was wretchedly wet, Romilly left Gloucester by the Regulator coach at 6 a.m., and travelled up to London with a drover who sang good comic songs. He reached town at 7 p.m. The fare was £1 4s. Some of his other expenses are worth quoting. He gave five shillings to the bellringers at Porthkerry (the four old bells have since been augmented to six), a shilling to a 'grunting old woman' and five shillings to the parish clerk. Sir Charles Tyler's servants received eight shillings, and the boy who rode his horse back on the 11th had half a crown. Romilly's bill at the Cardiff Arms came to £1 5s, with 8s 6d for the servants; the Castle at Merthyr charged 3s 6d (with two shillings for tips), and the George at Abergavenny seven shillings.

The coach from Abergavenny to Chepstow cost eight shillings and the stage to Gloucester a shilling more. The pins, at 7s 6d, seem surprisingly expensive. The real surprise, however, is to find Romilly hunting for Ilfracombe at Chepstow. Perhaps he hoped to see the north Devon village from here, and found that the coast of south Wales gets in the way.

## NOTES

**9 July** Francis Taynton, born in 1799, was made deacon by the Bishop of Salisbury in 1822 and priested by the Bishop of Bristol two years later, on letters dimissory from Llandaff. He was licensed to a curacy at Llancarvan in 1828, Eglwysbrewis (five miles west of Porthkerry) the following year, and Porthkerry itself in 1838. Since Romilly calls Taynton his Curate, presumably a previous licence, renewed by the Bishop for Romilly's successor, has been lost. Taynton went on to serve at Pendoylan and Ystradowen, and took over Talygarn chapel of ease in Llantrisant parish in 1846; he was still there in 1851, apparently living in Cowbridge. Here his father and namesake, married to Mrs Malkin's sister, was town clerk.[5]

Admiral Sir Charles Tyler K.C.B. (1760-1835)—he was promoted G.C.B. in 1833—was a veteran of Trafalgar (commanding *Tonnant*, captured from the French at the Nile) and a former C. in C. at the Cape of Good Hope. In 1795 his action in dealing with an insubordinate army lieutenant aboard H.M.S. *Diadem* led to soldiers in warships, considered by the army to be exempt from naval discipline, being replaced by marines. John Hensleigh Allen, Lady Tyler's first cousin, wrote in 1808 when Tyler got his flag, 'I was delighted with Tyler's promotion ... if he goes out again it will be in pursuit of a Peerage, this will completely reconcile him to losing the Colonelcy of Marines' (a sinecure which had eked out his half-pay as post captain and the £250 pension from Trafalgar). The peerage never came.[6]

Cottrell, near Bonvilston, had been in the hands of many related families. The Glamorgan antiquarian Rice Meyrick (died 1586), Admiral Sir Thomas Button (pioneer explorer of the Hudson Straits in 1612-3) and the Rev Samuel Gwinnett, whose brother signed the American Declaration of Independence, all lived here. The Allens had a long-standing connection with Cottrell: they were descended from the Buttons (which is why 'Button' occurs as an Allen Christian name), and called on their cousins there in the eighteenth century. Baugh's sister Jessie had cheerful recollections of visiting the Tylers, though her last day at Cottrell, as remembered in 1824, had been tedious: two hours turning over the girls' finery, four hours on the vices and follies of some titled lady, and then 'the long talking evening with no other change than the changes of dresses' and the 'flashes of endeavoured gaiety of the dear little Admiral'.[7]

Sir Charles had four daughters: Anne (who became Mrs Thomas Wedgwood in 1836), Caroline (Mrs Robert Ackland), Emelia and Jane. Miss Tyler should therefore refer to Anne. She had 'a most sweet and gentle nature as well as temper ... and is liberal as daylight'.[8]

Jumpers were Welsh Calvinistic Methodists. The custom originated in west Wales in about 1760: the congregation jumped for joy, with loud groans and violent gestures, sometimes ending in complete exhaustion.[9]

**10 July** Roper Trevor Tyler (1801-1885) was Sir Charles's second son by his second wife. Ordained in 1824, he became Rector of Llantrithyd, and held the living of Mynachlog-ddu from 1836 till his death.[10]

John Thomas Casberd D.C.L., son-in-law of Robert Jones of Fonmon, was Rector of Porthkerry from 1805 till 1823; he held other livings including Penmark. In 1819 he received the prebendal stall of Fairwell in Llandaff Cathedral. His son John Robert succeeded him at Porthkerry in 1823, having been priested that year. Romilly took over from him when Casberd became Rector of St Athan in 1829.[11]

Dr Benjamin Heath Malkin (1769-1842), author of *The Scenery, Antiquities, and Biography, of South Wales*, lived at Cowbridge. He married Charlotte Williams, daughter of the Curate and grammar school master there.[12]

Major (by 1836 Colonel) Taynton was Francis Taynton's uncle.

**11 July** Lady Tyler, Sir Charles's second wife, whom he married in 1788, was born Margaret Leach of Corston, Pembrokeshire; her mother was Baugh Allen's aunt. Leach may have been one of Lady Tyler's brothers, Abraham perhaps or John; or one of Abraham's numerous sons such as Henry, Edward or Charles, who was in the navy.[13]

Young Ackland was presumably a son of Robert James Ackland of Boulston, Pembrokeshire, and Caroline Tyler—perhaps Robert Dudley, born in 1820.[14]

Sir Charles was an old man and unlikely to have been steady on his legs: a small bone had been removed from the left one in 1777, leaving him lame, and a musket-ball had badly wounded his right thigh at Trafalgar.[15]

**12 July** Was Mr Whapham responsible for collecting the tithe for the absentee Rector? In 1851 Porthkerry had sixty-three acres of glebe.[16]

Wenvoe Castle (now demolished) was built in 1780 by Robert Jenner's maternal grandfather to a design by Robert Adam. It had three storeys with lower wings and a tower at either end. Malkin, aware perhaps that a genuine castle once stood here, deplored this pointless imitation; the only purpose of the towers was 'to aim at the convenience of a bow-window'.[17]

**13 July** Pontypridd's slim, single-arched bridge over the Taff, 140 feet wide, was erected at the third attempt by William Edwards in 1755. It still stands. The secret was the three holes that lighten each of the abutments and prevent the high arch from springing.[18]

**14 July** The Wedgwoods were John and Jane (Baugh's sister) and their eldest daughter, Eliza, born in 1795. On his return from Geneva the year before Romilly's visit, John had rented a handsome three-storeyed mansion at Abergavenny, called The Hill. It was rebuilt in 1904.[19]

**15 July** 'Shepley' is how I read the name here and in the next entry; but the name 'Shipley' occurs in the Allen letters—including a Miss Shipley.

Possibly the uncle, Mr Harrison, was related to John Harrison, a partner of the first Josiah Wedgwood.

Aunt Roget: Catherine (née Romilly) (1755-1835), mother of Dr Roget.

**16 July** Piercefield Park had been picturesquely laid out with more than three miles of walks by Col Valentine Morris, who entertained here too lavishly in the eighteenth century. Muffled bells tolled as he left Chepstow for another property in Antigua. He became Governor of St Vincent, but when the French captured the island he was ruined again; he spent seven years imprisoned for debt, his goods were sold and his wife became insane. He was buried at Chepstow in 1782. Piercefield has been the home of Chepstow Racecourse since the early 1920s.[20]

Why Harry Pearce should have been travelling on public coaches is a mystery, unless he was a discharged prisoner. Romilly called him 'the jailbird' as if he were notorious.

The Pin Manufactory was set up at Gloucester in 1626 by John Tisley. The process, as described in 1800, involved the following stages. Brass wire was stripped of its black coating and soaked in vitriol, drawn through a small orifice to reduce its thickness, straightened, cut into six-inch lengths and then to pin size, and sharpened on a grindstone. The head was made separately by spinning wire round a small rod; children with foot-operated hammers fixed head and shaft together on anvils. By boiling the pins in a mixture of pulverised block tin and the lees of port, the colour was changed from brassy to silver.[21]

John Phillpotts (c1775-1849), a barrister and elder brother of Henry, soon to be Bishop of Exeter (see note on 2 August 1840), won the Gloucester seat, and held it on and off till 1847. He died suddenly on a bus in Regent Circus.[22]

## SOURCES

1 G.R. Orrin, *Medieval Churches of the Vale of Glamorgan* (Cowbridge, 1988), 313-7, with photographs. I found the church locked, so had to peer through the windows. Mr L.S. Thomas, in his recent guide to the church, mentions the thatched roof. The evidence was a photograph which a worshipper at Porthkerry saw in a Bristol shop window; he could not buy it because the shop was shut. A case of mistaken identity? George's son J. Romilly Allen confirmed that the church was reroofed in 1867: article by him in *Arch. Camb.*, vol 7, 4th series (1876), 45-8. A search through *The Cardiff Times* for 1867 revealed nothing. My brother Gordon found the shop but not the photograph.

2 G. Eliot (W.J. Harvey, ed), *Middlemarch* (London, 1965), 563, 907, where Prof Harvey explains ''read himself' into the...church' as 'read and assented to the Thirty-Nine Articles'. A post captain 'read himself in' to assume command of his ship. Romilly may have been inducted by proxy before he arrived at Porthkerry. An unbeneficed curate was not competent to induct on behalf of the Archdeacon. Llandaff gained a second Archdeacon (of Monmouth) in 1844.

3 S. Baring-Gould, *A Book of South Wales* (London, 1905), 86. The full title of Harris's book is given as *A Treatise upon the Modes. Or, a Farewell to French Kicks.*

4 J. Williams, *Digest of Welsh Historical Statistics* vol I (Aberystwyth, 1985), 63.

5 *Crockford's Clerical Directory*, 1860; N.L.W., LL/O/533; LL/SC/1881-4; LL/P/2018-9; I.G. Jones and D. Williams, *The Religious Census of 1851 A Calendar of the Returns Relating to Wales* vol I (Cardiff, 1976) [hereafter Jones, *Census*], 157; B.L. James, 'A Cowbridge Society of 1831: The Society for the Improvement of the Working Population in the County of Glamorgan' in *Stewart Williams' Glamorgan Historian* vol 10 (Barry, 1974), 29. Mrs Bury quotes Romilly, 27 September 1837, writing to 'Taynton my Curate a letter of regret at parting with him'. In 1818 a Francis Taynton wrote from Cowbridge about land in Jamaica: N.L.W., Letters addressed to 'Taliesin ab Iolo', 745. Another Francis (c1731-1794), son of Nathaniel Taynton of Cowbridge, became Vicar of Farley in Kent: Foster, 1397. J.R. Guy, reviewing a new history of Ystradowen by Hilary M. Thomas in *J.W.R.H.*, vol 2 (1994), 125, says Taynton was non-resident there.

6 *D.N.B.*, LVII, 418-9; letter in Allen Papers.

7 C.J.O. Evans, *Glamorgan* (Cardiff, 1938), 145, 154, 202; letter dated 13 November 1824, in Allen Papers; F.S. Allen, *Family Records of The Allens of Cresselly, and Some Family Letters, &c* (London, 1905), 14, 23.

8  Burke, 1914; MS family tree in Allen Papers; H.E. Litchfield, *Emma Darwin* vol I (Cambridge, 1904), 381 (Fanny Allen quoted, 25 April 1836). Mr Roland Thorne confirmed to me that the daughters were Caroline and Emelia, and not Catherine and Amelia as he had written in *J.P.L.H.S.*, no 7 (1981), 45.

9  *O.D.C.C.*, 755; Leigh's *Guide to Wales and Monmouthshire* (London, 1835), 19.

10  Burke, 1914; N.L.W., LL/O/536; *W.W.H.R.*, III, 210. Roper's daughter married the son of Harry and Jessy Wedgwood. Is it a coincidence that 'Madam roper' is a marine? (So says I.H. Evans (ed), *Brewer's Dictionary of Phrase and Fable* (London, 1981), 964, though *The Shorter Oxford English Dictionary* does not give it.)

11  Burke (1853 ed), 658; N.L.W., LL/P/164-74; LL/RES/37; LL/NR/79, 81-2; LL/O/509. Foster, 227, says J.T. Casberd died 13 October 1830, but Romilly mentions him on 26 August 1838, and LL/RES/38 says he resigned Llanover, Mamhilad and Trevethin in 1842.

12  *D.W.B.*, 610.

13  Mr Roland Thorne pointed out the possibility that Leach could have been one of Abraham's sons.

14  Burke, 1914; H.Ref.Lib., Francis Green MSS, vol 27, 298-9; E. Walford, *The County Families of the United Kingdom* (London, 1880), 2.

15  *D.W.B.*, LVII, 418-9.

16  Jones, *Census*, 147-8. See also N.L.W., LL/TER/106-8, for terriers of Church property in Porthkerry; the oldest (106) dates from 1636.

17  J.B. Hilling, *The Historic Architecture of Wales* (Cardiff, 1975), 128, 225; B.H. Malkin, *The Scenery, Antiquities, and Biography, of South Wales* (London, 1804, reprinted 1970), 134-5; T. Lloyd, *The Lost Houses of Wales* (London, 1989), 86-7.

18  J.P.M. Pannell, *Man the Builder* (London, 1977), 220-2, with illustration.

19  B. and H. Wedgwood, *The Wedgwood Circle 1730-1897* (Ontario, 1989), 86-7; J.A. Bradney, *A History of Monmouthshire* part II, *The Hundred of Abergavenny* (London, 1906), 180.

20  J.T. Barber, *A Tour throughout South Wales and Monmouthshire* (London, 1803), 255-64; Mr and Mrs S.C. Hall, *The Book of South Wales, The Wye, and the Coast* (London, 1861, reprinted East Ardsley, 1977), 131-2; C.J.O. Evans, *Monmouthshire* (Cardiff, 1953), 268; I. Walters, *Chepstow Parish Records* (Chepstow, 1955), 30.

21  *The Cambrian Directory* (Salisbury, 1800), 3.

22  W.R. Williams, *The Parliamentary History of the County of Gloucester* (Hereford, 1898), 214; G.C.B. Davies, *Henry Phillpotts Bishop of Exeter, 1778-1869* (London, 1954), 94. I owe the first reference to Mrs Avril Kear of Gloucestershire Record Office and the other, which identified Mr 'Philpott', to Canon Richard Fenwick.

# 4  UNCHRONICLED VISIT

## 6—23 September 1831

On Tuesday 6 September 1831, Romilly entered in his diary, 'Here begins Journey to Wales'. Apart from two laconic references to current events—Warsaw taken by the Russians on 13 September and the third reading of the Reform Bill over, sent up to the Lords, six days later—that is all he recorded until Friday the 23rd, when the journey ended back in Dulwich.

The entries in his cash account enable us to piece together his itinerary. Although he was away for seventeen days, he spent only a week in Wales, apart from a quick drive up the Wye valley. Most of that week seems to have been devoted to visiting relations and friends around Porthkerry rather than to parochial duties there.

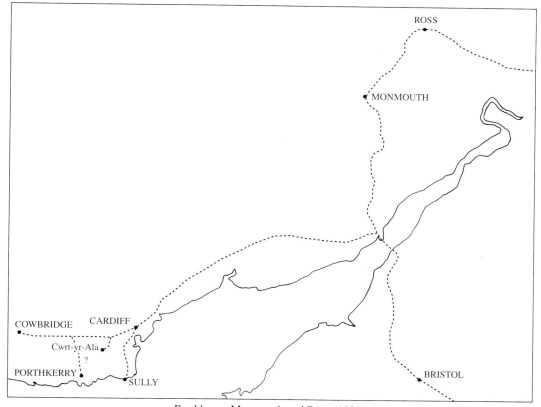

Porthkerry, Monmouth and Ross (1831)

Leaving Dulwich on the 6th, he appears to have taken what is now the A30, turning off just north of Winchester to have supper at Andover. Since he breakfasted next morning at Shepton Mallet, he must have travelled overnight, probably through Amesbury, Warminster and Frome. He went to see the ruins of Glastonbury Abbey, then on to Wells for dinner and a look at the Cathedral. That night he stayed at the White Lion in Bristol. On the 10th, for no clear reason, he took a stage coach all the way to Brighton[1] to spend a couple of nights at the Clarence, eating at Bath and Southampton on the journey down and at Chichester and Salisbury on the way back.

From Bristol, on the 13th, he went over to Cardiff and dined there; then he took a chaise to Sully, on the east side of Barry. Presumably he did duty at Porthkerry on Sunday 18 September, for on the 20th there is an entry for £1 3s 6d for the poor etc there, and a guinea subscription to 'Glamorgan Clergy'. He certainly went to Cowbridge (from Cwrt-yr-Ala) on the 17th. He returned to Bristol on the 20th, paying £1 3s for the mail and sixpence for the passage (by boat) across the Severn. The next day he took the stage to Monmouth (he did much the same in 1834). Perhaps he wanted to enjoy the Wye valley, though it was too early to see it at its autumnal best. That night he spent at the Swan in Ross, only to take another stage to Oxford on the 22nd. Dinner at the Mitre cost him 5s 6d, more than he usually spent. The stage coach charged him at the rate of between 3½d and 4d a mile. His expenditure on this curiously roundabout holiday included some purchases of black neckcloths, like the one he is wearing in his miniature portrait.[2]

## NOTES

1   Romilly paid several visits to Brighton. He has left an entertaining account of one in 1843: Bury & Pickles, 68-71. He visited a girls' school where 'each girl had a wooden machine (like a racket with the centre part taken away) stuck into her bosom & making a frame for her face: those that were handsome of course looked so much the more piquantes from the bizarrerie of this mask, but the plain ones looked frightful; wearing this machine to throw out their chest & keep their head back they were regularly drilled like soldiers'.

2   'I had (as usual) a black neckcloth on' (3 May 1836): Bury & Pickles, 166.

# 5  SWANSEA COPPER AND CARDIFF EISTEDDFOD

## 14—26 August 1834

Porthkerry was left to the Curate in 1832 and 1833. When Romilly came again, in August 1834, he made a much fuller record of his visit. He travelled down by coach along the great west road through Maidenhead and Marlborough. At Bath on the 13th he noted that they were raising the pinnacles of the Cathedral (he meant the Abbey) tower and restoring the building, having pulled down several houses that used to touch it. Next day he went on to Bristol, catching a distant view of Beckford's Tower—not the great tower of Fonthill Abbey, William Beckford's home in Wiltshire (it lay in ruins), but a folly he had built on the outskirts of Bath. It now serves as his tomb. Beckford, a rich and arrogant romantic, had the distinction of having had piano lessons from Mozart when the latter was eight and Beckford only five.[1]

Once in Bristol Romilly paused to patronise the Hotwells and then sailed for Swansea. Here he visited Havod Copper Works, run by the Vivian brothers. John Henry Vivian, as well as managing the works, sat as M.P. for Swansea for over thirty years. The scientist Michael Faraday has left a detailed technical account[2] of Havod, which he inspected on 17 July 1819. The ore, like Vivian, came from Cornwall, and contained no more than eight per cent copper. This was roasted in furnaces for up to two days. Further processes refined the metal, which was then cast into pigs, and, by a curious method called poling (the reheated copper was covered with charcoal and agitated with one or two green poles), made tough and malleable. Finally it was cast into small cakes an inch thick, ready for sale. A poisonous pall of smoke, laced with sulphur and arsenic, belched from the chimneys. Romilly must have been glad to get away for a swim and breathe the fresh air on the Gower. Next day he went on to his parish, where his cousin Edward had recently finished building Porthkerry House for himself. As yet it was not properly furnished, and Edward and his wife lodged in Barry.[3]

The highlight of this visit was the Gwent and Dyfed Royal Eisteddfod and Musical Festival, held in Cardiff under the patronage, but not in the presence, of the future Queen Victoria and her mother. Romilly left quite a full account, which it is interesting to compare with those in the local newspaper[4] and the journal of Lady Charlotte Guest,[5] who was also present. Surprisingly, Romilly does not mention her; they would have had a lot in common. Married to the Dowlais ironmaster John Guest, despite a twenty-seven-year difference in age and the social handicap of his being in trade and a Dissenter, she had learnt eight foreign or ancient languages, and published a scholarly translation of *The Mabinogion*, as she incorrectly called it, in 1846—a formidable achievement. She agreed that Lord Bute's opening speech was miserable; it made her nervous that she would be seen to smile. Reading the more or less verbatim account in the press, I thought the speech a fair specimen of its age. Perhaps it lost in the delivery. The Marquess, then in his forties, was handicapped by serious eye trouble and had to be led everywhere. He defended *Eisteddfodau* against the charge that they fostered 'an attachment to the Welsh language, it is said to the exclusion of the English'; 'if it be a general object to promote the cultivation of literature, assuredly that object is most promoted by drawing the attention of an ancient nation to the literature that by birth and language is essentially their own'. The audience applauded. He rounded off his long address with just one remark in Welsh: 'Oes y byd i'r Iaith Gymraeg', which the press helpfully translated in a footnote as 'May the Welsh Language flourish till the end of the world'.

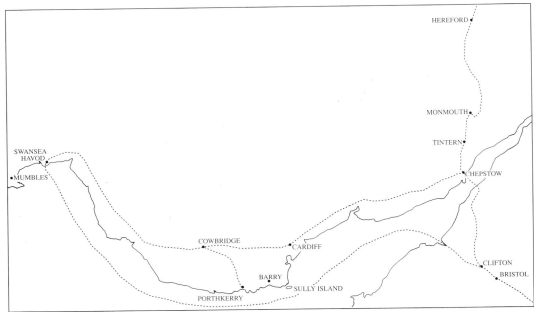

Swansea, Porthkerry, Cardiff and Hereford (1834)

**Thursday 14 August** ... At the Hotwell* at Clifton at 12½. Started by Glamorgan steamer at 1½. An invalid lady was so frightened at having to go down the ladder into the packet that she cried bitterly and screamed; it was with the greatest difficulty that another lady, her companion, and 2 gentlemen (who seemed relations) prevailed on her to go aboard. These 2 men sailed about 2 miles with us to talk to her, but she continued sobbing all the way. We were now only 4 cabin passengers, the 2 ladies, a gentlemanlike invalid youth and myself; the women didn't eat so captain had but 2 companions at dinner. A very delightful voyage, but I should have read a little less if my companions had been more entertaining. When off Barry looked in vain for Edward's house. Arrived off Swansea with magnificent moonlight at 10½; anchored for want of water. At 11 came a pilot boat and took me and the young man ashore. We slept in the same room (the house being full). I was a little surprised by the maid asking me how many beds we wanted; she thought one would do for us.

**Friday 15 August** Went to Mr Vivian's great copper works at Havod (1½ mile off). These are the largest works in the neighbourhood and employ above 300 men. I pitied greatly the men at the furnaces, and was myself dissolved into a pool by standing 2 minutes before one seeing a man rake out the dross. Most pleased with some grand fellows filling frames (like brick moulds) with liquid metal from iron ladles. These frames were then upset by a little boy into a trough, who seemed to enjoy prodigiously the hiss and the steam. Climbed the hill commanding the town and had a fine view of the bay, it being now high water; bathed and luxuriously, for they have machines.* At 3 I started by coach for the Mumbles (5 miles off) and was glad to find my young invalid sitting by me. We mounted the hills here and crossed to the small bay on the other side and picked up shells and rambled about for 3 hours in company with a sensible young copper merchant (whose guest he was at Swansea). This excursion was very picturesque, though the bay is not equal to that of Naples as they would fain persuade you.* Back to Swansea to dinner at 8.

Hafod Copperworks, Swansea, in about 1850

**Saturday 16 August** Left Swansea by the mail at 5½ and reached Cowbridge at 9; after breakfast wrote to the women and called on Taynton and Malkins. Francis Taynton dined with me at my inn (the Bear—Mrs Ballard's) at 3. At 4½ started [in] a car* for Porthkerry; found Edward and wife at their new house. We walked over to Barry and drank tea there at Jonathan Thomas's where they live (Mrs Garby's being full). Pleasant chat till bedtime. I had nice clean sheets, but there was a whole host of fleas and not a wink did I get before 5. In the bedroom was a ludicrous print of my uncle* with a brief in his hand, saying to a poor family, 'I have gained your cause'; in the back ground are those who brought the action: the devil is driving them and they are exclaiming, 'We shall all be hanged'.

**Sunday 17 August** Taynton read and I preached. 2 dogs of Edward's got into church: the younger thought the clerk turned over the leaves to amuse him and kept jumping up; the other trotted up and down with great gravity and was hailed by a child with the salutation of Pup, Pup. I made the clerk turn them both out; but they lay at the door whining and scratching. Called on the farmers; the Evans[es] very glad to see me. Had some bread and cheese with Edward in his new house; our table was a door laid on 2 forms. We dined with Dr and Mrs Malkin and met her nephew Mr Williams;* her other nephew, F. Taynton, came to tea.

**Monday 18 August** Yesterday received letters from the women; answered them today. Edward and wife and I in a chaise* to Cardiff; we here parted, they going to Liverpool and I to Mr Conybeare's. Arrived at 3; walked with W. Conybeare till 6 and saw some fishing with a drag net. Dined at 7. The party were Mr, Mrs, Miss, William and John Conybeare,* Mr and Mrs Grant* of Neath (and her little nephew), Mr and Mrs Rankin (very dull folks—he is Mrs Conybeare's brother), and a very agreeable lively young surgeon of Bristol, Mr Clarke. Mrs Grant is a languid fine lady and Mr Grant a silent country gentleman. There was however an abundance of agreeable conversation.

**Tuesday 19 August** Walked with Mr Conybeare and Mr Clarke on to Sully Island. Conybeare gave a short geological lecture. Same dinner party; the little nephew is a master Bushby and is nephew of the agreeable Miss Bushby whom I have met at the Wilkins'.* Mr Grant is Sheriff of Glamorgan and therefore a great man; he is also a dull one.

**Wednesday 20 August** The 1st day of the Eisteddfod. We went over in grand cortège—Mr and Mrs Grant, Mr and Miss Conybeare in the Sheriff's carriage; Mr Conybeare, William, Mr Clarke and I in the phaeton;* John Conybeare and young Bushby in the car. The scene of the bardic meeting was an inclosure in the castle* yard covered with an awning; it nearly touched the fine old keep. Lord Bute* presided, and at 12 opened with one of the clumsiest most break-down addresses I ever heard. Then came forward a very clever and eloquent clergyman of the name of Price;* he spoke admirably in praise of the ancient Welsh and made citations from the old bards. This was followed by the distribution of the prizes by Mr Bruce Knight* (brother of the king's counsel); his manner was very good indeed and he occasionally recited passages with great taste and animation. One of the volunteer reciting* bards was the tollkeeper* at Cowbridge; several were common labourers. The chief bard was adjudged to be Taliesin (something or other) Williams;* he was placed in a great antique chair crowned with laurel and wore a variety of prizes; he was a clever interesting young man. There were many reciters of stanzas (*englynion*) in honor of the Eisteddfod. I was much pleased with the blind old minstrel (Richard Roberts) from Carnarvon, who played several airs beautifully on the harp. Two minstrels had walked 150 miles to come to this Eisteddfod. The delight of the day was some awful howling which they called 'Singing after the manner of Gwent and Dyfed': 2 howlers* stood one on each side of the blind harper,* and sung (like Virgil's swains) alternately; it was irresistibly absurd, and anything but [a] musical treat. We lunched at Lord Bute's—same dinner party as yesterday.

**Thursday 21 August** The party to the 2nd bardic meeting consisted of Mr, Mrs and Miss Conybeare, Mr and Mrs Grant, Mr Rankin, Mr Clarke and I [sic!]. Met at 12 as usual. Mr Knight finished the adjudication of the prizes. 2 ladies gained prizes, Mrs Ha[ll]* (wife of the M.P.) and Mrs Barry Cornwall Wilson;* 2 gentlemen also, viz Col [?] Morgan* and one of the Secretaries (Mr Booker*), who made a villainous bawling rhodomontade* speech. Today the silver harps were contended for: we all rejoiced greatly at a blind youth being the victor. Mr Knight lost my good opinion today by making a most fulsome eulogy on Sir H.G. Harding,* whom he thought present on the hustings, but Sir H.H. fortunately escaped during this gross flattery. A beautiful little boy of 4 (named John Manuel*) was exhibited to us, who reads fluently Hebrew, Greek, Latin and Welsh; does it equally well when the book is upside down. One of the planks in the hustings gave way* and frightened Lady Bute prodigiously (she being an invalid); however, nobody was hurt. Of course the victors received their prizes with sound of trumpet from the hands of Lord and Lady Bute and other grandees. Rain came on and Mr Conybeare and I went back in the car to send the close carriage for the women.

**Friday 22 August** Find we missed the only female minstrel* yesterday; she sang after our departure. In the middle of breakfast this morning arrived a Mr and Mrs Eden, who staid breakfast and lunch. I went to Cardiff with the High Sheriff and drove back Mr Conybeare's phaeton in some pelting rain. Mr Clarke, W. Conybeare, little Bushby and I came to Cardiff in a hack chaise;* they were drest and staid in my bedroom. I spent 1½ hours in going to the sea lock and prying about. At 6½ Mr Clarke, W. Conybeare and I dined with Lord Bute. The High Sheriff and wife were there; they civilly sent their carriage for us, so we went in great state. At the dinner I met Roper Tyler, and Vaughan Edwards:* he (V.E.) has recently married his cousin; she was there. She is very pretty. Lord Bute is very nearly blind and is not as clever as the bats, for in introducing us to Lady Bute he ran against and upset a chair. The party was large, 24: Lady Brownlow,* Lord Willoughby,* Lord Ellenborough* &c. There was a band in the hall during dinner; and when the door opened, the swell of the music was very pleasing. I met Alexander Wood* yesterday and had much talk with him; saw Dornford* but avoided him. N.B.— In Cardiff Castle Robert, Duke of Normandy, was confined and died.* *Gwent* means Monmouthshire and *Dyfed* south Wales.

**Saturday 23 August** Left Cardiff at ¼ to 11 by Bristol mail. Miss Stephens and her niece Miss Johnson were inside. I saw her leavetaking with the little Brahams.* She stopped at the Passage (being bound for Chepstow); I crossed in a pouring rain and reached Bristol at ¼ to 4. Walking about for a couple of hours. The devastation* in Queen Square is still very glaring: about ⅔rds of the ruined houses are replaced. After dinner I wrote a very long letter to the women. Took up my quarters at the Bush.*

**Sunday 24 August** Went to St Mary Redcliff and found it shut up for repairs; went therefore to Christchurch and heard a very fair sermon from the old Rector, Mr Watson,* on the gospel of the day, 'the good Samaritan'; the Curate pronounced 'Sennachērib'.*

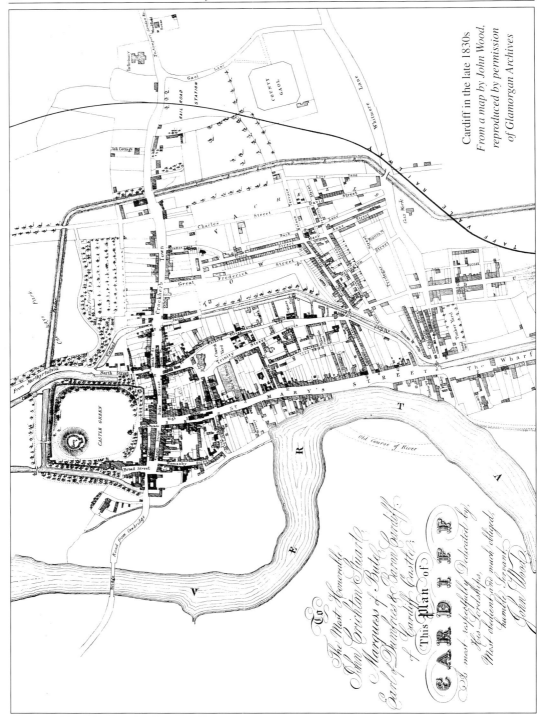

Cardiff in the late 1830s
From a map by John Wood,
reproduced by permission
of Glamorgan Archives

Dined at 4; at 5 went to the Cathedral; at 6 to hear a famous extempore preacher (Mr Seaton*) at St Thomas's. The church was crowded to suffocation, but I didn't think much like him: he was fluent, but full of repetition, and with little eloquence and no command over the feelings; not to compare to the Irvines* and Melvilles.* By good luck the 3rd Scotch Fusiliers are here, and their officers all staying at the Bush; so in the evening the band played for above an hour.

**Monday 25 August** Left Bristol at 10 by a 2 horse coach for Hereford; my companions behind the coach were an old lady Mrs Barnes (widow of a clergyman) and her daughter, who seemed about 35. She was awfully ugly but a tremendous flirt and talked unceasingly, with more zest than knowledge. She said of Mr Beckford, 'How odd it is of him always —ing* about with that little eunuch'—probably meaning *page*. The journey today was through a beautiful country along the Wye from Chepstow through Monmouth. At Tintern we took up for a little while [a] delightful enthusiastic young lady of 26 or 27, who had been staying 3 days at Tintern to enjoy the view; she was one of the maids who love the moon and she strongly advised me to stay an evening at Tintern to see it by moonlight.* At Monmouth saw Blunt* of Caius.* I had now the back of the coach to myself, but while I got down they had the impudence to put a large live pig (in an open wicker case) on the coach; I soon sent the squeaker off. At Hereford at 7; went to a very pleasant commercial house (the Mitre), where they gave me an excellent little fish (called salmon pink); it was very chill and I enjoyed the fire in company with some honest bagmen.*

**Tuesday 26 August** Left Hereford at 5 for Liverpool...

## NOTES

**14 August** The opening of the Hotwells (70°F) in the eighteenth century led to the development of Clifton.[6]

**15 August** Machines were those discreet booths which hid the bather as he or she changed; they could then be wheeled into the water to a convenient depth. Kilvert, who preferred to bathe naked, used one at Weston rather than strip openly on the beach as many other swimmers were doing. When on another occasion he had to wear drawers ('detestable custom') he lost them in the rough sea, and 'of course there were some ladies looking on'. 'If ladies don't like to see men naked,' he complained, 'why don't they keep away from the sight?'[7]

It was Walter Savage Landor (1775-1864) who compared Swansea Bay to the Bay of Naples. Whether the comparison extended to the Vesuvian plume of smoke from local industry I would not know.[8]

**16 August** A car was a two-wheeled carriage with two tip-up seats (see 26 July 1836).
'my uncle': Sir Samuel Romilly the lawyer.

**17 August** Mr (Charles) Williams: see note on 27 July 1836.

**18 August** A chaise was a light open carriage, generally with a pair of wheels and seating two passengers.

William Daniel Conybeare F.R.S. (1787-1857) was Rector of Sully and, from 1845, Dean of Llandaff. He was an eminent geologist, of Huguenot stock like Romilly, and married to Sarah Anne Ranken (not Rankin). Their son William became a Fellow of Trinity and the first Principal of the Liverpool Collegiate Institute; his brother John also went to Trinity and to Peterhouse.[9]

Henry John Grant of The Knoll, Neath, had married Mary Warde.[10]

**19 August** William Wilkins (1778-1839), the architect of the National Gallery, lived in Cambridge; he designed many college buildings in varied styles, the best known being the gothick screen in King's Parade adjoining King's College chapel. Romilly dined with him in 1838 on 'venison that stunk'.[11]

**20 August** A phaeton was designed for gentlemen to drive themselves: a light, fast, doorless carriage with four wheels (the front pair usually smaller than the rear); the high seating made it ideal for sight-seeing over hedges. It could be drawn by one horse or a pair.[12]

Cardiff Castle had been partly restored and extended by Henry Holland in 1777. The transformation we see now, by William Burges, did not come till 1867-90. A tourist in 1835 observed that the castle grounds were 'very pretty but badly kept', and though there were some family portraits the castle was 'by no means a fine place'.[13]

John Crichton Stuart (1793-1848), 2nd Marquess of Bute, married Lady Maria North, who brought him over £40,000 in cash and an estate worth more than £100,000, but no heir.[14]

Price Thomas Price (1787-1848), Vicar of Llanfihangel Cwm-ddu, was a notable Welsh historian and antiquary, who helped Lady Charlotte Guest translate *The Mabinogion*. His bardic name was Carnhuanawc. He lived at Crickhowell at this time. A few years later he had a barn at Llanfihangel converted into a vicarage, and erected a cromlech and menhir in the garden.[15]

William Bruce Knight (1785-1845) was Chancellor of Llandaff Cathedral. In 1843 he became Archdeacon of Llandaff and then the first Dean of Llandaff for seven hundred years. He had learned Welsh, and might have made a better Bishop of Llandaff than Edward Copleston.[16]

Romilly wrote 'victorious' and substituted 'volunteer reciting'.

The tollkeeper at Cowbridge seems to have been Edward Williams.[17]

Taliesin Williams (Taliesin ab Iolo) (1787-1847) ran a school at Merthyr. His father, Edward Williams (Iolo Morganwg), established the Gorsedd of bards in 1792; it was integrated into the Eisteddfod at Carmarthen in 1819, decorating the literary and musical festival with ceremonies of largely imaginary pedigree.[18]

According to the press, the two 'howlers' were William Davies of Merthyr and Richard Williams of Aberdare, with Thomas Davies, Merthyr, on the harp; though the blind harpist was Edward Watkins of Merthyr. Lady Charlotte Guest noted that the first harper was 'Daniel Du, an old blind man', who was too good to be allowed to compete. This could hardly have been the Rev Daniel Evans (Daniel Ddu) (1792-1846), former Fellow of Jesus College, Oxford, and distinguished Welsh poet; he was probably among the reciters of *englynion*.[19]

**21 August** Mrs Hall, the redoubtable Augusta Waddington, had married Benjamin Hall in 1823 (baronet in 1838, Lord Llanover in 1859; he gave his nickname, 'Big Ben', to the bell at Westminster). Though English, she had become a fanatical supporter of all things Welsh, ever ready to sting any person or institution that betrayed the language. Not for nothing was her bardic name Gwenynen (the Bee of) Gwent. She was elected to the Gorsedd in 1834. John Hensleigh Allen had wanted to marry her mother, but she had already become Mrs Waddington. The families kept in touch. His nephew George used to stay at Llanover, and George's daughter Rachel has left an account of a visit there in 1877, when four little boys sang Welsh songs to the music of a half-blind harpist.[20]

Mrs Barry Cornwall Wilson was in fact Mrs Cornwell Baron Wilson (1797-1846), wife of a London solicitor and born Margaret Harries. Poet, novelist, romantic dramatist and biographer, she won her prize with a poem on Princess (soon to be Queen) Victoria. Two hundred had entered.[21]

Col Morgan was from Llandough Castle.

Thomas W. Booker's speech is given in full in the newspaper.

'rhodomontade': bragging. The word is usually spelt 'rodomontade', after a boastful King of Algiers, Rodomonte.

General Sir Henry (eventually Field Marshal Viscount) Hardinge K.C.B. (1785-1856) was among the distinguished visitors at Cardiff Castle. An M.P., soon to be Chief Secretary for Ireland, he later served as Governor General of India and Commander-in-Chief of the British Army, responsible for introducing the Enfield rifle and for the shortcomings exposed in the Crimea.[22]

Lady Charlotte Guest mentioned the four-year-old Welsh prodigy, but not his name or his ability to read Latin. He seemed to her very playful and happy, and more wonderful than Sir Henry.

She was herself on the platform, and recorded the violent crash and rush for the door. Coolly, she stayed in her place.[23]

**22 August** The female minstrel must have been Miss Elizabeth Macfarlane of Merthyr.[24]

A hack, or hackney, chaise, was a light open carriage for hire.

Vaughan Edwards may have been a mistake for Mr Edwards-Vaughan of Rheola.[25]

Lady Brownlow was the third wife of Earl Brownlow. Lord and Lady Willoughby de Broke and the Earl of Ellenborough (later Hardinge's predecessor as Governor General of India) were also guests at the Castle.[26]

Alexander Wood was probably the Fellow Commoner at Trinity who acted as train-bearer to Lord Camden, the University Chancellor, on 4 July 1835.[27]

Dornford may be a misreading for Domford: Joseph Domford was a Fellow of Oriel College, Oxford, and a former Trinity (Cambridge) man.[28]

Robert of Normandy, William the Conqueror's eldest son, died in Cardiff Castle in 1134.

**23 August** Were the little Brahams connected with the tenor John Braham (1774?-1856)? He had a compass of nineteen notes of prodigious volume, but prostituted his gifts by showing off for money, though to his credit he sank £30,000 into building a London theatre, the St James's. Of his six children, one became an Anglican clergyman and another the Countess Waldegrave.[29]

The devastation in Bristol had followed the opening of the assizes in October 1831, when drunken rioters had burned down many houses and public buildings, including the Bishop's Palace, and left twelve dead and at least ninety-six injured. Unrest over the Reform Bill lay behind it.[30]

The Bush Tavern and Hotel in Corn Street was a famous coaching inn, where the London mail stopped and travellers could catch a coach for south Wales. Turtle and lime punch were sent from here to all parts of the country. In the 1850s an ornate classical bank replaced it.[31]

**24 August** The Rev R. Watson was Rector of Christ Church in Broad Street.[32]

Sennacherib: see, for example, II Kings 18, verse 13.[33]

William Seaton, Rector of Lampeter Velfrey (see note on 19 August 1838), had to live for a while in Bristol, or so he claimed, because of his wife's violent internal complaint (she lived to be ninety-one); so this was almost certainly he.[34]

Irvine was the Scottish preacher Edward Irving (1792-1834), whose early appeal turned sour;

he was convicted of heresy by teaching that Christ's humanity was sinful, and his emphasis on Christ's Second Coming led his followers (Irvingites) to form the so-called Catholic Apostolic Church. Its success notably diminished when the last of its 'Apostles' died in 1901, with Christ still not returned.[35]

Henry Melvill was incumbent of Camden chapel, Camberwell. Romilly heard him preach on Christmas Day 1833, and again, for one hour and a quarter, in 1836. Reputedly he took sixty hours to prepare every sermon.[36]

**25 August** The word '—ing' has not been censored—even though Beckford was a notorious homosexual. I cannot decipher Romilly's handwriting.[37]

Tintern Abbey's romantic reputation may be said to date from the publication of Wordsworth's poem, *Lines composed a few miles above Tintern Abbey*, in 1798; not that he ever mentioned the Abbey.[38]

John Elijah Blunt (c1796-1856), a former Fellow Commoner of Trinity and by now a Commissioner in Lunacy, helped to drum up votes for Romilly in the election for Registrary in March 1832; but this may have been Walter Blunt (c1810-1882), who was a Caius man, and later ordained.[39]

Caius: Gonville and Caius College. The royal physician Dr John Caius—thought to be a Latinised form of Kaye—refounded Gonville Hall in 1557, giving medical students there special privileges. He was himself a specialist in sweating sickness.[40]

'bagmen': commercial travellers—what we would call 'reps'.

## SOURCES

1 *Enc. Brit.*, vol 3, 355-6; (A.A.) *Illustrated Road Book of England and Wales* (London, 1966), 512.

2 D. Tomos, *Michael Faraday in Wales* (Denbigh, no date), 33-6, 116-7; see also Mr and Mrs S.C. Hall, *The Book of South Wales, The Wye, and the Coast* (London, 1861, reprinted East Ardsley, 1977), 339-40, for another description of the copper process at Swansea—the poling was done with a rod of birch.

3 D. Moore (ed), *Barry The Centenary Book* (Barry, 1985), 206, note 11, with reference to B.L. James, *The Vale of Glamorgan, 1780-1850* (University of Wales M.A. thesis, 1971), 58, note 46.

4 Cardiff Central Library, *The Glamorgan Monmouth And Brecon Gazette and Merthyr Guardian* [hereafter *Guardian*], 2, 23 and 30 August 1834.

5 J. Davies, *Cardiff and the Marquesses of Bute* (Cardiff, 1981) [hereafter Davies, *Bute*], 20-1; Earl of Bessborough (ed), *Lady Charlotte Guest Extracts from Her Journal 1833-1852* (London, 1950) [hereafter Bessborough, *Guest*], 4, 7, 8, 33.

6 *Enc. Brit.*, vol 4, 220.

7 W. Plomer (ed), *Kilvert's Diary* (London, 1978) [hereafter Plomer, *Kilvert*], 199, 221, 249-50.

8 W. Vaughan-Thomas, *The New Shell Guides: South and Mid Wales* (London, 1987), 177.

9 *D.N.B.*, XII, 61-3; *D.W.B.*, 81; B. Colloms, *Victorian Country Parsons* (London, 1977), 249; G.M. Jones and E. Scourfield, *Sully* (Sully, 1986), 26-8; Bury, 240.

10 E. Walford, *The County Families of the United Kingdom* (London, 1880) [hereafter Walford, *County Families*], 428.

11 Bury, 137, 256.

12 *Enc. Brit.*, vol 4, 962; S. Walrond, *Looking at Carriages* (London, 1980), 28-63.

13 J.B. Hilling, *The Historic Architecture of Wales* (Cardiff, 1975), 128, 181, 224; Wiltshire Record Office, 473/387, 7 October 1835 (I owe this to Mr S.D. Hobbs).

14 Davies, *Bute*, 2, 15.

15 R. Haslam, *Powys* (Harmondsworth and Cardiff, 1979), 315-6; J. Davies, *A History of Wales* (London, 1994), 386-7. *Guardian*, 23 August 1834, simply says he was of Crickhowell.

16 *D.W.B.*, 537; E.T. Davies, 'The Church in the Industrial Revolution', in D. Walker (ed), *A History of the Church in Wales* (Penarth, 1976) [hereafter Davies, 'Revolution'], 126-7.

17 *Guardian*, 23 August 1834.

18 *D.W.B.*, 1071; *Enc. Brit.*, vol 8, 103; C. Wilkins, *The History of Merthyr Tydfil* (Merthyr Tydfil, 1867), 311-3. See also N.L.W., Letters addressed to 'Taliesin ab Iolo', 26-36, for correspondence about the 1834 Eisteddfod from Thomas Booker.

19 *Guardian*, 23 August 1834; Bessborough, *Guest*, 34; *D.W.B.*, 222 (I owe this to my brother Peter; his wife, the Rev Beti Morris, is Vicar of Pencarreg, where Daniel Ddu is buried).

20 C.J.O. Evans, *Monmouthshire* (Cardiff, 1953), 344-5; Davies, 'Revolution', 127, 130-3, 143 note 10; H.M. Vaughan, *The South Wales Squires* (London, 1926), 128-34; N.L.W., Letters addressed to 'Taliesin ab Iolo', 206; Pembs R.O., HDX/132/2. For another theory on the naming of Big Ben, see F. Barker and P. Jackson (ed), *London 2000 years of a city and its people* (London, 1979), 299.

21 *D.N.B.*, LXII, 87.

22 *Enc. Brit.*, vol 11, 94.

23 Bessborough, *Guest*, 34 and note, 35; *Guardian*, 30 August 1834.

24 *Guardian*, 23 August 1834.

25 Walford, *County Families*, 607.

26 *Guardian*, 23 August 1834; Debrett's *Peerage* (21st ed) (London, 1836), 152, 196; *Enc. Brit.*, vol 8, 294.

27 Bury, 78, 256.

28 Bury, 47, 241; but Bury & Pickles, 211, has Romilly referring to a Mrs Dornford.

29 *D.N.B.*, VI, 195-7.

30 W.H. Somerton, *A Narrative of the Bristol Riots* 2nd ed (Bristol, no date); G.M. Trevelyan, *A Shortened History of England* (Harmondsworth, 1959), 467.

31 Robson's *Commercial Directory of London and the Western Counties* (London, 1840?) [hereafter Robson, *Directory*], Bristol section, 70; G. Harries, *Early Bristol Paddle-Steamer Shipwrecks* (St David's, 1993), endpaper with annotated plan of Bristol, c1820; C. Crick, *Victorian Buildings in Bristol* (Bristol, 1975), 33.

32 Robson's *Directory*, Bristol section, 104.

33 Presumably Romilly pronounced the name 'Sennachĕrib', though not perhaps (as now) with the stress on the second syllable. The same argument occurs in G. Huntington, *Random Recollections of Some Noted Bishops, Divines and Worthies of the 'Old Church' of Manchester* (London, 1893), 260.

34 P.M.S. Jones, 'The Diocese of St David's in the Nineteenth Century: A Comment Based on the Life and Career of the Rev W. Seaton', *J.H.S.C.W.*, 26 (1979), 69-70, 76. Dr Jones (Seaton's great-great-great-grandson) kindly gave me a copy of his original typescript and other information. I had thought the preacher might have been Seaton's eldest son and namesake, Curate of Bedminster, but he was not yet ordained: Somerset Record Office, D/D/BO no 63 (I am grateful to Miss Sue Berry for checking this). The second son, John, worked for a while with the Rev Patrick Brontë at Haworth. Abdiel, later their father's Curate at Lampeter Velfrey but also not ordained at this time, was the youngest son.

35 *O.D.C.C.*, 251, 702. Kilvert wrote, 29 November 1872, 'The Irvingites are all in a flutter of expectation and excitement. They believe that Christ has already come and is at Glasgow working miracles': Plomer, *Kilvert*, 203.

36 Bury, 43-4, 97, 146, 248.

37 R. Porter, *English Society in the Eighteenth Century* (Harmondsworth, 1982), 282. The index does not distinguish between Beckford and his father of the same name. William *fils* did marry and have children—like Oscar Wilde.

38 *Enc. Brit.*, vol 22, 9.

39 Bury, 8, 238; Venn, vol I, 304. Walter was perhaps John Elijah's brother.

40 J. Steegman (B. Little, rev), *Cambridge* (London, 1954), 20-1; *Enc. Brit.*, vol 4, 588.

# 6  GLAMORGAN CALLS

## 15—28 July 1836

This was Romilly's last visit to Porthkerry as Rector. While at Cambridge he seems to have put the parish out of his mind; after all, few lived there, and they were provided with a priest who, if not himself resident, lay within easy reach. No doubt Romilly thought of it less as a cure than as a family possession, and came to see his cousin rather than his parishioners. They were Edward's tenants, and, now that Porthkerry House was habitable, Edward could spend more time on the estate.

The plan had been for Romilly to sail from Bristol to Swansea and then drive down. Failing to find a boat, he decided to stay overnight in Bristol and travel round the opposite way by road. This meant crossing the Severn at the Old Passage, where the suspension bridge now stands. In 1827 a six-hundred-foot pier had been opened here to make it easier to board the boat at low water.[1] The mail, which had been using the New Passage downstream, three miles wide and subject to delays, changed to the Old Passage not long before this visit. It could be a dangerous crossing, but Romilly negotiated it safely.

His beloved sister Margaret had preceded him by about a fortnight, and with greater inconvenience: her boat had been driven back by contrary winds within sight of

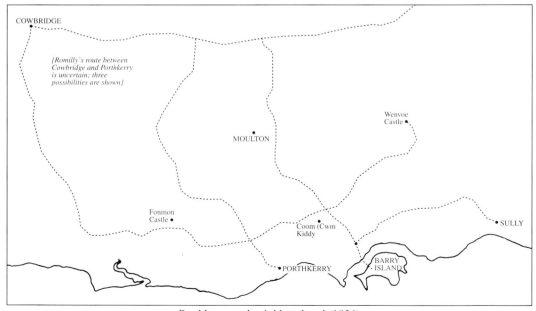

Porthkerry and neighbourhood (1836)

Porthkerry, so she had had to post twenty miles by road. The experience cannot have helped her recover from the pleurisy which had dogged her through the spring, leaving her with a troublesome cough.[2] Anxiety about her health clouded this visit, and Romilly did not like to stray far from Porthkerry. He did manage a half-naked paddle and a bathe at Barry Island (then undeveloped), and some social calls, on the Conybeares and the Malkins and at Fonmon and Wenvoe Castles. At Fonmon he was much taken with the charms of Robert Jones's teenage sister.

**Friday 15 July** ... Reached Bristol dinnerless at ¼ to 8. Went off to Clifton to enquire about steam-boat for Swansea tomorrow; found there was none till Monday. Took a hot bath; got some tea and a mutton chop at 9½ at the Cumberland Hotel at Clifton and then went back in a fly to Bristol, where I slept at that nasty Bush Inn.

**Saturday 16 July** Left Bristol at ¼ to 8 by Welsh mail: the 2 Miss Nevils* inside, I and their brother and Crawshay* (the iron master) outside. A man (name unknown) lent me Mary Howett's *Seven Temptations*;* read the 1st 2 with some pleasure. The 1st is an attempt of the evil spirit in the shape of a philosopher to seduce a poor scholar who is dying; he is defeated. The student is strong in affection for his mother and in real religious feeling. The 2nd is a case of avarice and the foul fiend wins the day. The poetry is occasionally good, and the tone of feeling always. Calm passage by the old ferry. Reached Cowbridge at 2¼; called on Mrs Malkin, where I saw Col Taynton. Started for Porthkerry at ¼ to 3. Postboy didn't know the way; lost himself 2 or 3 times. At last he said to me, 'You were never in Porthkerry'. 'O yes though, but I have: I'm the Rector'. 'Then you can tell me the way'. 'No I can't, but I can describe the church tower to you, and you can steer by that'. Arrived at Porthkerry at 4½. Found Margaret (thank God) looking much better than expected; think her appearance decidedly improved. Dined at 5½; in the evening Edward read loud Wraxall's *Posthumous Memoirs.**

**Sunday 17 July** To the Sunday school, where Taynton and I examined the children; thought they did vilely. Read prayers, and preached from the epistle of the day (7th Sunday after Trinity), 'What fruit had ye then &c'.* A little child was making its first efforts to speak during the whole of the sermon; as loud though not so distinct (I hope) as the preacher. Would not let Margaret go as the weather was very cold and comfortless. After service Edward, Taynton and I walked over the estate to see the farm buildings at Coom Kiddy* and other improvements. Edward holds a large farm in his own hands and is trying all manner of experiments of drainage &c. We dined at 5½ and [?] in the evening Edward read loud.

**Monday 18 July** After breakfast Edward, Taynton and I went to superintend cutting down trees. I then wrote to Cuthbert and Lucy saying that I could not give them the satisfaction of reporting Margaret's cough to be gone as she had coughed 3 or 4 times in the evening and felt a soreness in her side as if she had received a hard blow. After lunch Edward, Taynton and I walked along the cliffs to Roose to call on Evans the farmer; we walked with him over the glebe. A tolerable day with sunshine. 6 vessels came ashore to load with limestone; Margaret and Mrs Edward went down to see them. One poor fellow fell from off a plank about 12 feet with his head on the stones; he was very seriously hurt. In the evening we plaid 3 penny whist: Taynton and I against Edward and his wife; we lost 28 points in 4 rubbers.

**Tuesday 19 July** Taynton left us before breakfast. Edward and I went after breakfast to Barry to enquire after the man who had fallen; found him alive and likely to recover. Hard blowing rainy miserable day; we got thoroughly wet through. Home again at 2. Edward read Wraxall loud till dinner time. I read Auguste la Fontaine's* domestic tales with amusement. I also read von Raumer* in Mrs Austin's* translation and found it insufferably dull. In the evening Margaret and I plaid whist against Edward and wife.

**Wednesday 20 July** Another miserable wet day. Edward and I and Mrs Edward contrived to drive over to Fonmon Castle* during an interval of storms; we got well washed however during our drive back. Much struck with the information and talent of Mrs and Miss Jones.* The latter is one of the prettiest and most attractive girls I have ever seen. She is about 16: a light fairy figure, an oval face with laughing eyes and beautiful auburn hair in ringlets. Mrs Edward thought she pronounced her criticism of books in too decided a way; I on the contrary was delighted with the quantity of knowledge she exhibited and with the spirit of her conversation. Mrs Jones (her mother) is a clever well informed woman strict in her religious opinions, and therefore disliked by her neighbours and called a Methodist.* Her son* (the laird) is about 21: very goodlooking and apparently an amiable quiet man. In the evening Wraxall.

Fonmon Castle from the east in 1828

**Thursday 21 July** Edward and I drove over to Sully and experienced only one heavy shower. He returned to Porthkerry but I staid. Found Mrs Conybeare with a bad cough. Went to Sully Island, where I found Conybeare and Miss Conybeare and his cousins Major and Mrs Olivier.* We dined at 5½: Mr and Mrs Conybeare,* Miss Conybeare and 3 of her brothers* and Major and Mrs Olivier and I. In the evening Conybeare had a bilious attack and we did not see him for the rest of the day. After tea Mrs Olivier sung 'What though I trace' tolerably well. I read prayers at bed time.

**Friday 22 July** Read prayers for Mr Conybeare, who came to breakfast however, but was looking extremely ill. I took a walk with little Crawford along the beach for 2 hours: a pretty amusing child of 7 years old, who expresses himself remarkably well. At 3 o'clock came Edward and wife in the car; we got back to Porthkerry through an awful road and found Mrs Malkin arrived. No reading loud this evening; we plaid a little whist.

**Saturday 23 July** Scrambled up a nasty dangerous rock hunting for Miss Wilcox's* fern; got filthily dirty and found nothing like it. Mrs Malkin, Edward and wife, Margaret and I then walked to the farm at Cwm Kiddy; rather too far I thought for Margaret; however the day was not hot nor did it rain—the most tolerably genial day we have yet had. The Conybeares and Oliviers came for a morning call: Mr and Mrs Conybeare, Major and Mrs Olivier and son in a phaeton, Miss Conybeare and Charles Conybeare* on horseback. We took them down to the beach and showed them the view from the churchyard.

**Sunday 24 July** Children did rather better at the Sunday school. Preached and read prayers in afternoon: text I John 2.16, 'He that saith he abideth in Christ ought himself also to walk even as he walked'. The day was too cold and miserable for Margaret to stir out. She still, alas! coughs a good deal, but in strength and general health is decidedly improved; she says too her side is much less sore.

**Monday 25 July** Finished Auguste Lafontaine's novel *St Julien*. It is a tale of horrors of the French revolution. It is far too long and is full of ridiculous improbabilities, especially that of Louis St Julien falling in love with his sister Adelaide without either discovering their relationship till they come into the church to be married. This said Adelaide was led out for execution and also Borde (her sister Anne's lover), but they are both saved, most absurdly, and the novel ends most matrimonially. Wrote home. Margaret and Mrs Edward and I went along the beach to visit Mrs Marcet's* cave. After lunch Edward and wife and I went in the car to call on the Jenners* at Wenvoe Castle;* saw Mrs Jenner, who is very pretty (though her nose is so acqueline) and has some beautiful children. The house and grounds are very striking. Mrs Malkin returned home today on horseback. Read aloud *Major Downing.**

**Tuesday 26 July** Went before breakfast to bathe; mizzling rain all the time. The bathing was just detestable to the feet as the sand lasted only a few yards and then came those horrid stones. After breakfast I went for 2½ hours along the western cliffs hunting fruitlessly for fern. After lunch Edward and I went over to Moulton* to see farmer Smith and go through the farm. Smith is an intelligent active handsome old man and his sons peculiarly goodlooking; Edward thinks him a clever rogue. Came back through narrow lanes, which scarcely admitted the car with its 2 seats turned up. Whist in evening.

**Wednesday 27 July** After breakfast went to explore Barry harbour and Island. Though the tide was out I found there were little streams in the harbour beyond the power of shoes and stockings, so I took them off as also my trowsers and with said clothes under my arm went across. Bathed from the Island; the sands here are firm and quite delightful. At luncheon today we had Mr Halket (Edward's man of business) so Edward couldn't come over to dine with the Malkins. Left Porthkerry at 2¼ in the car. I thought Margaret's cough not at all better than when she left home a month ago; but her side is much less sore and her general health very much improved. Mrs Edward has got a slight cold and sore throat. Her little errand-boy William drove me over in the car. Dined with the Malkins and met Dr Williams* and his agreeable daughter, Mrs Howell. I was also much pleased with his son Charles Williams.* My Curate, Taynton, and his uncle, Col Taynton, were also there. The rest of the company were a pretty Miss Jenkins and brother, a Mr Edmondes* (Vicar of Cowbridge) and Mr Redwood, a coxcombial* young lawyer, who talked political economy. The party was very agreeable indeed; all the guests were in perfect good humour though we discussed Dr Hampden,* whom I defended against Mr Charles Williams; I was in a minority of one on this question. Played whist with Mr Edmondes, Col Taynton and my Curate.

**Thursday 28 July** Breakfasted with Col and Francis Taynton and met a Mr Rawes and his sister Miss Rawes (possibly Mrs—about 50) and a young redhaired niece of the same name. The man is an invalid with a bad cough. He is much of a humourist and from his constant censures of every thing and every body reminded me of Matthew Bramble.* Called on Mrs Malkin to take leave. Off from Cowbridge at 12 by the mail; obliged to go inside from want of outside room. A hot close day, but without rain. Reached Bristol at 6½...

Romilly went on to Bath, where he noted a new illuminated clock in the 'Cathedral' transept, a new and beautiful Early English church (St Michael's) and a new bridge being thrown over the river. Next day he returned to London.

NOTES

**16 July** Romilly (4 January 1838) refers to the Miss Nevilles, daughters of the Hon George Neville Grenville (1789-1854), Master of Magdalene College, whose country seat was in Somerset. They had six brothers, the two eldest, Ralph and William, born in 1817 and 1818 respectively. This may have been the family.[3]

William Crawshay (1788-1867), grandson of Richard who founded the Cyfarthfa Ironworks at Merthyr, built Cyfarthfa Castle (see note on 30 August 1854). It was not unusual for distinguished men to travel outside the mail—for one thing, it was less stuffy; but Crawshay could afford his own transport.

Mary Howitt (so spelt) (1799-1888), born a Quaker but a Roman Catholic after 1882, published *Seven Temptations* in 1834.[4]

Sir Nathaniel Wraxall (1751-1831), an amusing Bristol-born braggart, wrote *Posthumous Memoirs of his Own Time*, published—hence the title—in 1836.[5]

**17 July** 'What fruit had ye then &c': Romans 6, verse 21.

Coom Kiddy (Cwmcidy) was the Romilly's model farm. This detached part of Porthkerry parish once had its own chapelry, perhaps the ruined one mentioned in 1781.[6]

**19 July** August Heinrich Julius Lafontaine (1758-1831), not to be confused with the much earlier author of the *Fables*, was a German clergyman of French descent, who wrote numerous moralising novels.[7]

Mrs Sarah Austin, wife of the Professor of Jurisprudence at University College London, had published the previous year a translation of Prof Friedrich von Raumer's *England in 1835*.[8]

**20 July** Fonmon Castle, late Norman but much added to and domesticated, became part of the considerable estates of Col Philip Jones in 1658. He was a confidant of Oliver Cromwell, whose contemporary portrait adorned the hall. (Malkin confused him with Cromwell's brother-in-law, Col John Jones, who was hanged, drawn and quartered in 1660 for having signed Charles I's death warrant. Philip died in 1674.) Upstairs in the 1760s a long saloon or library was created, its rococo plasterwork in marked contrast with the house's plain exterior.[9]

The widowed Mrs Robert Jones (born Maria Antonia Swinburne) had two sons, Robert Oliver (1811-1886), 'the laird', older than Romilly thought, and Oliver, who became an admiral. They had two half-sisters, Louisa and Laura, by Mr Jones's first wife, and a younger sister, Rosa Antonia. Louisa and Laura must have been in their late twenties in 1836, so the teenage beauty was Rosa. She married John Montague Cholmeley of Easton in Lincolnshire (c1813-1860), Fellow of Magdalen College, Oxford, and bore him a daughter on 11 July 1840 at Lower Beeding, Sussex. The Cholmeleys were related by marriage to Jane Austen. Rosa reminds me of Elizabeth Bennet at Rosings: 'you give your opinion very decidedly for so young a person'.[10]

Mrs Jones's Methodism was nothing new at Fonmon. Robert Jones, her husband's grandfather, had been at Oxford with Charles Wesley and became in 1741 the first of the Welsh gentry to be converted to it. The Wesley brothers and Howel Harris, founder of Welsh Calvinistic Methodism, were welcome visitors at Fonmon, where Robert turned the dining room into a chapel. John Wesley recorded in his journal on 2 October 1741: 'We rode to Fonmon Castle. We found Mr. Jones' daughter [five-year-old Catherine] ill of the small-pox, but he could cheerfully leave her and all the rest in the hands of Him in whom he now believed'. She survived—but Mr Jones died next year.[11]

**21 July** Henry Stephen Olivier (1796-1866) of Potterne Manor House, Bedfordshire, married Mary, daughter of Rear Admiral Sir Richard Dacres, in 1823. He became a lieutenant colonel, so may have been the officer referred to here.[12]

For William Daniel Conybeare, his wife and their sons William and John, see note on 18 August 1834; for their son Charles, see note on 23 July below.

**23 July** Romilly inserted a note: 'Miss [Alison Allen] Marshall married to Mr Castendieck!!!'[13]

The 1844 diary has the address of a Miss Wilcox (Rose Cottage, Northam, Devon) written inside the front cover; similarly in the 1854 diary, where it is given as 4 Croft Terrace, Tenby.[14]

Charles Ranken Conybeare (c1821-1885), William Daniel's third son, became a Student (i.e. Fellow) and Tutor of Christ Church, Oxford.[15]

**25 July** Mrs Marcet (Edward Romilly's mother-in-law): see note on 25 August 1838.

Robert Francis Jenner of Wenvoe Castle (1802-1860) married Elizabeth Jenner-Fust and had fifteen children. Two boys died young. By 1836 the family was far from complete: Algernon Romilly Jenner, who married Alice Jones of Parc Glas (daughter of Anna Maria, née Eaton), was not born till 1845.[16]

For Wenvoe Castle, see note on 12 July 1830.

Major Downing was the humorous creation of a U.S. editor, Seba Smith (1792-1868). His 'letters' first appeared in 1830.[17]

**26 July** Moulton is near Porthkerry. An undefended settlement has been found here, underneath a Roman villa.[18]

**27 July** William Williams (1765-1847) had married Elizabeth, Mrs Malkin's sister, and was Headmaster of Cowbridge Grammar School.[19]

Charles Williams (1807-1877), his third son, was a Fellow of Jesus College, Oxford, and in 1857 became its Principal.[20]

Thomas E. Edmondes (1806-1892), Vicar of Cowbridge, married a sister of Charles Williams, and was the father of Archdeacon Charles Edmondes, Principal of St David's College, Lampeter, and of Archdeacon Frederick Edmondes of Llandaff.[21]

'coxcombial': foppish or vain.

Renn Dickson Hampden (1793-1868) had just been appointed Professor of Divinity at Oxford amid loud protests about his orthodoxy. A similar outcry attended his nomination to the see of Hereford in 1847 (he had applied for St Davids in 1840).[22]

**28 July** Matthew Bramble is a character in *The Expedition of Humphrey Clinker* by Tobias Smollett (1771).[23]


SOURCES

1 H. Williams, *Stage Coaches in Wales* (Barry, 1977), 109-11.

2 Bury, 101-3.

3 Bury, 137 and note 2. Burke's *Peerage* (1970 ed), 341, says Neville Grenville (he added 'Grenville' in 1825; his children dropped it) was also Dean of Windsor. Lodge's *Peerage* (1853 ed), 72-3, names five girls (born 1820-30). His brother Lord Braybrooke was hereditary Visitor of Magdalene and (says Bury, 238) the first editor of Pepys's *Diary*, one of Magdalene's treasures. Braybrooke's daughters, the eldest of the three aged fifteen at this time, also appear in the diaries: Bury & Pickles, 258. Another possibility lies with the children of William Nevill, 4th Earl of Abergavenny; as he had not yet succeeded his brother, his girls did not at this time bear the courtesy title Lady. Dr Pickles, who kindly supplied Lodge's *Peerage*, pointed out that the Abergavenny children were too young to be travelling unchaperoned, and that Romilly would probably have mentioned a companion. He thinks one of the Magdalene families the likeliest; Romilly knew them well. 'Nevils' may have been a slip.

4 S.A. Allibone, *A Critical Dictionary of English Literature and British and American Authors* (Philadelphia and London, 1900) [hereafter Allibone, *Authors*], 905-6; S.J. Kunitz and H. Haycraft, *British Authors of the Nineteenth Century* (New York, 1936) [hereafter Kunitz, *Authors*], 311-2 (with portrait).

5 Allibone, *Authors*, 2856-7; Kunitz, *Authors*, 673.

6 D. Moore (ed), *Barry The Centenary Book* (Barry, 1985) [hereafter Moore, *Barry*], 170; J.R. Guy (ed) *The Diocese of Llandaff in 1763 The Primary Visitation of Bishop Ewer* (Cardiff, 1991), 70, 72 (with further references; I owe this source to Canon Richard Fenwick).

7 *Nineteenth Century Short Title Catalogue Series I Phase I 1801-1815* vol 3 (Newcastle-upon-Tyne, 1985), 120; H. and M. Garland, *The Oxford Companion to German Literature* (Oxford, 1976), 503.

8 J.F. Kirk, *A Supplement to Allibone's Critical Dictionary of English Literature and British and American Authors* vol I (Philadelphia, 1900), 62.

9 C.J.O. Evans, *Glamorgan* (Cardiff, 1938), 152, 251; H. Thomas, *A History of Wales 1485-1660* (Cardiff, 1972), 235; A.G. Vesey, 'Colonel Philip Jones, 1618-74', *Trans. Cymmr.*, 1966, 337-9; H.M. Vaughan, *The South Wales Squires* (London, 1926), 60-1; B.H. Malkin, *The Scenery, Antiquities, and Biography, of South Wales* (London, 1804, reprinted 1970) [hereafter Malkin, *South Wales*], 131; J.B. Hilling, *The Historic Architecture of Wales* (Cardiff, 1976), 127-8, 137; plans and elevations in *Arch. Camb.*, vol VII 3rd series, 1861, opposite page 8.

10 G.T. Clark, *Limbus Patrum Morganiæ et Glamorganiæ* (London, 1886), 216; Burke, 1060; Foster, 249; Carmarthen Reference Library, *The Carmarthen Journal*, 24 July 1840. Jane Austen's mother's brother married a Cholmeley: W. and R.A. Austen-Leigh (D. Le Faye, rev), *Jane Austen A Family Record* (London, 1993), 301. Several portraits of Rosa's family have been reproduced and are publicly available, but if one of Rosa herself exists in private hands I have not been able to find it.

11 *D.W.B.*, 507; A.H. Williams (ed), *John Wesley in Wales 1739-1790* (Cardiff, 1971), xxii-iii, 8.

12 Venn, IV, 591.

13 C.U.L., Add 6839 (12 August 1859, where Romilly recorded her death), gives her first names.

14 C.U.L., Add 6823, 6833.

15 Foster, vol I, 287.

16 Burke, 1045.

17 *Enc. Brit.*, vol 20, 696.

18 Moore, *Barry*, 40.

19 Malkin, *South Wales*, v (foreword by T.J. Hopkins); *D.W.B.*, 1027-8; T. M. Rees, *Notable Welshmen 1700-1900* (Carnarvon, 1908), 219. Williams became Headmaster in 1788, Prebendary of Llandaff Cathedral in 1797 and D.D. (Oxon) in 1814.

20 *D.W.B.*, 1027-8. 1807 was the year of his christening, so he was most probably born then. Like Lord Bute, he was handicapped by very poor eyesight.

21 *D.W.B.*, 179.

22 O. Chadwick, *The Victorian Church* part I (London, 1966), 112-21, 241 note 2.

23 *Enc. Brit.*, vol 20, 702.

# 7   GRAND TOUR FROM BRISTOL

## 2—31 August 1837

So we come to Romilly's most extensive tour of Wales. This time he ventured back to Pembrokeshire, and stayed with his brother-in-law, Baugh Allen, at Cilrhiw. After more than a fortnight calling on relatives and friends and exploring the neighbourhood as far as Pembroke Dock and Laugharne, he set off with Baugh and his two Allen nephews for the north of Pembrokeshire and into Cardiganshire. Near Lampeter they parted company. Romilly took in Aberystwyth and Devils Bridge, and then made his way to Liverpool.

Accompanied by his young nephew George Romilly, he had left Cambridge on the last day of July, enjoying outside but dust-free seats on the Telegraph coach. It took seven and a half hours to reach Baugh's house at Dulwich in south London, roughly sixty miles away. Next morning it was again a ten o'clock start, but the weather had broken. George was put on a steamer for Herne Bay, with a paid inside seat on the Dover coach to follow. Romilly wrote some letters at the Athenaeum, dined at Simpson's and whiled away an hour playing billiards till a quarter past seven, when he left London on the Bristol mail with two dull men and a sharp, clever boy, who was going by himself all the way to Swansea.

The four days Romilly spent in Bristol before sailing to Tenby are worth including, for they are full of interest and colourful detail.

**Wednesday 2 August** Reached Bristol at ¼ to 8. Went immediately to Clifton and found the Tenby steamer had sailed ½ an hour. Ordered breakfast at the Cumberland Hotel, and took a boil at the Hot Well. Directly after breakfast drove to the Deanery. 'La!' says the coachman, 'the Dean* is dead and a nice little man he was'. 'I am heartily glad of it,' said I, 'for he has made way for a friend of mine, who though not a little man is yet a nice one'. At the Deanery I found Musgrave at breakfast, with Archdeacon Thorp* and Mr Tate* (the Canon of St Paul's). Musgrave received yesterday a letter from Lord Melbourne* offering him the see of Hereford (vacant by the death of Lord Grey's brother). I rejoice much at this appointment, and think Musgrave will make an excellent bishop. To the Cathedral* morning and afternoon. A most miserable wet day. About 4 it was tolerably fine, and Musgrave, Thorp and I walked to Clifton. Mr Tate (who had been making a visit a few miles off) joined us at dinner at 6.

**Thursday 3 August** Musgrave off to town at 7 to see Lord Melbourne. Another complete rainy day. To the Cathedral at 11. Wrote to George Allen at Kilrhew. Thorp hired a carriage and in spite of the dismal wet took Mr Tate and me out driving. He took us in the 1st place to a place called Compton, to see a Mr Shepherd, who had an excellent house here and some beautiful views of the Severn and the Welsh hills. In spite of the rain he took us into his grounds and showed us some of his best points of view. We

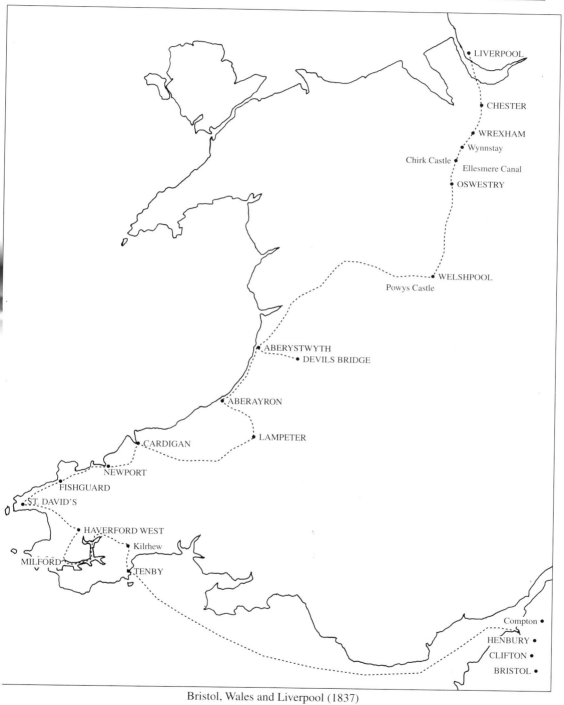

Bristol, Wales and Liverpool (1837)

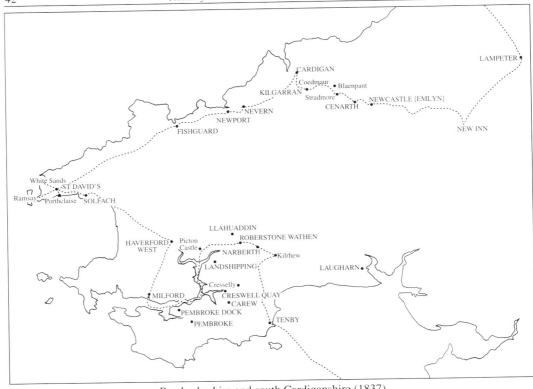

Pembrokeshire and south Cardiganshire (1837)

had however to draw a good deal on our imagination as the mist was heavy in the back ground. Mr Shepherd is a man of an active fidgetty mind and a feeble body; he is constantly employing himself cutting out fresh views and making improvements, and now that the plan is almost perfect he is sick to death of it and wishes to part with it. His wife and daughter joined us at lunch; they are very amiable people.

We next went to Henbury church.\* This and its churchyard are complete bijoux; there is indeed a fund of £200 a year for keeping it in repair, but independently of this, part of the population is very wealthy and they take a great pride in having handsome marble monuments and keeping up the whole plan with magnificence. The inside of the church is very striking from the handsome columns that support the nave and divide it from the aisles. Perhaps ornament has been too much studied in the inside, and the vases and hanging drapery look rather theatrical. The vestry is a separate building and is (like the chancel) furnished with Early English windows; it is very handsome. The churchyard is very striking from its having on part of 2 sides a high wall overgrown with ivy, in which monuments are interspersed. The church tower is also partly overgrown with ivy. The school is one of the boundaries of the churchyard and is in harmony with the church and the vestry. We went in with Mr Gray the Curate, and the Archdeacon made the boys read a chapter and examined them in it; they acquitted themselves very well. We next went to

Blaize Castle and left cards on Mr and Mrs Harford,* who were from home. We drove through the grounds, and were much delighted with the beauty and the views, and more particularly with a certain well-wooded glen which we crossed.

At dinner our party was reinforced by Dr Howell and Mr Bromby; the former is Thorp's physician and had been through the Peninsular War with [the] Duke of Wellington. He is an agreeable conversible man; he showed us the ring he wore, which bore this inscription, 'Margaret Howell mother of 36 children'. He himself was her 33rd. She married at 18 and died at 47. A large proportion of her children were twins. Mr Bromby has a school of 110 boys here. He is a very young A.M.* of St John's, and is prodigiously shy; among the few words he uttered he called Mr Tate 'doctor', for which the Canon good-humouredly reproved him. Mr Bromby also breakfasted with us, and then had a closeting with Mr Thorp to receive hints on the craft of pedagogues.

**Friday 4 August** A prodigious knocking at the Deanery at 3 this morning: it was by the policeman, who found the garden gate open. At 6 Mr Tate left us; he went to Cardiff by the steamer. Last night Mr Tate read a chapter in the Bible (viz, the 12th Romans), and Mr Archdeacon Thorp made an extempore prayer on it. He did it very well indeed, especially on the 10th verse, 'Be kindly affectioned one to another with brotherly love', because he knew the 2 men had quarrelled. This morning Thorp read the 27th of Proverbs; I did not like his prayer this morning as well as last night's. I should have said that on Wednesday Musgrave took me to the Institution* and wrote down my name, so that I may go there and read for a month. We also went on Wednesday to the Mayor's chapel,* which is a building far too narrow for its length. No expense has been spared on the interior; it is just fresh from the workmen's hands and is rather too ornamented. It is however a very handsome Gothic room with a flat cieling. There is here some good painted glass from Fonthill* brought by Beckford from Cologne.

Today (Friday) I went directly after breakfast to St Mary Redcliff. I found the transept very narrow, but it is (in spite of that) a noble building. At the altar are 3 indifferent pictures* by Hogarth. Today was a glorious sunny day and I went up to the top of the tower of St Mary Redcliffe and had a fine panoramic view of the city. I was in agreeable company, viz a gentleman and his daughter who had travelled a good deal abroad and spoke French and German well. I at 3 went with Thorp to the Cathedral and we dined tête à tête at ½ past 4. We then went to see the Blind Asylum* and Charity School* (for the Red Maids, so called because the girls wear red gowns); these buildings at top of Park St are by Rickman* and are a pretty specimen of Early English. After this we went to the Zoological,* which is in Clifton and commands a fine view; the show of animals is very indifferent. I was much amused by seeing an elephant in the principal walk taking his evening exercise; he had a keeper on each side of him, and all the people made way for him as respectfully as if he had been a king. His gait was very shuffling as might be expected from so unwieldly a beast, and at one time he excited some slight alarm by backing at the sudden barking of a dog. We met here a very pleasant friend of Thorp's (Mrs Morris), who was kind enough to send me in the course of the evening a letter of introduction to Col and Mrs Ferrier* at Tenby.

**Saturday 5 August** Breakfasted early and started by fly* for Clifton at ¼ to 8. Just as I was driving off up drove another fly containing the new Bishop of Hereford, who was just returned by the mail. About ¼ to 9 we moved off in a dirty Tenby steamer of 80 horse power named the *Palmerston*.* We had not got 100 yards before we were inveloped in steam, which escaped in a most unexpected manner; there was a slight explosion, and by and bye the engineer came to inform us that they had put on too great a pressure of steam and that something in the boiler had given way, that they must pump out all the water, repair the damage and endeavour to sail by the next tide. It was most happy for us that we escaped with so slight inconvenience from so great a danger, and we had every reason to be most thankful to God.

We all quitted the steamer and amused ourselves at our discretion. I took a hot bath, wandered about Clifton and played some billiards. When we met again at 5½ at dinner in the steamer some of my companions said that they had seen a man go over the iron wire at the St Vincent Rocks* in a basket. I should like very much to have seen this aerial transit. I heard that the fare is reduced from 5s to 2/6. There were but a few cabin passagers, an old Mr and Mrs Penney and their son (with whom I played billiards) and a little granddaughter (by another son), Edward Leach* (a redhaired cousin of Baugh's, who made love to Miss Liddiard unsuccessfully, and has just left his sick wife* at Gloster), a Mr Protheroe of Magdalene, whom I had met in Magdalene combination* [room], and 2 other gentlemen. We set off at 8 and I smoked one of Mr Leach's cigars. We had an hour's moonlight, which lasted us as long as we were in the Avon and had any scenery worth looking at. When it was pitchdark we had tea and talk till bed time or rather sofa time, as we had to lie down on certain black horse-hair sofas, where I slept very well.

**Sunday 6 August** Had a very calm and good passage of 11 hours; got up at 6 and reached Tenby pier a little after 7. The bay, and the islands and the cliffs overgrown with green and all that nature has done is very fine here, but the houses and all that man has

*Palmerston* landing passengers at St Catherine's Island, Tenby, 4 September 1828

done is ugly enough. There is not an attempt at architectural design, no two houses are alike in any thing except in having their walls and roofs whitewashed, and they seem to me placed on the heights in the most tasteless disorder possible. It was mortifying to find that our arrival 12 hours after our time created no excitement whatever in the calm phlegmatic Tenbyites; there was no crowd to welcome us and to ask a thousand questions, and not a syllable expressive of surprise was uttered by the few watermen who plied with boats.

I went to Mrs Faulkner's* hotel (the Castle) at Baugh's recommendation. The hostess was abed and had my letters in bed with her. I walked till 8 on the soft firm sands, which are quite delightful; she was still abed however. So I had breakfast and began writing to the women. At 9 the hostess sent me 2 letters from Baugh and George saying they would breakfast with me in a private lodging (the hotel being full), and while I was dressing there Baugh and George and Edward came and finding I had breakfasted went to Col Wedgwood's* and breakfasted there. They afterwards took me up at my hotel and we went to church together. The church is a fine large one with a nave and 2 aisles and a long flight of steps up to the altar; the interior of this church is very striking from its spaciousness—I should think it would hold 2000. A redfaced Mr Humphrey* (the Rector) read prayers tolerably well, and a redfaced Mr Mirehouse* (brother to the Common Serjeant) preached upon 'Salvation remaineth for the people of the Lord'.* It was extempore and far too long and very full of dull repetition, and his head scarcely appeared above the cushion, and he worked one arm like a pump handle, and he affected a tremulous voice and had the bad taste to talk about the sick and dying friends of many there who had come in the vain hope of being cured.

I called today on Archdeacon Musgrave* and saw him and wife and children; they wanted me to dine with them, but I could not. I ought to have called on Col Ferrier but forgot it till too late. After church Baugh and I and the boys walked into the caves of St Catherine's Island and on the southern sands till dinner time at 3 at Col Wedgwood's. We met here, besides our host and hostess (born Ann Tyler), our host's father (John Wedgwood the inventor* of the Wedgwood ware) and his sister Mrs Harry Wedgwood (born Jessy Wedgwood), who married her 1st cousin. After coffee the phaeton came to the door and Baugh drove me and his boys to Kilrhew, a distance of about 8 miles. The house is a small one and, like all the houses of the country that are not stone,* whitewashed. After tea Baugh asked me to read a chapter of Burton's* *Church History*; dull work it was and produced a most sleepy effect on my hearers. Found very agreeable letters from the women.

**Monday 7 August** Baugh went off early to Newcastle [Emlyn] (25 miles) to vote.* After breakfast, finished my yesterday's letter to the women, and then visited the stables (which are very neat and commodious) and went with George and Grim into the woods, and was much pleased with the walks and views Baugh has made here.* We then amused ourselves for an hour making a dam in the brook. As we were reading *Pickwick*\* (i.e. Grim reading loud and George and I listening) after lunch, Mr Allen* drove up and offered to take me with him to Cresselly. I told him that I was his brother's guest and did not know how Baugh would like my being kidnapped. He agreed to settle all that, wrote an explanatory note, took me into his phaeton and away we drove to Cresselly (about 7 miles) and arrived there about 4½. At 5½ we dined, a party of 6: viz Mr Allen and his sister Fanny and daughter Isabel and brother-in-law John Wedgwood and niece Mrs Harry Wedgwood; these last two I had met yesterday at Col Wedgwood's. After dinner we all took a walk into the woods, and saw a most beautiful sunset. After tea Miss Isabel gave us some music, to which we attended as little as people usually do to pianoforte playing.

**Tuesday 8 August** Cresselly* is a largish mansion of grey coloured stone, without any pretence to architectural beauty; it has 5 windows of a row and is 3 stories high. In the back there are bow windows commanding a very pretty view of an arm of the sea. I read prayers to the family and read a chapter of the Bible; it is the practice here to have morning prayers, but not evening. Mr Seymour joined us this morning (having been out on a fishing party yesterday). After breakfast I wrote a 3rd letter to the women. I then made a solitary excursion to Carew Castle at the distance of 2 miles; it is a most picturesque ruin. The castle was built in 1100; it was added to in the time of Henry 7th and was dismantled by Oliver Cromwell. I found here 2 different sets of artists making drawings. A lovely day. I then walked on to Carew church (½ a mile further). At dinner by the addition of Seymour we became a party of 7. Walk in the woods in the evening; and music and chat after tea.

Cresselly, with Seymour and Lady Catherine Allen, in about 1845

H.M. Steam Frigate *Gorgon* lying in Hamoaze, Plymouth

**Wednesday 9 August** Took a little walk before prayers; the practice here this lovely weather is also to walk after prayers for ½ an hour before breakfast, which is about 9¼. Today Mr Allen drove Mrs Harry Wedgwood, his sister Fanny and myself to Pembroke Dock &c. I sat behind with Fanny and enjoyed very much her talk about Wordsworth, Mackintosh* and Campbell.* Pembroke Dock is on an estuary 2 miles from the town at a place called Pater. All the buildings here are of stone and are in very handsome stile and on a grand scale; there are 600 people at work in the dock yard. We went over a large steamer (the *Gorgon**), which is to be launched in a month; her deck is near 200 feet long, her tonnage about 1100, and she is to mount I know not how many guns. We also went into a 60 gun frigate (the *Collingwood**), which is not got at all forward and the works in her are suspended. We saw here Capt Crombie,* who has the command of the dockyard and who did not join us till after we had seen every thing we wished to see. We then drove to Pembroke; I was much pleased with the splendid ivy-grown ruins of its castle. At dinner we were joined by Baugh and his boys and made now a party of 10. After dinner Baugh, George and Edward and I called on Mr and Mrs James Allen (the parents of Tom Allen); she is a Roman Catholic but not very strict. This house* (which is one mile from Cresselly) has a pretty view of the estuary. After tea, Mr Wedgwood, John and Baugh Allen and I plaid some whist.

**Thursday 10 August** Lessons with George and Edward till lunch. We then walked down through the woods to the ruins of Creswell Priory and to Creswell Quay; the views here are pleasing from the abundance of wood, and would have been much more so if it had not been low water. Our dinner party today was reduced to 9 by the departure of Mr Seymour to the Haverford raceball.* In the evening Baugh and George and Edward and I walked by a different path to Creswell Quay and returned through the woods. Creswell has a good spring of water; and I suppose this water was famous in the days of old as Creswell is said to be a corruption of 'Christ's well';* Cresselly they say is *Creswell-way*.* After tea, John and Baugh Allen, Mr Wedgwood and I plaid whist.

**Friday 11 August** Lessons to George and Edward. Mr Meares* rode over from Haverford West (10 miles to see me). He came at 10. I had rather a headache, so after the boys' lessons were over (at 1) I started for a solitary walk down to Creswell Quay and along the water. I contrived to take a wrong turn when near Carew and was going exactly in the wrong direction. I made enquiry at a cottage where I stood up for the rain and was there told the way to the 'great house'. The day had now turned out diluvial, and as I had no umbrella and walked for an hour in the pouring rain I got sufficiently wet. Home at 4; went to my room and read Johnsoniana* till dressing time. At dinner (besides Meares) we had Mr and Mrs James Allen; but (as Seymour was not returned) we were a party of 11 only. The rain ceased after dinner, but as it was very sloppy, we walked up and down before the house a little, Mr Allen in caloshes,* and I in a pair of the women's clogs. At eight I suffered for my gallantry by offering to take as my partner that agreeable conversible lady, of the Roman Catholic persuasion, called Mrs James Allen. Her playing was ludicrously bad; so lost both rubbers, and she then wisely declined playing any more. I then took Mr Wedgwood as my partner and won 2 rubbers and cleared 1s.

**Saturday 12 August** After breakfast took a walk with Miss Fanny and enjoyed her conversation very much. At 11 Baugh and his 2 boys and I took our departure for Kilrhew and arrived at 1. We did lessons. Then walked in Mr Allen's woods till dinner time. After dinner Mr Allen, George and I walked to see a talkative pleasant lady (Mrs Eaton) with a large family of daughters.* Saw but one of these ladies, and that by owl's light, so I could not appreciate her beauty. We paid a long visit and did not get home to tea till 9½. Found at Kilrhew pleasant letters from the women, which they had ingeniously pasted into a letter of the Duke of Northumberland's* thanking me for Graham's* sermon which I had sent him lately.

**Sunday 13 August** A very nasty wet day. I read prayers and preached to the household, consisting of our 4 selves and 5 servants. I had no sermon with me, but there was a volume of sermons printed by subscription of a living Welshman named Fenton* in the house. I selected one of these, and by altering and shortening it accommodated it to my audience. The cook (as George told me afterwards) was in tears the whole time though the sermon was by no means calculated to affect in that manner a person whose nerves were not peculiarly excitable. She had lost a son 2 months ago in a very shocking manner—in blasting the rocks he was killed by an explosion. The weather became dry above in the evening; so we walked from 6½ to 8½ in the high grounds to have a view of the sea. At night I read to the family and servants a chapter in the Testament (18 Matthew), which I expounded briefly and then read a short selection from the evening prayers. Wrote part of letter to the women.

**Monday 14 August** Finished my 4th letter to the women. After lessons George and I made an excursion on horseback through a very beautiful country to see the ruined castle of Llahuaddin.* We turned our horses loose and passed an hour in clambering up the towers and on the walls of this ruin; it was rather dangerous and slippery work. I sprained my back a little from my footing giving way. Our horses gave us a grand chase before they would let us catch them. Today Meares dined with us and seemed to be more at his ease a great deal than he was at Cresselly. The weather being delightful we took a good walk of 2 hours in the evening. We then had tea and talk till it was time for Meares to mount his horse and ride home the 11 miles. I had the luxury of a hot bath, as there is a very comfortable bath-room here at Kilrhew.

**Tuesday 15 August** Baugh and Edward and I drove over to Picton Castle, the seat of Sir Richard Philipps.* There is a fine view of the Haven from the park. The castle was a Norman one of the time of Rufus built soon after the Conquest (not dismantled by Cromwell). There are however no external appearances of antiquities. There is a very modern entrance in the Norman style, and one half of the whole building was built by the late tenant Lord Milford. Lady Philipps* is a very pretty youngish woman (of 26 or 27) with beautiful teeth. She has an abundance to say for herself and is very gay and good-humoured. She has no children and is absurdly fond of a huge hideous poodle dog that she has had shorn like a lion. A certain Lady Matthias* is a constant inmate of the house and is a patroness of the abominable dog. We had lunch here, and then walked to the conservatory and over the ground with Sir Richard Philipps and a 2nd cousin of Baugh's (a clergyman named Morgan*). We got home again to dinner about 6, and walked in the evening as usual. Chess with George.

**Wednesday 16 August** Received a letter from the new Bishop of Hereford offering me one of his chaplaincies;* wrote to him to accept it. As we were walking in the woods we were joined by Fanny Allen, Isabel and Seymour, who had rode over from Cresselly. They staid dinner with us; and when they had gone we walked to Kilrhew farm, where we had the amusement of seeing the gambols of 2 beautiful kittens. In the evening I read Mme Sévigné.*

**Thursday 17 August** Lessons as usual. At 3 o'clock Baugh drove me over to Cresselly; at the foot of the hill before Cresselly he met an old woman with a basket, to whom he kindly gave a lift. We found at Cresselly the people whom we had left, viz the Allen and Fanny, Isabel, Seymour, Mr Wedgwood, and Mrs Harry Wedgwood. After dinner we men folks sallied out and walked till dusk. After tea we played 6 rubbers; I won 4 of them with my usual luck.

**Friday 18 August** Baugh Allen and his brother off at 7½ to Pembroke to attend the funeral of their cousin Mr Leach.* I read prayers as usual to the rest of the family at 8. After breakfast I walked out into the woods with the *Edinburgh Review** and read that brilliant article of Macaulay's* on Montagu's* edition of Bacon; then had a tête à tête walk with Miss Fanny for an hour. At dinner Baugh and his brother made their appearance: their spirits were not in the slightest degree affected by the ceremony of the morning. At 7 Baugh and I drove back to Kilrhew and had tea with the lads at 9.

**Saturday 19 August** Baugh and the boys and I drove over to a place 11 miles off called Larn (but written Laugharn), I enacting coachman. This place (in Carmarthenshire) is picturesquely situated on the confluence of the Tâf with the sea; it of course has a castle ruined by Cromwell. Fish is vastly cheap here: Baugh bought 8 flounders for 6 pence. We called on a prettyish Mrs Watkins here and had wine and cake; her husband* is a nephew of Mr Watkins the owner of the great edition* of Shakspere that Baugh keeps at Dulwich. This pretty lady had a foolish trick of laughing at the end of every speech she made: 'Have you seen the castle? hi! hi! hi!' 'I hear there are to be races at Tenby, hi! hi! hi!' We returned to dinner at 6. Walk in the evening to Castle Merrion* to look towards the sea.

**Sunday 20 August** A fine day. We all went to church* at Narbeth. The service was very respectably performed by the Rector, Mr Lloyd.* He pronounced some words singularly: *Yea* he pronounced ye-a, and *Great* he called greet. His sermon was from Ps. 90 v. 8, 'Thou hast set our misdeeds before us'; his object was to show that we have no certain possession of any thing but our crimes, which we should carry away with us. So he said in a loud solemn voice, 'Have you any money?', and made a long pause. I was afraid somebody would answer him, 'La! no! not we'. He repeated his question in a louder voice, 'Have you any money?' Fortunately nobody took the word out of his mouth, so he went on to tell them that however much they might have they could take away none. After church we examined the ruins of the castle, which suffered much some months ago from lightening [sic]. We then called on Mrs and the Miss Eatons, who promised to come and drink tea with us tomorrow. Today I received very agreeable letters from the women and began writing my 5th letter to them. Gale of wind today and some heavy rain for 2 hours. We walked a little in the evening. At night I read and expounded a chapter in St Matthew and made a selection of different prayers and collects for family prayers, as I did last Sunday.

**Monday 21 August** After lessons I finished my letters to the women. To day it rained till 3 o'clock. Took a hot bath. At 6 arrived an excuse from the Eatons on account of the badness of the day. We however (as it was fine overhead) marched out for a walk, and in the walk called on the said Eatons. We drank tea at home at 9.

**Tuesday 22 August** Left Kilrhew in a very misty dull chill morning with Baugh and George and Edward in the phaeton, Baugh acting coachman, and I sitting bodkin* behind between the 2 boys to keep them from fighting, and hard work I had with the obstinacy of the one and the bullying of the other. We called at Roberstone Wathen on one of Baugh's cousins (named Leach*). Reached at 11½ Picton Ferry (10 miles) nearly opposite Landshipping. We got into a stout seaboat rowed by 5 men of the Revenue cutter *Skylark* (Capt Ðeans), because Baugh's friend Harry Leach* (of Tenby) could not send us the Custom House cutter (the *Endeavour*), which happened to be out of repair. The mist gradually turned into heavy rain and we got very wet. However, in spite of the haze I was struck with some of the reaches of Milford Haven and had an indistinct impression of how fine it must be in good weather. We past several brigs &c and their white sails were well relieved on the dark clouds. We arrived at 2½ at Milford in heavy rain and went to the Nelson Inn, where we had lunch. There was a billiard table in the house, so I played 3 games with Capt Deans and 2 with another man; lost them all 5.

At 6 we went to dine with Mr Harry Leach and met his wife*, and his sister Miss Leach* (who is an intimate friend of the Knoxes and had met Margaret at Mrs Fisher's,* and she said she had experienced much kindness from Margaret), and a medical Dr McMillan. Before dinner we saw for ½ an hour 3 grandchildren* (by a daughter in India, Mrs Elliott*): they were very pretty children, 2 girls of 8 and 10 and a boy of 6. Little George was a delightful fellow and I had a grand game of play with him. At tea we had the governess (Miss Wilks): she was neither handsome nor conversible, but she seemed an attentive listener. At 10 it was pitch dark and rained hard, so we were escorted to our inn by the footman bearing a lantern.

**Wednesday 23 August** Grim and I investigated the town before breakfast. It is a miserable dull place going to the dogs as fast as it can ever since the packets and the dock have been transferred to Pater. George 4th put in here in a storm when coming from Ireland. The event is commemorated by a tablet against the Custom House, and also by 2 brass imitations of shoes let into a step of the quay. The artist had an odd idea of royal feet, they are both *right.** We breakfasted at 9 with Mr Leach, and went off at 10 in a considerable haze. As the day advanced the weather improved, but the scenery all the way to Haverford West was not at all remarkable.

Haverfordwest: High Street and Castle Square in about 1850, the Courthouse extreme left

We stopped here a couple of hours to bait* the horses, and walked over the town with Baugh's solicitor (by name Evans, formerly of Jesus College, Cambridge). He took us over the Jail;* by the way, the view of this up and down town from its gate is very striking. He also exhibited to us the Courts (which are new and handsome), and St Mary's church. The interior of this is striking, the arches of the aisle are in good early stile; some of the capitals very grotesque—rabbit playing on fiddle, &c. We went into the belfry, which has 8 bells. The inscriptions on some of them amused us: 'Hope, faith and grace Dwell in this place'; 'For Harford West We'll ring our best' &c. We walked at top of the roof of the church. Our guide had been making me stoop down to observe the great steepness of the street, when on a sudden George laid hold of the battlement and sprung up as if he were going to leap over. Our guide was convinced he was going to destroy himself. He hid his eyes, screamed out and rushed back. I scolded George well for his folly. The streets of Haverford West are generally very narrow and precipitous and must be murder to horses in winter.

From Haverford West we drove to St David's. The approach to St Brides Bay and all the views of the sea and the coast are very fine. About the center* of the bay we drove for a few hundred yards along the fine firm sand of the sea, and had a noble seascape. We afterwards past through a very pretty neat village called Solfach (with a new National school,* and a very snug little harbour bosomed in rocks). Solfach is situated on a steep hill. We walked up this as usual, and asked leave to go into a house to see the seaview from the back window. We were very civilly received by a young lady, and saw a guitar lying on the ground—I should as soon have thought of seeing the Coran* on the table. She showed us 2 portraits of her brothers painted in Italy; it appeared that their father had been a sea captain, and that now they let lodgings. Their names were Cormac.* I heard afterwards that they were most respectable people, and that one daughter (from their reduced circumstances) was desirous of being schoolmistress at the village National school.

We reached St David's about 5. This city is a collection of a few most miserable hovels. We drove by the principal inn* not thinking it possible that it could be our resting place. Upon returning to it we found the hostess had never received our letter ordering dinner and beds; the post did not think it worth while to send to her, and she never sent to the office as she hardly ever had a letter. We ordered dinner in 2 hours and in the mean time walked down about a mile to the seaside, where the boys bathed and Baugh and I strolled about the rocks and enjoyed the grand sea view. This spot was called White Sands.* Upon reaching our inn at 7½ we found dinner ready; we dispatched it with all speed and went to drink tea with the Canon Residentiary, Mr Davis (Archdeacon of Brecon).*

He is a singular man and has the repute of sometimes being scarcely in his right mind. He sometimes keeps his room and even his bed for months, then he thinks he cannot possibly be too much in the open air and take too much exercise. He was in this latter state, and now gets up every morning before 4 and walks at least 10 miles before breakfast. He was about Baugh's standing at Westminster.* We found him very kind and very entertaining. Besides his brother-in-law and his wife and sister there were other 3 ladies staying in the house* with him. They were all sitting very formally against the wall round 3 sides of the room to receive us. After the 1st introduction we got on very well. The females were neither young nor handsome, but our hostess and one other were very conversible. She was a jolly roundabout redfaced dame, who took to patronising a diminutive terrier called Wasp. She was expatiating on the sweetness of his temper when she happened to touch him with her foot; he flew at her with great fury, upon which she said, 'Poor fellow! He cannot endure being kicked, he can bear anything but that'. Our host was an enthusiast and a humourist: he told some good stories, one about himself. He had to preach the assize sermon and chose for his text, 'Cain, where is thy brother Abel?' The judges were George Richards and Abel Moisey,* and the latter happened not to have come to church. He told us also that upon the charge to the grand jury being delivered, a working man remarked upon it that it was a very good discourse, but he thought the text an odd one and he didn't know where in the Bible it was, 'Gentlemen of the jury'.

**Thursday 24 August** Got up at 6; walk with Archdeacon Davis at 7. He took us to a fine point of view of the bay, the Cathedral,* Vaughan's chapel (part of the Cathedral), St Mary's chapel,* the ruins of the Bishop's Palace (which must have been a noble structure). The Cathedral is in so miserable a state that it is enough to make a lover of church buildings mad. Formerly St Davids was held in that degree of veneration that 2 pilgrimages to it were thought equal to one to Rome. 'Roma semel quantum bis est Menevia tantum'*—to which hexameter some good antipapist has tacked a pentameter: 'Mercedem similem reddet uterque locus'. At 8 we breakfasted with the Archdeacon and met the same party as yesterday. At 9½ we embarked with the Archdeacon in a very indifferent boat at the snug little harbour of Porthclaise. The Archdeacon took also with him his servant, John Fortunatus, bearing a large basket of provisions. John Fortunatus was picked up out at sea in a small boat near Java; he had been turned adrift. He looks like a New Zealander and is an excellent servant. There was a freshish gale, but we could not sail as the mast was out of order. We were rowed to the isle of Ramsay and here disembarked and walked across to the western extremity where several rocky

St Davids Cathedral: the nave looking east in 1836

islets* made a most beautiful scene. The Archdeacon pronounces it the most striking spot in the world; that is rather a bold dictum, but it is certainly very fine. When we re-embarked, a grand luncheon was spread before us; poor Grim was too qualmish to touch it. We were pulled across Ramsay Sound and landed at the ruins of St Justinian's chapel* (a miserable affair with a mud cottage tacked on to it) in a lovely lake-like-looking bay, and got to the Archdeacon's house at 2 after a delightful excursion.

We set off at 2½ in the Archdeacon's carriage drawn by 3 horses. The coachman whisked us over 16 miles of awful road up-hill down-dale in 1 hour 50 minutes to Fishguard. It was near here that 1400 Frenchmen under General Tate* landed in 1797; they had expected to find all the natives ready to support them. They surrendered next day to Lord Cawdor (with 500 militia &c), who gave them 24 hours to make up their mind to be cut to pieces or to lay down their arms. The situation of Fishguard is very picturesque. We here fell in with Mr Fenton* (clergyman of the place), son of the historian of Pembroke; he is an ingenious mechanic and has made improved locks and snuffers. He did the honors of the place to us. The hill out of Fishguard is one of the steepest and worst I ever saw: we all helped shove the carriage up.

We reached Newport at 6. We went to Mrs Lloyd's (at the Castle): she is a very neat, cleanly, talkative, healthy looking dame of 76, who broke her leg 4 years ago. Her daughter is a civil, tidy young woman. They are both especial favorites of Baugh's. He had written to order dinner. While it was setting on the table we walked up to the ruins of

Newport, Pembrokeshire, in about 1832

the castle, which are well situated on a hill. The dinner deserved all Baugh's previous praises: the things were admirable of their kind and deliciously cooked. The kind hostess (in spite of her lameness) came in every now and then to urge us to eat, recommending each dish in order for some peculiar excellence. The dinner consisted of trout (the best I ever ate), boiled leg of mutton and tongue (they are eaten together in Wales), roast chickens and ham, and 7 sorts of vegetables, viz, potat, french beans, cabbage, cauliflower, parsnips, cucumber and salled; pastry of course. Only 3s a head. After dinner by starlight we walked to the harbour; it was low water, and was nasty uncomfortable walking, as we had to flounder through several rills in the sand.

**Friday 25 August** Up at 6. Started on foot at ¼ to 7. We walked through the very pretty village of Nevern (on the river Nevern) 2 miles from Newport. Having to ascend a very long hill, we walked 2 more miles before the phaeton overtook us. We reached Cardigan (11 miles) at 9½ and breakfasted there. Good part of this stage was very wild like the Highlands, with bare mountains and rocks and the rough roads covered with loose stones. Cardigan is a small clean town (with a gaol) on the Tivy (famed for salmon). Grim and I perambulated the town together and saw its 5 arch bridge &c.

About 11½ while the tide was still lowish we set off in a boat* pulled by 3 lazy men. We ran aground 2 or 3 times from the shallowness of the water, and were at last obliged to anchor for an hour till the tide rose sufficiently. We had a small waterfall to ascend near the slate quarries: it seemed only a fall of a few inches, but it offered very stout resistance. We therefore were obliged to get out (all but the steersman) and pull away at the rope; we called in the assistance of 4 workmen from the slate quarry, and they and we pulled the boat for about ¼ [of] a mile over this and 2 other lesser waterfalls. We then got into the boat again and were pulled about 2 miles through most lovely scenery. The place is called Coedmaur (from the *great woods* on each side), and is singularly beautiful from the number of reaches of the river, which form so many lakes surrounded by wooded hills. At Kilgarran Castle we left the boat and ascended the hill upon which this castle is situated. The situation is a delightful one, but the ruins have very little interest. George however and Edward and I clambered up the tower and every accessible part.

Upon descending this hill we walked along the Tivy for about a mile to a bridge where the phaeton was waiting for us. We had the pleasing excitation during this very pretty walk of seeing a salmon caught* by 2 men paddling themselves down the stream in 2 coracles holding a net stretched across the stream. The coracle is a sort of wicker basket covered with a tarred blanket; it merely goes with the stream, and the fisherman carries it (as represented in the *Penny Magazine*) when going up the river. The fish weighed 9 lb and it was offered us for 4s. As we were getting into the phaeton the mail drove by and Baugh desired the coachman to order dinner and beds for us at Newcastle Emlyn.

When we were about 4 miles from Newcastle and Baugh was pointing out the beauty of certain grounds (called Stradmore*) belonging to Mr Brigstock*, a voice from an orchard greeted him. 'Baugh, I'm very glad to see you'. He pulled up, and presently Mr Brigstock came to us and insisted on our all going to his house (Blaenpant* or Black Grove) 4 miles off the road. Baugh consented if he would send a man and horse to

Newcastle to countermand the beds and dinner. This was complied with and we immediately got out and walked into the orchard, where Baugh forthwith kissed Mrs Buck.* We were introduced to Mrs Brigstock,* and Miss Sophia Buck* (a red-eyed white-haired fat albino sort of a girl); Mr Leach* (of Roberstone Wathen) was also here. 'Pray', said I to George, 'what relation of your father's is Mrs Buck that he kisses her?' 'O', said he, 'governor kisses a great many who are no relations at all'. So it was here: Mrs Buck is a sister of Mr Brigstock's, but no relation of Baugh's. We all went back (by means of 2 carriages and sundry horses) to Blaenpant, so called from its avenue of dark firs. We walked about the grounds and garden till 6 o'clock. It is a good large house the front of which is covered with ivy; considerable additions are making to it though the lord and lady of the mansion are childless. Mr Brigstock is a man of large landed property (7000 acres). He has an easy fortune of £3000 a year and he farms himself about 500 acres. He is a goodnatured farmerlike man. His wife is about 25, redhaired, not pretty; seems amiable. She is a daughter of Admiral Parry,* for whom she is in deep mourning. Besides ourselves and the orchard party we had at dinner Mr Augustus* (the host's brother), a clergyman who lives 4 miles off. After dinner we looked over a prettily illuminated copy of *La Nef des Fous.**

**Saturday 26 August** Left Mr Brigstock's at 10½. About 3 miles came to a beautiful place called Cennarth Bridge: here are 3 or 4 little water falls, which were well supplied with water, as there was some heavy rain last night and this morning. The road all the way to Newcastle [Emlyn] is pretty, having the Tivy on one side and woods on the other. A little beyond Newcastle saw an old woman with soap most carefully washing a huge swine! Reached New Inn* about 4: it is a miserable little hamlet 2 miles from Grim's farm of Lan.* We had some eggs and bacon for dinner, and I then took my leave of Baugh and the boys, and set off in a very shaky phaeton (drawn by one horse) for Lampeter (11 miles off). At the end of 5 miles the pin fastening one of the shafts was found missing. The driver walked back a few yards to look for it, and not finding it, tied on the shaft with cord. By and bye this would not do, and he produced a stout leather strap, which succeeded perfectly.

Reached Lampeter at 7¼; it is a poor miserable place of very few houses.* Called on Ollivant;* not at home—at his living. Went over the establishment* with the porter: found it very neat. The library of 7000 volumes has just had an important addition of 9000 left by Bishop Burgess; his widow has given £500 towards enlarging the library, which is now doing. The establishment is far from flourishing: it has a government annual grant of £400. It was chartered for 5 professors, but it can only afford to maintain 3, viz, the Principal (Llewellyn*), the Vice Principal (Ollivant) and the Welsh teacher (Rees* I think). They have never had more than 45 students though they have accommodation for 70. One great drawback is the smallness of their Church preferment, and another is that very few of the bishops will ordain the Lampeter students. All this I learned afterwards from Ollivant at Aberystwyth. Ollivant means to solicit the new Bishop of Hereford (Musgrave) to ordain them. Took a chaise at Lampeter and reached Aberayron at 10; tea and then to bed.

**Sunday 27 August** Walk on the pier before breakfast. This little town has been increased by several new houses and a chapel. Directly after breakfast in a chaise to Aberystwyth, 15 miles. Arrived at 11½; went to the Belle Vue,* which is charmingly situated opposite the sea. They were so full that they could not take me in to sleep but billeted me on a lodging house called Cambridge House. I walked on the shore and climbed the hill bounding the town to the north. Just before dinner had a hot bath. At 6 went to church. It is a new building* without tower or spire. It is built in the form of a cross and is very capacious. I hear it is a difficult church to preach in, more particularly in winter and stormy weather as it is close to the sea and the noise of the wind and waves is too much for ordinary lungs. It is well accommodated with free seats. A stranger, Mr Digby,* with a red face 2 feet long read prayers very indifferently. Mr Hughes* (the Vicar) preached a powerful evangelical sermon on Isaiah 58.1: 'Lift up your voice as a trumpet'. His object was to show how utterly wicked we were. He exerted himself very much and though a stoutlooking man seemed a good deal exhausted. He has told Ollivant that without he sends him an efficient curate the labor will soon kill him. After the service the organist played us out with a chorus of Handel's, and amused him self by showing off the instrument for ½ an hour. In the evening wrote my 6th letter to the women.

**Monday 28 August** Directly after breakfast set off in company with one of the visitors at the Belle Vue in a one horse phaeton to the Devils Bridge. As we were setting off our driver met the Duke of Newcastle's* gamekeeper, so we inquired if strangers were admitted to Hafod,* and he told us that they were not in consequence of the recent intrusion of some visitors into the house without leave. Of course the Duke of Newcastle of all men 'may do what he will with his own', but this was very annoying to an innocent traveller like myself. The day was beautiful and I was much delighted with the waterfall at the Devils Bridge (11 miles from Aberystwyth). The bridge itself is not much but the waterfall is really beautiful, and we saw it to great advantage as the sun shone most brilliantly and the cascade was very full of water from the recent heavy rains. This was almost the only waterfall I ever saw without feeling disappointed. My companion and myself past 2 hours rambling about this beautiful spot. There were a great number of visitors and with true English feeling several had brought provisions. I was invited to share one of the picnic parties but declined. The river is called the Mynach (or Monk), and just opposite to this fall is a small but pretty one of the Rheidol, the river which runs into Aberystwyth through a charming valley.

We returned home by the other side of the valley by certain peatbogs and leadmines,* a route of 14 miles and not so picturesque as our outward bound one. Dined at my inn at Aberystwyth at 6. Then walked out on the beach and was amused by the eagerness with which several of the ladies were rummaging among the shingle to see if they could find any agate or other hard polishable stone.* For my part I had neither patience nor judgment for such a search and therefore went to a lapidary's and bought a very pretty wafer-seal. When I returned to tea at 9 I found Ollivant in the coffee room and talked with him till bedtime. He told me that my host at St David's (Archdeacon Davis) was not always (if indeed ever) quite in his right mind. Sometimes he has fits of keeping his room and lying abed for months; at others (as when I saw him) of walking for very many hours. Sometime ago he gave Ollivant a draft of £1000 for Lampeter College, which Ollivant has carefully locked up and intends returning to the wife. At the Belle Vue the harper came every day at 1 and played incessantly[?] till 10 at night.

**Tuesday 29 August** Took a hotbath; walked for 3 hours on the beach. This morning at breakfast time Ollivant brought his 2 eldest children, a girl of 5 and a nice little boy of 3, to see me. He drove them and their 2 maids off in his phaeton to Lampeter, where there is to be an examination for next Sunday's ordination in the chapel. Bought wittles* &c as presents to the women. Played billiards at the Assembly Rooms* for an hour with a person who was a good match: we played 5 games and I won 3. Wrote up the arrears of my journal.

Today there were grand doings 10 miles off at Aberdyfy, viz a boat race (at which the Aberystwyth boat *Victoria* won), pony and donkey-races, the classical sports of climbing greasy poles and catching pigs with soaped tails and jumping in sacks, and the day's amusements wound up with a ball. I had no inclination to go over.

**Wednesday 30 August** Left Aberystwyth at 8 by the Queen of Trumps coach, engaging to deposit me at Liverpool tomorrow at 2, sleeping on the road (at Welchpool). By the way, Aberystwyth should be called Aberrheidol* as that is the river which one sees; the Ystwyth also runs here into the sea, but one sees nothing of it. My companions inside were an old lady and her daughter, who has been 5 weeks at Aberystwyth for health. The joy of the younger (about 25) amused me very much; she turned to me and said, 'Dear me, I am so glad to be going home; I can hardly contain myself for joy'. The scenery of the Dyfy was rather pleasing, but otherwise nothing worth recording. Reached Welsh Pool (about 65 miles) at 4. Here, I and a lad (Crompton) of 14 stopped. We dined tête à tête off venison and salmon and then walked to Powys Castle, the seat of Lord Clive;* it is a deer park and is really beautiful, but the castle is of red stone and is worth little. It was anciently called Pool Castle and sometimes Castle Coch. The evening turned out diluvial. I wrote a letter to Baugh this evening. This lad Crompton was a talkative good humoured chap passionately fond of riding.

**Thursday 31 August** Got up at 5½ to start at 6. The coach however did not move off till 7. We went at a prodigious rate. We breakfasted at Oswestry at 8½. Parted from young Crompton at Wrexham. Today passed through a land of collieries, at Chirk &c. Near Chirk saw 10 arches of the aqueduct of Ellesmere Canal.* Two miles beyond Chirk Castle one of the most beautiful views I have seen on this tour: the castle of Wynnstay* (Sir W.W. Wynn's* place) in a wood on rising ground with its flag flying, a long line of the aqueduct, &c &c. On entering Chester I was much struck with the beauty and magnificence of a new lodge of Lord Westminster's,* which is nearly finished. Reached Woodside (opposite Liverpool) at 2. This is a thriving suburb, and the entrance to the steamer quay is got up in grand stile. Dined in Liverpool at I know not what hotel. Reached the railroad station at 4; the skreen is superb with grand columns &c. Started at 4½ in what is called a mixt train*: it had 5 carriages each holding 18 people very loosely, might have held 24. In one carriage the fare was 21s, in the other 4 (which had no cushions) 14s; as my money was running low I went in the cheap conveyance. The distance from Liverpool to Birmingham is 97¼ miles. We arrived at Birmingham at 10 minutes to 11; we ought to have arrived at 10, but not finding water at one of our stations we had (to my amusement and to the dismay and anger of many) to travel back 4 miles to water...

Romilly was back in Cambridge on 2 September. In the second week in November he wrote to the Bishop of Llandaff resigning* his living at Porthkerry.

## NOTES

**2 August** Henry Beeke (1751-1837), Dean since 1814 and an expert on income tax, had died on 9 March and been replaced by Thomas Musgrave.[1]

Thomas Thorp had succeeded Romilly as Senior Dean of Trinity; in 1836, while remaining Tutor there, he had become Archdeacon and Chancellor of Bristol. A High Churchman, he agreed (in 1839) to be the first President of the Cambridge Camden Society, better known under its later name of the Ecclesiological Society, the architectural counterpart to the Oxford Tractarians. It dogmatically encouraged narrow principles of medieval church design. Though suspended in the 1860s, its influence on church restoration and lay-out has been immense, lasting and in some ways disastrous.[2]

James Tate (1771-1843) was Prebendary of Consumpta per Mare in St Paul's Cathedral from 1833; he died at Clifton.[3]

Lord Melbourne, the Prime Minister, was facing an election caused by the death of William IV on 20 June; he narrowly won.

Bristol Cathedral then lacked its Victorian nave and western towers.

**3 August** Henbury parish church, striking now with its tall nave arcade and brass chandeliers, had been altered between 1830 and 1836, Rickman being one of the architects. G.E. Street was to transform it again in 1876-8, rebuilding the chancel and porches. One of the monuments is attributed to Grinling Gibbons. It is surprising that Romilly does not mention the tombstones of Scipio Africanus (1702-1720), negro servant of the Earl of Suffolk. They caught my eye as I walked through the churchyard.[4]

The Harfords were Bristol bankers. They bought the Peterwell estate at Lampeter in 1819 and provided a site for St David's College.[5]

'A.M.': Master of Arts (Artium Magister). Cambridge University abbreviates many of its degrees (such as Litt.D. and Mus.B.) in the opposite way to Oxford, but 'A.M.' was used by both at this time.

**4 August** The Bristol Philosophical and Literary Institution, founded in 1822, was housed in a building (now Freemasons' Hall) by C.R. Cockerell, at the bottom of Park Street.[6]

The Mayor's (since 1899 the Lord Mayor's) chapel beside College Green belonged to Gaunt's Hospital until the city bought it after the dissolution. In 1721 it became, uniquely, the corporation's official place of worship.[7]

Fonthill Abbey was an extraordinary gothick erection designed by James Wyatt and begun in 1796. It housed Edward Gibbon's library, which Beckford had also bought. The tower, variously put at 260 and 278 feet high, collapsed soon after 1822, and the rest of the building was pulled down.[8]

Hogarth's huge paintings covered 750 square feet on three sides of the present ambulatory. When the wall blocking the eastern arch was taken down in the 1850s, the pictures were removed; they now hang in the tourist information centre in St Nicholas's church.[9]

The Asylum and School of Industry for the Blind, instituted in 1793, had moved from a site near the Royal Infirmary to Queen's Road. Rickman's buildings (1834) have been replaced by those of the University and the city's Museum and Art Gallery.[10]

The Red Maids' School had been founded in 1634 under the will of John Whitsun of Bristol, originally as a hospital for 'forty poor women children, daughters of Burgesses deceased and decayed', who were to be 'apparelled in red cloth', a uniform which the girls still wear, in modernised form; on special occasions they add a traditional tippet, apron and bonnet. Housed at College Green at this time, the school had planned to move to new premises near the Asylum, but the design (1834, not by Rickman) was thought inappropriate. Bishop Monk bought the building for a college of his own. The Red Maids are now at Westbury-on-Trym.[11]

Thomas Rickman (1776-1841), doctor turned architect, coined the terms Early English, Decorated and Perpendicular to describe the phases of English gothic architecture.[12]

Romilly was a very early visitor to the Zoological Gardens at Clifton; they were opened in 1836. 'The gardens are laid out with fine taste', observed a local directory in 1880, 'and are very attractive. They contain a choice collection of beasts, birds and reptiles, also a marine aquarium'.[13]

Col Charles Ferrier was living at the Norton, Tenby, in 1850.[14]

**5 August** A fly was a light, covered carriage, drawn by one horse (originally by a man, like a rickshaw), and sometimes let out on hire. The word was also applied to a fast stage-coach.

The *Palmerston*, 115 tons (eventually 170), was one of the first sea-going paddle steamers to be built in Bristol (in 1822). Intended for the Dublin run, she became one of the Bristol General Steam Navigation Company's vessels plying between her home port, Swansea and Tenby. The Tenby trip in summertime usually took twelve hours. The fare was advertised in 1835 as £1 2s 6d; even steerage class cost a great deal more than Romilly's five shillings or half a crown.[15]

Thomas Jenkins of Llandeilo visited St Vincent Rocks on 25 July 1841 to see the piers for Brunel's new Clifton suspension bridge. 'There is now an iron bar 3" diameter and 800ft. long stretched across with a basket sliding by ropes along it. The distance between the piers is 630ft.'[16]

Edward Leach (1802-1855), a solicitor, and son of Abraham Leach of Corston (the late Lady Tyler's brother), married Elizabeth Thomas, widow of Henry Parry.[17]

'combination room': the Cambridge name for a common room.

**6 August** Mary Faulkner kept a boarding house in the High Street in 1850.[18]

Col Thomas Wedgwood was living at St Mary's Hill in 1850.[19]

John Hunter Humphreys LL.D. had been Rector of Tenby since 1831.[20]

John Mirehouse of Brownslade and Angle, Common Serjeant of London, had two brothers: Thomas Henry (1790-1867), a Lincolnshire clergyman, and his twin, William Squire (1790-1864), also a clergyman and, since he was a Pembrokeshire J.P., probably the one Romilly heard. His text appears to have been Psalm 3, verse 8.[21]

Musgrave was Charles, Archdeacon of Craven, younger brother of Romilly's friend Thomas. He was a year behind Romilly at Trinity, tenth wrangler and sometime Fellow.[22]

John Wedgwood was in fact a banker. The inventor was his father, Josiah.

Cilrhiw is built of rubble; Romilly meant the walls were not ashlar.

Edward Burton (1794-1836), Regius Professor of Divinity at Oxford before Hampden, published two volumes of *Lectures on Ecclesiastical History*.[23]

**7 August** Property in Carmarthenshire qualified Baugh to vote in the county election (see note on 26 August).

A friend wrote to Baugh at Cilrhiw in 1841, urging him to go on improving his château, verges and boskets: 'your wood is perfection, and wants only a few more openings, and a walk beside the streamlet', adding, 'if you will pay me ten shillings a week, and find me a pretty Welsh soubrette to cook for me, I will come and execute my plans'.[24]

*The Posthumous Papers of the Pickwick Club* by Charles Dickens were issued in twenty weekly parts, each costing a shilling. The first came out on 31 March 1836. The June number in 1837 did not appear because Dickens's sister-in-law died suddenly.[25]

Mr Allen: John Hensleigh, Baugh's elder brother.

**8 August** Cresselly had been rebuilt on higher ground by Baugh's dark and moody father, John Bartlett Allen. The present bay-windowed wings were built in 1870. Elisabeth Inglis-Jones called it a 'spacious, uncompromisingly plain grey stone house', and quoted Fenton's observation that it was 'in the midst of a colliery'. Coal provided some of J.B. Allen's wealth, and, indirectly, his second wife. Romilly made a very crude sketch of Cresselly in his diary (see page xxviii).[26]

**9 August** Mackintosh: Sir James, Catherine Allen's husband.

Campbell was the Scottish poet Thomas Campbell (1777-1844).

H.M.S. *Gorgon* was launched on 31 August: 'the first true fighting steamship', of 1,111 tons, 178 feet long and costing £54,306. Laid down as a 32-gun frigate but later rated as a paddle sloop, with a change of armament, her guns bombarded Acre in 1840. In 1858 she tried to lay an Atlantic telegraph cable.[27]

The *Collingwood*, in fact an 80-gun third rate launched on 17 August 1841, was not much longer than the *Gorgon*, but wider in the beam and more than twice the tonnage. She served as a flagship in the Pacific, and was later fitted for steam and screw propulsion.[28]

Capt William Pryce Cumby C.B. was Captain Superintendent from March 1837 till his death on 27 September. He served at Trafalgar as First Lieutenant in H.M.S. *Bellerophon*—the ship to which Napoleon surrendered ten years later—and took over command when her captain died in the battle; indeed, he saved the ship by throwing overboard a smouldering enemy grenade.[29]

Mr and Mrs James Allen lived at Freestone Hall, near Cresselly.

**10 August** Haverfordwest was the chief centre for racing in south-west Wales. The races were first held in 1726, on Portfield Common. Balls rounded off the evening.[30]

Cresswell, from cress growing round the spring, once had a chapel which as early as 1390 led some to call it Christ's Well. Cresselly, however, may be from the Welsh *croes*, cross, and someone named Eli or Heli.[31]

**11 August** Samuel Owen Meares was at Trinity in 1828 and ordained in 1833. After curacies at Rudbuxton and Holton he became (see 5 August 1840) Perpetual Curate of Uzmaston and also (from 1856) of St Martin's, Haverfordwest.

'Johnsoniana': writings by, or about, Dr Samuel Johnson (1709-1784).

'caloshes': galoshes or waterproof overshoes—a sensible fashion worth reviving.

**12 August** Mrs Eaton and her daughters: of Parc Glas (see the Introduction).

Hugh Percy, 3rd Duke of Northumberland, became High Steward of Cambridge University in 1834 and Chancellor in 1840.[33]

John Graham, Master of Christ's College, was talked of as a possible Dean. When Peacock accepted the Deanery of Ely in 1839 (Lamb of Bristol having been offered it), Professor Whewell of Trinity produced a new scale of notation: denary, Peacock; undenary, Graham; duodenary, Lamb. In 1848 Graham became Bishop of Chester.[34]

**13 August** Fenton the sermon writer would appear to be Samuel, Vicar of Fishguard, whom Romilly met on 24 August. He was son of Richard Fenton, whose published travels round Pembrokeshire are a valuable historical source. It apparently did not occur to Romilly to compose a sermon of his own.[35]

**14 August** Llahuaddin (Llanhuadain or Llawhaden) Castle was once a seat of the Bishops of St Davids.

**15 August** Richard Philipps, Lord Milford, died childless in 1823. His cousin Richard Bulkeley Phillipps Grant succeeded to the estate of over 20,000 acres (but not to the original baronetcy or to the barony), and took the surname Philipps. He was himself created Lord Milford in 1847. The first Lady Philipps was born Eliza Gordon.[36]

Lady Matthias may have been the widow of Sir Henry Mathias of Fernhill; she died in 1848 aged eighty-three.[37]

Was Morgan the Vicar of Talgarth (see note on 24 July 1840)?

**16 August** Musgrave seems to have appointed Romilly to be an examining chaplain, that is, one who examined candidates for holy orders, not a domestic chaplain; or perhaps the post was purely honorary.

Marie de Rabutin-Chantal (1626-1696), Marquise de Sévigné, was granddaughter of a saint and mother of a sensationally beautiful daughter, Françoise, Comtesse de Grignan, to whom she wrote letters as brilliant as her conversation.[38]

**18 August** John Leach (1764-1837), dead since 11 August, was the younger son of Abraham Leach and Baugh Allen's Aunt Margaret.[39]

Basil Montagu (1770-1851), despite a superficial knowledge of philosophy, had edited the works of Francis Bacon in sixteen volumes; the last appeared in 1837. Macaulay (who had held a Trinity fellowship with Romilly till 1831) was out in India at this time; history had not yet replaced politics as his chief occupation. Though he himself has been called entirely uncritical in historical method, he protested at Montagu's shortcomings in the July issue of the *Edinburgh Review*. This was a Whiggish quarterly which appeared between 1802 and 1929.[40]

**19 August** Apparently Lloyd Watkins lived at Hurst House just outside Laugharne, and was related to the family at Pennoyre (see 30 August 1854).[41]

John Boydell (1719-1804) of Hawarden moved to London (where he became Lord Mayor) and published an edition of Shakespeare in nine volumes, illustrating it with a sumptuous book of engravings chosen from over a hundred pictures which he had commissioned from leading artists.[42]

Castle Meherin, variously spelt, is the summit south of Cilrhiw.[43]

**20 August** Narberth church had been cruciform till the chancel was widened in 1829 and extended northwards. Fifty years later, Thomas Graham Jackson, noted for 'the elegance of his ornament and the ineptitude of his planning', rebuilt all but the tower and north wall as a longer church with a wide nave and cramped chancel.[44]

William Lloyd, a Carmarthenshire man then aged about forty-nine, had been Rector of Narberth since 1826; he held the living till 1863.[45]

**22 August** 'bodkin': squeezed in between.

For Mr Leach of Robeston Wathen, see note on 25 August.

Captain Henry Leach (1770-1848) was from 1806 till 1842 Collector of Customs at Milford Haven. The late Lady Tyler was his second cousin.[46]

The *Endeavour* was built in Rye in 1823, and sold by auction by H.M. Customs and registered at Milford twenty years later, at which time she was recorded as being of nearly twenty-seven tons burthen, a little under forty-three feet long and nearly fifteen in the beam, clinch-built (that is, clinker, with overlapping planks), with a square stern, single mast and deck and a running bowsprit but no figurehead. Her registration was transferred to Bristol in 1849. Such cutters—and *Skylark* was doubtless similar—usually carried up to ten long nine-pounder guns and were designed for speed, to prevent smuggling. Two Revenue cutters of 122 tons, *Racer* and *Sprightly*, were built at Pater by 1818, and two more were on order.[47]

Harry Leach's wife was Mary Brand Jones of Brawdy (1771-1849). Their eldest daughter, Thomasina, married George Lettsom Elliot (1797-1871), a judge in India, and gave him four children; Romilly did not meet the youngest girl. Miss Leach, Harry's sister, was Elizabeth (1772-1840). They were both second cousins of Lady Tyler.[48]

Mrs Fisher may have been the wife of Thomas Fisher the Cambridge banker.[49]

**23 August** George IV landed (13 September 1821) on the steps by the Customs House, now the Museum. The plaque has been moved to the Hakin bridge, and the brass shoes have disappeared.[50]

'bait': give rest for food.

If Romilly meant the town's Jail, it was on St Thomas's Green; the county Jail was in the Castle.[51]

'the center of the bay': Newgale.

A National school was one supported by the National Society for the Education of the Poor in the Principles of the Established Church—that is, a Church of England rather than a Nonconformist school.

'the Coran': the Koran or Qur'an, the holy book of Islam.

Moses Cormack lived on the main road, in Portland Square. His daughters, Mary and Hephzibah, were then in their late twenties; they died in 1840 and 1850 respectively.[52]

The only inn at St David's mentioned in a guide-book two years before this was the Black Lion. The Twr-y-Felin was still the original windmill (1806), which ceased working in 1904. Grove House was not converted into an hotel till just before 1870. The following year, Kilvert had been warned that the inns here were 'dirty and uncomfortable', so he stayed at a private house.[53]

White Sands, now written as one word, was the beach where Kilvert left his notebook; 'I found it happily for it was full of people's names and notes and private matters'.[54]

Richard Davies, a handsome man then aged about sixty, was Vicar of Brecon, and, from 1805 to 1859, Archdeacon of Brecon. (He also served as a major in the militia.) Since 1665, the four Archdeacons in the diocese had been inhibited from carrying out archidiaconal visitations—no help to a Bishop whose diocese stretched across the English border and whose duties often kept him in London.[55]

'Westminster': the public school, whose boys were entitled to three annual scholarships at Trinity. Baugh's son George was Westminster scholar in 1839, the only one elected that year.[56]

Davies presumably stayed in the predecessor of Brecon House, in the Cathedral Close. The site had been a perquisite of the Archdeacons of Brecon since 1278. William Walter, Archdeacon from 1504, had built a house with a large dining hall and a porch decorated with heraldry, set in a courtyard with a covered gateway. It survived till well after Romilly's visit. (The present Canonry next door was then the Chancellor's house, erected by Chancellor William Stradling between 1511 and 1539 but rebuilt c1846.)[57]

Abel Moysey was a Somerset man, M.P. for Bath, Deputy Remembrancer of the Exchequer and, in 1777, a Welsh judge. He died in 1831.[58]

**24 August** The Cathedral still had its much-buttressed west front by Nash. The nave was bare inside except for some stalls and a lofty pulpit; the walls had recently had the 17th-century whitewash removed (under Archdeacon Davies). No organ stood on the screen; to strengthen the tower, the west and south arches of the crossing had long ago been largely walled up, and the aisles of the presbytery and most of the eastern chapels were in ruins.[59]

St Mary's chapel belonged to the College founded here between 1364 and 1379 by Bishop Adam Houghton, with the support of John of Gaunt, Duke of Lancaster, and his wife, for a Master, seven priests and two choristers. The College was dissolved in 1549, and one explanation for the royal stall at St Davids is that the Master had previously held this Cursal prebend. However, the last Master was Prebendary of Caerfai. The chapel, nearly seventy feet long, has been restored as a hall.[60]

'It was esteem'd as meritorious to visit St. David's twice, as to visit Rome once' and 'It is as meritorious to visit one, as the other' (translation by Browne Willis's correspondent 'M.N.', who had 'reddit' for 'reddet'; literally, 'Each place brings [or, will bring] the same reward').[61]

The rocky islets are the Bishops and Clerks.

Nicholas Roberts, Vicar of Llanddewi Velfrey, writing to Edward Lhwyd at Oxford in 1693, mentioned St Justinian's chapel, 'whereof now are to be seen only ye walls, battlements & Tower, & some of ye yard wall'. Charles Norris's engraving (1811) shows what appears to be a lean-to at the end of the chapel nearest the road, extending beyond the north wall. Was this the mud cottage?[62]

William Tate was an American soldier given command of the smallest part of a three-pronged French attack. The first two forces had already failed when Tate set sail for Bristol with four ships, ending up (near his alternative destination) between Fishguard and Strumble Head.[63]

Samuel Fenton was Vicar of Fishguard from 1825 to 1851 (see note on 13 August).[64]

**25 August** Perhaps Malkin put the idea of the river trip into Romilly's head: 'there is ... a very pleasant excursion by water, from Cardigan to Kilgerran'.[65]

Cilgerran was one of the four villages on the Teifi (Cenarth was another) where the local fishermen had a monopoly of their stretch of water, with elaborate unwritten rules—one of which was that August was a close season for salmon fishing.[66]

The *Penny Magazine* was the brain child of Charles Knight (1791-1873), publisher to the Society for the Diffusion of Useful Knowledge, which had been founded (by Dr Roget amongst others) to provide affordable books for the working classes. By the end of its first year, 1832, it was selling two hundred thousand copies. It lasted till 1845.[67]

Stradmore was on a bend of the Teifi below Cenarth, about one and a half miles south of Blaenpant. The house was demolished a few years after Romilly's visit.[68]

Blaenpant had a mid-eighteenth-century core and delightful gardens. The later extensions to the mansion are in ruins. The name means the upper end of a hollow or valley—nothing to do with dark firs.[69]

William Owen Brigstocke (1784-1861) married twice but had no children; his wedding to Maria Webley-Parry was in 1835. Mrs Buck was his sister Sophia (1788-1871), widow of a Yorkshireman. Young Sophia would be their daughter—as they were married in 1812, probably not very young. Another sister, Elizabeth (1800-1861), had married Henry Leach (1794-1864), son of Abraham Leach of Corston, Lady Tyler's brother and Baugh's first cousin. Henry lived at Robeston Wathen; Romilly had called on him there on 22 August. Maria's father, William Webley-Parry, had been promoted Rear Admiral of the White on 10 January, so he had not lived long to enjoy it. Augustus (1792-1852) was Vicar of Cenarth (and his elder brother John, Rector of Burton).[70]

*La Nef des Fous* (*Das Narrenschiff*) was a popular allegorical poem by Sebastian Brant of Alsace (1458?-1521), published in 1494 with woodcuts thought to be by Albrecht Dürer. It was adapted as *The Shyp of Folys of the Worlde* by Alexander Barclay in 1509 and translated into French as *La grand nef des fols du monde* by J. Drouyn in 1579. *The Ship of Fools* is the common English title.[71]

**26 August** New Inn, on the Carmarthen-Lampeter road, is not on any direct route from Newcastle Emlyn to Lampeter. Romilly made a detour to allow Grim to go to his farm. In fact Lan (in Llanfihangel-ar-Arth) belonged to Grim's father: the copyhold qualified Baugh to vote on 7 August. He was descended from John Lewis of Lan through John Bartlett Allen's first wife, Elizabeth Hensleigh.[72]

How small Lampeter was in 1822 can be judged from the inscription on the College's foundation stone, which calls it St David's College 'near Lampeter'.[73]

Alfred Ollivant (1798-1882), sixth wrangler and Fellow of Trinity, was Vice Principal at Lampeter (1827-43), Regius Professor of Divinity at Cambridge, and from 1849 until his death a distinguished and reforming Bishop of Llandaff. Lady Charlotte Guest found him an excellent bishop because he 'sets his face entirely against Puseyism [the High-Church Oxford Movement], which is a great blessing'. 'Which' did not refer to Puseyism![74]

The establishment of St David's College by Bishop Burgess in 1822 (students were first admitted five years later) was to lead to Lampeter having the oldest degree-giving institution in Wales.

Llewelyn Lewellin, besides being Principal (and Vicar of Lampeter), was from 1840 the first Dean of St Davids; previously, since 1224, the head of the Chapter had been styled Precentor, an office the Dean still holds. Lewellin began the great work of restoration which, amongst other things, saved the tower from collapse.[75]

Rice Rees was Professor of Welsh from 1827 to 1839.[76]

**27 August** The Belle Vue, half-way along Marine Terrace overlooking the beach, was a popular hotel with the upper classes. In 1824 two lords and seven baronets were staying there, and the Duke of Gloucester was expected.[77]

The church was St Michael's, near the castle ruins. Designed by Edward Heycock of Shrewsbury to replace a smaller building nearby, it was opened in 1833 and cost over £3,700. Money did not suffice for a tower, so a vestry was substituted; its ruins are all that survive. A third church was built in 1890. The organ is now in St Mary's.[78]

Digby may have been the Rev G. Digby, Curate of Glasbury.[79]

John Hughes (1787-1860), Vicar of St Michael's in 1827 and of Llanbadarn Fawr from 1833, and briefly Archdeacon of Cardigan, was a famous Evangelical preacher; Newman used to go to listen to him when Hughes held a curacy near Oxford. He was instrumental in having St Michael's rebuilt.[80]

**28 August** Hafod Uchtryd was an extraordinary house, mostly oriental gothick at this period, and partly by Nash. Henry Pelham, 4th Duke of Newcastle, an autocratic and unpopular old bachelor, bought it for £62,038 in 1832. He removed the contents, even the fireplaces which had come from Fonthill. Anthony Salvin designed a vast extension in 1846-51, dwarfing the old house. The whole irregular ensemble no longer exists, but the grounds are being restored.[81]

Lead mining in Cardiganshire prospered again after 1836, and in 1841 one firm alone was paying out £40,000 in wages.[82]

Thomas Turner, who visited Aberystwyth earlier in the month, noted that the beach abounded with valuable pebbles. Experienced lapidaries advised collectors, and polished specimens of stones like jasper and agate.[83]

**29 August** 'wittles': whittles—woollen shawls or blankets.

The Assembly Rooms, at the junction of Laura Place and Church Street, were designed by Repton and opened in 1820. The gentry and their ladies met here for balls, cards, billiards, reading and refreshments. Romilly does not mention a ball, though one was held every Tuesday in the season from nine in the evening till an hour after midnight. One of the rules excluded gentlemen (except the military) who were wearing boots; perhaps Romilly had the wrong footwear on.[84]

**30 August** The reason why Aberystwyth is not called Aberrheidol, as Romilly contended it should be, lies in its military past. A castle had been built at the mouth (*aber*) of the Ystwyth, but it was superseded by a stronger one, near which the town grew up, beside the lower reach of the Rheidol further north (the two rivers meet, at least today, at the estuary). It seems that the name of the earlier castle, properly Aberystwyth, came to be transferred to its successor, which had originally been known as Llanbadarn Castle, this being the parish of Llanbadarn Fawr. Humphrey Lhuyd compounded the muddle in 1584 by exchanging the names of the rivers on his map.[85]

Lord Clive (1785-1848), grandson of 'Clive of India', inherited Powis Castle on his uncle's death in 1801. His father was still alive at this time; on his death in 1839 he would also inherit the Earldom of Powis.[86]

**31 August** The Ellesmere Canal, part of a complex linking the Severn, Dee and Mersey, was built by Thomas Telford between 1793 and 1805. His aqueduct at Chirk spanned the valley by means of a channel floored in cast iron and carried on ten masonry arches, each forty feet wide. Romilly seems to have missed the much longer and loftier aqueduct of Pontcysyllte.[87]

Wynnstay, home of Lord Clive's brother-in-law, Sir Watkin Williams Wynn, whose family arms (seen in St Asaph Cathedral) display forty-six quarterings, was rebuilt by James Wyatt in 1789. Many other architects, notably C.R. Cockerell, had a hand in it. In 1858 the house and its valuable contents, including unique Welsh manuscripts, were destroyed by fire. Benjamin Ferrey designed a new house in 1861.[88]

Lord Westminster: the dukedom dates from 1874. From the lodge (since rebuilt) a five-mile drive led to Eaton Hall.[89]

A mixed train carried both passengers and goods. Shunting the goods wagons slowed it up, so the system fell out of favour in this country.[90]

Romilly's resignation as Rector of Porthkerry was dated 11 November. He did not forget his old parish. In May 1845 he spent £1 13s on books from the S.P.C.K. for a lending library there.[91]

SOURCES

1 J. Ross, *The Cathedral Church of Bristol* (Gloucester, 1947), 54; *D.N.B.*, IV, 124-5; J. Haydn (with H. Ockerby), *The Book of Dignities* (London, 1894, reprinted Bath, 1969) [hereafter Haydn, *Dignities*], 440.

2 Bury, 254; *O.D.C.C.*, 222; H.S. Goodhart-Rendel, *English Architecture Since The Regency* (London, 1953) [hereafter Goodhart-Rendel, *Architecture*], 90-100; O. Chadwick, *The Victorian Church* part I (London, 1966), 212-4; G.W.O. Addleshaw and F. Etchells, *The Architectural Setting of Anglican Worship* (London, 1948), 203ff. For the controversy that led to 'Camden' becoming 'Ecclesiastical', and Thorp's part in it, see Bury & Pickles, 126, 132.

3 W.S. Simpson, *Registrum Statutorum et Consuetudinum Ecclesiæ Cathedralis S. Pauli Londinensis* supplement (London, 1897), 149; A. Morrison, *Memorials of St Paul's Cathedral* (MS, c1980, copy in the possession of Canon Richard Fenwick).

4 Church guide.

5 D.T.W. Price, *A History of Saint David's University College, Lampeter* vol I (Cardiff, 1977) [hereafter Price, *Lampeter*], 17.

6 C. Crick, *Victorian Buildings in Bristol* (Bristol, 1975) [hereafter Crick, *Bristol*], 1.

7 *Treasures of Britain* (London, 1973), 102; *Enc. Brit.*, vol 4, 221.

8 *Enc. Brit.*, vol 3, 355-6; vol 10, 606B-C (with illustration); A.H. Gardner, *Outline of English Architecture* (London, 1949), 91.

9 R.F. Cartwright, *The Pictorial History of Saint Mary Redcliffe* (London, 1963), 12, 16, 20; Crick, *Bristol*, 24. The unrestored church still had a truncated spire.

10 Slater's *Royal National Commercial Directory of North & South Wales, Monmouthshire, Shropshire, and the Cities of Bristol and Chester* (Manchester, 1880) [hereafter Slater, *Directory*], Bristol section, 4; G. Harries, *Early Bristol Paddle-Steamer Shipwrecks* (St David's, 1993) [hereafter Harries, *Shipwrecks*], endpaper with annotated plan of Bristol, c1820; Crick, *Bristol*, 9, 10 (with illustration).

11 School prospectus; Crick, *Bristol*, 9; information from Mrs Gillian Gammage, referring to J. Vanes, *Apparelled in Red* (Bristol, 1984).

12 Goodhart-Rendel, *Architecture*, 86; M.S. Briggs, *Everyman's Concise Encyclopædia of Architecture* (London, 1959), 275.

13 Slater, *Directory*, Bristol section, 5.

14 Hunt & Co's *Directory* (London, 1850) [hereafter Hunt, *Directory*], 161.

15 G. Farr, *Shipbuilding in the Port of Bristol* (London, 1977), 3, 7, 37; Harries, *Shipwrecks*, *passim*; Leigh's *Guide to Wales & Monmouthshire* (London, 1835) [hereafter Leigh, *Guide*], 325.

16 D.C. Jenkins (ed), *The Diary of Thomas Jenkins of Llandeilo 1826-1870* (Bala, 1976), 31.

17 Information from Mr Roland Thorne. He has written an exhaustive account of 'The Leach Family of Castlemartin' in *J.P.L.H.S.*, no 7 (1981), 29-51.

18 Hunt, *Directory*, 165; Leigh, *Guide*, 325, which lists Faulkner's Hotel among the principal inns.

19 Hunt, *Directory*, 162.

20 *W.W.H.R.*, IV, 221. Possibly a good whist player: Bury & Pickles, 186, 254.

21 Burke, 1324; Haydn, *Dignities*, 493.

22 Venn, IV, 504; *D.N.B.*, XXXIX, 426.

23 *O.D.C.C.*, 210.

24 Letter from J.(?) Mitford, 202 Sloane Street, in Allen Papers. The Rev John Mitford (1781-1859), editor of the *Gentleman's Magazine*, lived in that street: *D.N.B.*, XXXVIII, 78-80. See also B. Colloms, *Victorian Country Parsons* (London, 1977) [hereafter Colloms, *Parsons*], 98-111.

25 A.L. Hayward, *The Dickens Encyclopædia* (London, 1924, reprinted 1969), 125 (which says *Pickwick* appeared March 1836 to October 1837); *D.N.B.*, XV, 22 (which gives April 1836 to November 1837); G. Gissing (rev), *Forster's Life of Dickens* (London, 1903), 43-56 (which gives 31 March 1836, closing in December 1837! I am grateful to Col Andrew Man for this last source).

26 E. Inglis-Jones, 'A Pembrokeshire County Family in the Eighteenth Century', *N.L.W.J.*, vol XVII no 2 (1971), 136-7.

27 D.K. Brown, *Before the Ironclad* (London, 1990), 61-4; S. Peters, *The History of Pembroke Dock* (London, 1905), 17, appendix I. Mrs Peters (or her printer) named the ship *Gordon*, but Mr (now the Rev) Clive Hughes pointed me in the right direction, and Miss J.M. Wraight of the National Maritime Museum furnished details and an illustration.

28 Information from Miss J.M. Wraight. The *Collingwood* was an 80-gun third rate, and the almost identical *Centurion* (see 7 August 1840) a second rate.

29 Pembs R.O., HDX/1204/1: G. Mason, *Pembroke Dock, Royal Dockyard, and Neighbourhood* part 1 (Pembroke Dock, no date), 51-3; letter from Ted Goddard, *Western Telegraph*, 25 August 1993; P. Carradice, *The Book of Pembroke Dock* (Buckingham, 1991), 75.

30 D. Howell, 'Society, 1660-1793' in B. Howells (ed), *Pembrokeshire County History* vol III *Early Modern Pembrokeshire, 1536-1815* (Haverfordwest, 1987) [hereafter Howells, *Pembrokeshire*], 262-3.

31 B.G. Charles, *The Place-Names of Pembrokeshire* (Aberystwyth, 1992), 493-4.

32 Venn, IV, 382; Bury, 248.

33 Burke, 1970; Bury, 62, 202.

34 Bury, 170; Bury & Pickles, 252.

35 Information from Mr David Bleines of Tenby Museum. He pointed out that Samuel's father, Richard, died in 1821 and that Richard's grandson, Ferrar, was also ruled out for 1837. Roger Fenton had sermons published, but he could not qualify as a living Welshman, having died in 1615: *D.N.B.*, XVIII, 327. Possibly Romilly confused his Fentons.

36 *D.W.B.*, 753; M.M. Philipps, *The History of the Family of Philipps of Picton* (London, 1906), 26-7; D. Williams, *The Rebecca Riots* (Cardiff, 1955) [hereafter Williams, *Rebecca Riots*], 7.

37 D. Miles, *Sheriffs of the County of Pembroke 1541-1974* (Haverfordwest, no date), 57.

38 The saint was Jeanne Françoise de Chantal, who founded the Order of the Visitation. *Enc. Brit.*, vol 5, 275; vol 20, 280.

39 Information from Mr Roland Thorne (and see ref 17 above).

40 *D.N.B.*, XXXVIII, 217; *Enc. Brit.*, vol 14, 494-5; M. Drabble (ed), *The Oxford Companion to English Literature* (Oxford, 1985) [hereafter Drabble, *Literature*], 306.

41 According to Mr Thomas Lloyd. The surname Watkins appears but rarely in the Laugharne registers of the period, and never prefixed Lloyd. T. Jones, *A History of the County of Brecknock* (Brecknock, 1898), 266-7, says Pennoyre Watkins of Brecon left the Broadway estate, Laugharne, to his eldest son.

42 *Enc. Brit.*, vol 4, 46; S. Lee, *A Life of William Shakespeare* (London, 1898), 341; D. Moore (ed), *Wales in the Eighteenth Century* (Swansea, 1976), 132. The artists included Reynolds, Romney, Fuseli, Benjamin West and Angelica Kauffmann.

43 M.G.R. Morris, *Princes Gate* (Lampeter Velfrey, 1987), 4, 5.

44 M.G.R. Morris (ed), *The Story of Narberth* (Narberth, 1990), 31; Goodhart-Rendel, *Architecture*, 176-7.

45 *W.W.H.R.*, III, 212.

46 Information from Mr Roland Thorne (and see ref 17 above). This was the Capt Leach mentioned in ref 5 to the note on 16 October 1827.

47 Pembs R.O., HT/SHIP/2/5; P. Kemp (ed) *The Oxford Companion to Ships and the Sea* (Oxford, 1988), 700; R. Thorne, 'Pembrokeshire in Wartime 1793-1815 1. Social and economic change' in Howells, *Pembrokeshire*, 37.

48 Information from Mr Roland Thorne, who says Thomasina's sister Mary died allegedly of boredom: *J.P.L.H.S.*, no 7 (1981), 35.

49 Bury & Pickles, 98.

50 Information from Wing Commander Ken McKay, the historian of Milford. The brass shoes were new to him. Helen Palmer has written an entertaining account of the seasick King's visit in the Dyfed Archives Service *Quarterly Newsletter*, winter 1994-5, again without mentioning the shoes.

51 R. Fenton, *A Historical Tour Through Pembrokeshire* (Brecknock, 1903, reprinted Haverfordwest, 1994) [hereafter Fenton, *Pembrokeshire*], 115, 122.

52 Pembs R.O., HPR/84/2, 8; Whitchurch census, 1841; T. Broom, *Notes for a History of Solva: the 19th Century* (Bristol, 1995), 23, with map inside back cover.

53 Leigh, *Guide*, 300; H. Evans, *Twr-y-felin History and Guide to St. David's* (1923) [hereafter Evans, *Twr-y-felin Guide*], 17-9; D.W. James, *St. David's and Dewisland: A Social History* (Cardiff, 1981) [hereafter James, *St. David's*], 195; W. Plomer (ed), *Kilvert's Diary* vol 2 (London, 1939) [hereafter Plomer *Kilvert*], 63.

54 Colloms, *Parsons*, 185; Plomer, *Kilvert*, 65.

55 *W.W.H.R.*, IV, 290; E.M.N. (née Lewellin), *Pleasant Memories of Eminent Churchmen* (Carmarthen, no date), 41-2; D.T.W. Price, *Yr Esgob Burgess a Choleg Llanbedr: Bishop Burgess and Lampeter College* (Cardiff, 1987) [hereafter Price, *Burgess*], 37. Was Davies the 'eccentric Archdeacon ... who gave his dog his sermon to carry to church'?—G. Huntington, *Random Recollections of Some Noted Bishops, Divines and Worthies of the 'Old Church' of Manchester* (London, 1893), 99. The dog once forgot, so the people had no sermon that morning.

56 G.M. Trevelyan, *Trinity College* (Cambridge, 1946), 49; Bury, 166. Since 1775 these Westminster scholars had lost their prescriptive right to Trinity fellowships.

57 Fenton, *Pembrokeshire*, 38; W.B. Jones and E.A. Freeman, *The History and Antiquities of Saint David's* (London, 1856) [hereafter Jones, *Saint David's*], 219 (this gives *David* Stradling), 221; *W.W.H.R.*, IV, 290; V, 133-5; E. Yardley (F. Green, ed), *Menevia Sacra* (London, 1927) [hereafter Yardley, *Menevia*], 5 and plan facing, 8; Evans, *Twr-y-felin Guide*, 96-7; James, *St. David's*, with plans of the houses in 1720 and 1840.

58 Foster, 995.

59 Evans, *Twr-y-felin Guide*, 75; W. Evans, 'St Davids Cathedral: The Forgotten Centuries', *J.W.E.H.*, vol 3 (1986), 73-92; W. Evans and R. Worsley, *St Davids Cathedral 1181-1981* (St David's, 1981), 43, 50, 85, with illustrations. One, Parker's painting of 1836, shows no wall above the screen. A watercolour of about the same date by E. A. Leyson, in M. Wight, *The Pilgrim's Guide to St David's and its Cathedral* 4th ed (Gloucester 1939), 31, lent me by Mrs Kay Halliwell, also omits the wall. Jones, *Saint David's*, 84, says it was partly taken down in 1847-8, so the artists must have used some licence. The 7-stop Father Smith organ stood under the north tower arch till rebuilt there by Lincoln in 1843 (A. Lamb, *The Organs of St. David's Cathedral* (1992), gets this wrong).

60 Yardley, *Menevia*, 372-6, with plan of the College; *W.W.H.R.*, V, 203-4; VI, 34-8.

61 B. Willis, *A Survey of the Cathedral Church of St David's* (London, 1717), 55. Non-Latinists can get the rhythm of a hexameter and pentameter (an elegiac couplet) by reciting, 'Down in a deep dark ditch lay an old cow munching a beanstalk. Out of her mouth came forth yesterday's dinner and tea'.

62 Oxford, Bodleian Library, MS Ashmole 1817A, f 309; C. Norris, *Saint David's, in a Series of Engravings, Illustrating the Different Ecclesiastical Edifices of that Ancient City* (London, 1811). Jones, *Saint David's*, 225, mentions a ruined cottage adjoining the chapel's *west* end in 1856.

63 R. Howell, 'Pembrokeshire in Wartime 1793-1815 2. Military activity' in Howells, *Pembrokeshire*, 391-6.

64 *W.W.H.R.*, I, 297.

65 B.H. Malkin, *The Scenery, Antiquities, and Biography, of South Wales* (London, 1904, reprinted 1970), 406.

66 J.G. Jenkins, *Life and Tradition in Rural Wales* (London, 1976), 176-9.

67 Drabble, *Literature*, 538; *D.N.B.*, XXXI, 246; XLIX, 149-51; *Enc. Brit.*, vol 4, 281.

68 According to Mr Thomas Lloyd.

69 T. Lloyd, *The Lost Houses of Wales* (London, 1989) [hereafter Lloyd, *Lost Houses*], 53.

70 Haydn, *Dignities*, 823; Burke, 233; information from Mr Roland Thorne.

71 *Short-title Catalogue of Books printed in France and of French Books printed in other countries from 1470 to 1600 now in the British Museum* (London, 1924), 323; *Enc. Brit.*, vol 4, 105-6; *Enc. Brit.* (15th ed, 1990), vol 2, 477.

72 *Ancestral Tablets*, 5 (in Allen Papers); Carmarthen Record Office, Dynevor Records, 160/7.

73 Price, *Burgess*, 57 (with illustration). Alas, the College now calls itself the University of Wales, Lampeter; goodbye to St David.

74 Price, *Lampeter*, 47; Earl of Bessborough (ed), *Lady Charlotte Guest: Extracts from Her Journal*

*1833-1852* (London, 1950), 251. For a memoir of Ollivant see J. Morgan, *Four Biographical Sketches* (London, 1892), 1-60, and for Romilly's description of his election as Regius Professor (he thought him the least striking candidate) see Bury & Pickles, 41-3.

75 *W.W.H.R.*, IV, 286, 288. Jones, *Saint David's*, 84-5, says that in 1840 the stall formerly (and again today) inscribed *Dom[inus] Epi[scopus]* on the south side of the choir was renamed *Decanus* when Lewellin occupied it as Dean; before 1840, the Bishop sat here as Dean. When—and why—did the Dean move back to the Precentor's stall? The present Dean thinks it happened after the stalls were removed during Scott's restoration and their titles repainted (the Precentor's stall being relabelled *Decanus*) He suggests that the Bishop—Thirlwall—wanted his stall back.

76 Price, *Lampeter*, 35.

77 W.J. Lewis, *Born on a Perilous Rock* (Aberystwyth, 1980) [hereafter Lewis, *Perilous Rock*], 13, 196.

78 Lewis, *Perilous Rock*, 13, 37-9; I.G. Jones, *Communities Essays in the Social History of Victorian Wales* (Llandysul, 1987), 70-87; I.G. Jones and D. Williams, *The Religious Census of 1851 A Calendar of the Returns Relating to Wales* vol I (Cardiff, 1976), 533, where the cost of the second church is given as £4,335; further information (also on John Hughes) from the Rev D.B.G. Davies.

79 N.L.W., SD/SC/408.

80 Lewis, *Perilous Rock*, 38.

81 E. Inglis-Jones, *Peacocks in Paradise* (London, 1950), 242; E.D. Evans, 'Hafod in the Time of The Duke of Newcastle (1785-1851)', *Ceredigion*, vol XII no. 3 (1995), 41-61; J.B. Hilling, *The Historic Architecture of Wales* (Cardiff, 1976) [hereafter Hilling, *Architecture*], 129, 131 (with drawing); Lloyd, *Lost Houses*, 51 (with photograph).

82 Williams, *Rebecca Riots*, 88. See also A. Francis, *History of the Cardiganshire Mines from the Earliest Ages, and Authenticated History to A.D. 1874, with their Present Position and Prospect* (Aberystwyth, 1874, reprinted Sheffield, 1987).

83 T. Turner, *Narrative of a Journey, associated with a Fly, from Gloucester to Aberystwith, and from Aberystwith through North Wales* (London, 1840), 25.

84 Lewis, *Perilous Rock*, 197. Lewis, 38, says it was George Repton. Perhaps he meant Humphry Repton, the landscape architect, who collaborated with John Nash and argued with Uvedale Price, for whom Nash designed Castle House in Aberystwyth: *Enc. Brit.*, vol 19, 191; Hilling, *Architecture*, 132. Humphry Repton died in 1818; his son John Adey Repton (1775-1860) was an architect.

85 Lewis, *Perilous Rock*, 2, 3.

86 National Trust guide to Powis Castle, 57-8, 60-1.

87 J.P.M. Pannell, *Man the Builder* (London, 1977), 68-70.

88 Hilling, *Architecture*, 126, 179; Lloyd, *Lost Houses*, 24.

89 I owe this to Fr John Barnes. The Marquessate of Westminster was created in 1831.

90 J. Simmons, *The Victorian Railway* (London, 1995), 312.

91 N.L.W., LL/RES/288; Bury & Pickles, 132.

# 8   SOUTH WALES CIRCUIT

## 8—28 August 1838

No longer Rector of Porthkerry, Romilly still had a cousin there. That summer he combined a brief visit to him with a longer one to Baugh Allen in Pembrokeshire. Instead of making Bristol his base, as he had between 1830 and 1837, he retraced (in the opposite direction) the route he had taken in 1827 along what we now call the A40. The return journey, mostly by way of the southern turnpike past Swansea, took in Cowbridge and Porthkerry; then, from Newport, he went to Hereford to stay with his friend Bishop Musgrave.

Again accompanied by young George Romilly, he had left Cambridge by fly on 6 August. They sat outside and had the full benefit of three very heavy showers of rain. Next day he saw George off by the Dover coach from London. After a steamer trip to Greenwich, he himself returned by railway, looked in at the National Gallery (the new building in Trafalgar Square, with its pleasureless dome and secondhand portico, opened to the public in April), visited the United Service Museum, and then walked to the House of Lords with Musgrave, who had clumsily lamed himself by dropping a penknife on his knee. He dined at the Athenaeum.

The journey to Wales began next day. This time Romilly took advantage of the new technology; as yet, however, the Great Western Railway had stretched out its broad-gauge steel tentacles only as far as Maidenhead. Thereafter it was back to the coach, averaging eight miles an hour instead of twenty-one.

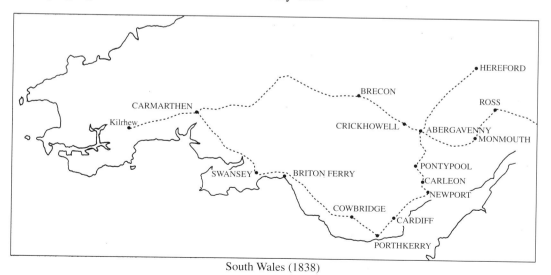

South Wales (1838)

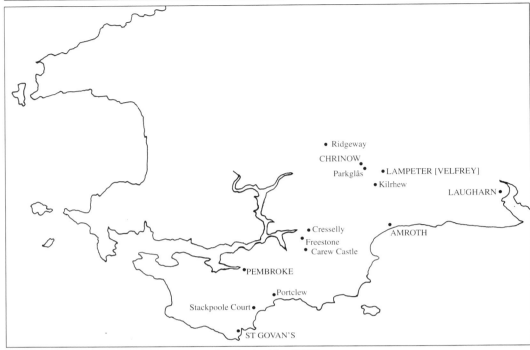

Pembrokeshire (1838)

**Wednesday 8 August** Reached Regent Circus at ¼ to 8, where I met Swabey* and Edward Allen. Got to the Paddington Railway Station* a little before 9. Our stage was put on the train and we ourselves deposited in the train carriages. Our engine was most absurdly called the Apollo.* One talks indeed of the *singing* of a teakettle, but there is little music in the harsh rush of steam from an engine; it is more like the hideous roar of a wild beast. We did not go very fast: we were 70 minutes travelling the 25 miles. At Maidenhead we resumed our places outside the coach. Dined at Star at Oxford, and reached Gloster about 8. During the day we had a few showers but altogether the weather was very bearable. After tea we walked about the town by moonlight in company with an agreeable fellow traveller.

Apollo railway engine

**Thursday 9 August** Fortunate enough to get 3 places by the Carmarthen mail: 2 outside for the boys, 1 inside for myself. Left the Bell* at Gloster at 8½. Occasional showers and mist through the beautiful country of Ross and Monmouth. After that the weather settled into an incessant rain, so that we could see but little of the fine scenery from Abergavenny through Crickhowell, Brecon, and Carmarthen. We dined very comfortably in the grand Concertroom* at Brecon. Reached Carmarthen at 8 and had tea; here the lads got quite dry and we luckily obtained 3 inside places for Kilrhew,* but (though the rain came down fast) Grim went round to the outside passengers and easily prevailed on a large fellow to come inside. We reached Kilrhew at 11½ and found George and the servant waiting for us with a wheelbarrow.* Found Allen pretty well, but he is by no means free from cough. More tea and to bed by 12½.

Cilrhiw in 1884: the conservatory and far wing added after 1840

**Friday 10 August** Miserable wet day. Baugh, George and I went over in the phaeton to Laugharn to dine with the Lloyd Watkinses.* We met here old Mr Watkins: I found him very affable and courteous, extremely choice in his language and an admirable reciter of poetry in general and Shakspere in particular; Baugh has his Boydell's Shakspere* at Dulwich. He is an old man past 80 but (bating* a slight deafness) in the full enjoyment of health. Our dinner party was raised to 10 by the presence of Mr Utterson (brother to the 6 Clerk*) and Col and Mrs Browne* and her great niece, Miss

Woodcock.* Mrs Browne calls her husband her *Legacy*. The colonel had proposed several times unsuccessfully; she married another man, who on his deathbed begged her to marry her old admirer the colonel. In the midst of a rubber the colonel got up in much pain and left the room. 'Ah', said his wife, 'this is one of his attacks of cramp; but it is very slight. Sometimes he will hollow enough to frighten you out of your wits'. In a quarter of an hour he returned and finished his game. In the evening an old Mrs Shekell* with a preposterous headdress came in; she played backgammon with George, beat him shamefully and greatly scorned his play, which she said was very loose—he just hated her [?].

**Saturday 11 August** George and I slept last night at the inn at Laugharn. We of course breakfasted with the Watkins. After breakfast we went to call on the Uttersons. Mrs Utterson (born Jones) is 1st cousin of Dr Griffith; so I had much conversation with her about him. Back to Kilrhew by about 4½. In the evening we walked in the woods; at night I had a hot bath. Today very satisfactory letters from Margaret and Lucy. Helped George and Swabey in cutting down a largish tree before dinner. Today the weather very cold and dull, but very little rain.

**Sunday 12 August** Today most mournfully wet. Baugh and George and I went to the little church* at Chrinow (at the back of Mrs Eaton's house). A dull monotonous Mr Jones* preached very lamentably from the 1st lesson,* 'How long halt ye between 2 opinions?' After he had given it out in English he repeated it in Welsh; I expected every sentence of the sermon to be in the 2 languages, but I had not this opportunity of taking a lesson—he confined himself entirely to English. Wrote to the women. In the evening the rain ceased and we walked as far as the post office. At night the servants (6 in number) were had in, and I read them the 2nd lesson* of the morning (Cornelius) and gave them a short lecture upon it, and ended with a few prayers which I read from the prayer book.

**Monday 13 August** Every day I do lessons with the boys. At 1 Grim and I walked to Amroth to bathe. George and Swabey rode to Amroth for same purpose. The distance about 4 miles: the last mile and ½ through a beautiful wellwooded valley.* On the sands George lent me his horse and I had a good gallop; he and Swabey riding on the other. I suppose it was here that a telescope (put by Grim into my pocket) must have dropped out. I could not find it again, and gave him a sovereign to buy another. This was the 1st bathe in the open sea I have had for these 2 years. Home to dinner at 6¼. Met James Allen* (son of Bird Allen*) on horseback; he had been calling on us at Kilrhew.

**Tuesday 14 August** Baugh, George and I rode to see a Mr and Mrs Gonn,* who live in a very pretty house some 6 miles off: they are a good looking couple, who have been married some 2 or 3 years. Baugh rather perplexed the lady by asking after her little one—there being no such a creature. Mr Gonn is a Trinity man, who instantly recognised me. We met here a merry bouncing Miss Philips with no personal charms. We staid luncheon. In the evening Baugh, George and I and Swabey drank tea with Mrs Eaton and her two youngest daughters (Dora and Bertha). Their house is called Parkglâs (i.e. Green Field). Mrs Eaton gave us a long account of an operation (cutting out a tumour from her shoulder), which has been lately performed by Lawrence. Grim of course declined this party. In coming home it was pitch dark and we had the greatest difficulty in finding our way through Mrs Eaton's trees and over the brook.

**Wednesday 15 August** Baugh, George and I rode over to Ridgeway* (5 miles), Mrs Foley's. The house is beautifully situated, looking over Caniston woods. We staid lunch here. This lady's husband was brother of Sir T. Foley.* While we were out Mr Allen of Cresselly and Miss Allen and Harry called. In the evening we walked. Played chess with Swabey and found him a very young player.

**Thursday 16 August** Rode to Amroth to bathe. I was to have met Swabey and George there and they were to have rode back; but after I had had a good bathe and staid an hour and saw nothing of them I rode home. I went today on the left side of the pretty valley leading to Amroth and came back the usual road. On my road was a stone fence: I was told by a damsel that I must leap my horse over it. I with becoming consciousness of my bad riding dismounted and led the horse over. Walk in evening.

**Friday 17 August** Got up at 5. Started a little before 6, all 5 of us (viz Baugh, George, Edward, Swabey and I) in the phaeton, Baugh being the charioteer. We reached Pembroke, 15 miles, at 8½. We had been somewhat frightened by the dulness of the morning and the rain for the last ½ hour; the weather however cleared up now, and we had a most lovely sunshiny day with a gentle breeze. We were shown over the ruins of this once magnificent castle by an active dame, who pronounced Grim to be the most timid youth she had ever seen. She pointed out to us the room in which Henry 7th was born. We visited also the kitchen, climbed up all the staircases, and went into the great cavern under the castle. We then breakfasted at the Dragon at Pembroke and went in a hired phaeton through Lord Cawdor's park (Stackpoole Court*). We went under the guidance of the housekeeper on the terrace, which looks down on a fine artificial piece of water; on the terrace are 2 long Spanish cannons mounted. I did not at all admire the outside of the house though it has a double flight of steps; it wants a portico.

We called on Mr William Allen* (who married his 1st cousin Miss [Frances] Allen, daughter of Mr James Allen and his Roman Catholic lady, and a sister of Tom and Mary Allen). Met here Miss Mary Allen. Much amused with William Allen's little boy, who has been taught to tell the following story: a man and his wife were on the sea; the lady dropped her ring into the water; sometime after, a dozen herrings were given to her, and when the cook opened the 1st she found nothing in it but the guts; when she opened the 2nd, &c &c. Mr William Allen mounted his horse and escorted us to St Govan's Rocks (said to be named from an Italian prince Giovanni, brother to King Arthur's wife*). There is a superstition attaching to the spring here, that it will cure almost any bodily ailment and even mental imbecility: so that it is a current joke to say of a silly person that he must be dipped at St Govan's. One of the stones here (close to the chapel) when struck produces a ringing noise like a silver bell; some very idiotic people believe that the chapel bell is inside it. The limestone rocks here and all along this part of the coast are very lofty, and from forming arches, and caves, and from the great indentations of the shore, the effect is highly picturesque. In one of the snug little bays Swabey and George and I bathed. We of course visited all the different objects of curiosity, such as the

Devil's Cauldron,* the Stacks and Adam's Leap* (where a man so named is said in a foxchase to have leaped over a chasm 10 feet broad; the legend states that he followed a black figure mounted on a black horse, both of which disappeared at this rent in the rocks). We returned to the Dragon at Pembroke (after [?] a road of 17 or 18 miles) by a different road at 5, and after a cold dinner at the inn we went to tea at Cresselly, where we found Mr Allen and his son Harry and daughter Isabel and sister Emma. Home a little before 10 after a very successful day's pleasuring.

**Saturday 18 August** Clumsily sprained my ancle jumping out of windows; could not therefore walk with the rest of the party either morning or evening.

**Sunday 19 August** Nasty wet morning. We all sallied forth however for Lampeter [Velfrey] church (2 miles off). When we had got a little way in the woods we met Mrs Eaton's servant, who was come on a message; he was dismounted and I got up in his stead. The church at Lampeter has been for a 12 month undergoing a thorough repair and beautifying.* Service is therefore performed in the clergyman (Mr Seaton's*) kitchen. It is a capacious one, but from the thickly packed crowd it was insufferably close till Mr Seaton wisely ordered the windows to be opened. He read prayers very well and preached a capital extempore English sermon on 'Harden not your hearts'.* He read the 2 lessons and the text in Welsh. After service we went into the drawing room with Mr and Mrs Seaton, and son;* they afterwards exhibited to us their very pretty church, which is to be reopened next Wednesday. Wrote my 3rd letter to the women. In the evening Grim and I went to the post office. This morning a letter from Edward;* wrote to him and also to the Bishop of Hereford offering to come to him. In the evening I read a chapter (17 Acts) and expounded it and then read prayers. After dinner Baugh, George and Swabey went to Mrs Eaton's.

**Monday 20 August** 2nd letter from home: Margaret left off abruptly in her letter, which has frightened me a good deal, but Lucy does not say a word of her being taken ill, so I hope that my fears are groundless. Lucy writes me word that poor Dunford* has broken his leg in returning from a feast given by the College cook to the servants; he is in the hospital. Today a most stormy day, so that we kept house. Harry and Tom Allen kept their appointment however to dine with us; so did Mrs Eaton and her 2 daughters Dora and Bertha. We had a neck of venison given by Tom's brother-in-law (William Allen). Mrs Eaton's phaeton in bringing her today broke a spring, so the servant came in the evening with a pony and lantern. Baugh of course had out his own carriage and horses and sent them home, though Mrs Eaton begged hard to be allowed to walk. The party was very agreeable.

**Tuesday 21 August** Started from Kilrhew at 4½ with Baugh in his phaeton to dine at Freestone. We arrived at 6 and met (besides our host (Mr James Allen) and his Roman Catholic wife and their son Tom and daughter Mary) John Allen and Emma and Isabel and Harry, Mr and Col Wedgwood. A haunch of venison was the plea on which we had been called together; it was so high that almost every body sent their plate away. In the evening we played whist. Yesterday the 20th my customary letter was to be forwarded to Frank.* Mr James Allen read prayers at night.

**Wednesday 22 August** Walked over the grounds with my host. The view of the Haven from his kitchen garden very beautiful. Mrs James Allen was summoned that morning to her daughter Mrs William Allen, who is ready to cry out.* Went to Cresselly for 3 days. Took 2 books off the table and went out for a 5 hours ramble. The books were Talfourd's *Captive of Athens** and a volume of Madame Junot's (Duchesse d'Abrantès) *Salons de Paris.** I thought the *Captive of Athens* inferior to the Ton:* the character indeed of Creusa is drawn with tenderness, and her affection for her brother Hyllus and her love for Thoas (the Athenian captive) are touching; but the whole plot of the play is unnatural. Creon (King of Corinth) is an absurdly feeble twaddling old man, and his 2nd wife Ismene (who turns out to be mother of Thoas) a preposterously hateful and wicked woman, and Thoas is unaccountably and quite in opposition to his own generous nature made her tool in the murder of Creon. I was occasionally offended with bad English, such as 'Whence *drew thou* these reflections?' The *Salons de Paris* I found highly interesting, part 1 the account given by Koschiousko* at Madame de Stael's.* Today an old woman of 82 came up to me as I was sitting reading on a bridge. I gave her 6d and was much struck by her saying, 'The poor have one friend, God Almighty, who puts it in people's heart to be kind to them'. At dinner we had a party of 8 consisting of John Allen, Emma, Isabel, Harry and John, Baugh, Grim and myself. Whist in the evening.

**Thursday 23 August** Letter from Edward so pressing that I altered my plans and determined to go there on Saturday. Took another volume (that about Josephine) of the *Salons de Paris* and strolled to Carew Castle &c, enjoying the fine air and sunshine for 5 hours. At dinner we had 10 by the addition of George and Swabey. Whist in the evening. Won 41 [?] points.

**Friday 24 August** At ¼ to 6 this morning a great hollowing under my window for Grim: it was the voice of his cousin Tom summoning him for a day's fishing. I went into his room and roused the sleeper. Baugh drove Emma, George and me over to Portclew to call upon Col and Mrs Wedgwood; both out. We saw however the colonel's father, Mr John Wedgwood, and his [the colonel's] two sisters Jessy (Mrs Harry Wedgwood) and Eliza. We staid lunch. Baugh, George and I went down to the seabeach and had a cold bath. Today most lovely, with infinite variety of beautiful clouds and fine warm sunshine; the air was so singularly clear that we seemed close to Lundy Isle, a sure symptom of approaching bad weather. The dinner company increased to 12 by the addition of Mr James Allen (of Freestone) and his amiable clever daughter Mary and young James Allen (son of Bird Allen), clergyman of Castle Martin. In the evening played chess till past 12 with Isabel; won 2 games against her one. She plays so well that I found it necessary to give all my best attention. We are now even as I played a game with her on Wednesday night which she won. George and John (or little John* as he is called because he is 6 feet 3 inches) sat up with me and saw me safely deposited at 1½ in the mail, which very comfortably drives up to the door.

**Saturday 25 August** A most dismal foggy rainy day. It happened to be high water as we past Briton Ferry and I was much pleased with the beautiful* view—a happy contrast to the abominations of the copper works at Swansey. Got to Cowbridge at ¼ to 11. I paid a visit to the Malkins at Cowbridge and found that Mrs Arthur Malkin* had been very near dying. Took a chaise from my friend Mrs Ballard, the hostess of the Bear. Passed Edward and wife on the road. Found Mrs Marcet* in the act of writing sermons for the poor, she declaring with very great justice that most discourses in villages are unintelligible to the audience. I enjoyed very much a long chat with her about Geneva. In the evening we had a rubber of whist after some reading aloud of *Slick of Slickville.**

Briton Ferry in 1819: travel by foot, horse, carriage and sail

**Sunday 26 August** Very much pleased with the improved state of Porthkerry church; I hear that the Rural Dean (Dr Casberd*) says we have made it almost like a cathedral. Mrs Marcet [?] and Mrs Edward and self went to church, where Taynton read prayers very well but preached a dull ineffectual sermon on confirmation. There was a general expectation of my preaching and the church was very full. The clerk (Rees) had got from Penmark 3 brother singers and they really sang capitally. Edward had gone over to Barry to give notice of a meeting he means to hold there tomorrow to inquire into the state of Welsh knowledge. The old Rector is just dead, and the Curate Morgan (a Welshman) wishes to be the new one and has occasioned the presentation of a memorial to the Bishop of Llandaff.* Edward has sent a statement also much at variance with the memorial, saying that almost all the parishioners speak English. His wish of course is to present Paul Ashmore,* and there is at present a feud with the Bishop. After service I went down to the shore and had a bathe, and then walked till dinner time. Edward has been making great improvements in the laying out of the grounds.

**Monday 27 August** Left Porthkerry directly after breakfast in Edward's carriage. Reached Cardiffe a little before the mail; no place till Newport. They engaged to produce me a car which should keep up with the mail this one stage of 12 miles. The car was brought out in a minute and kept up famously for the 1st 3 miles; at the end of which the driver pointed to his horse and said, 'Tommy'll never do it'. I said I was of his opinion and therefore desired that Tommy might forthwith go along at a gentle trot. Got to Newport a little before 2 and got on to the Abergavenny mail. The road is a very beautiful one along the valley of the Usk, passing through Carleon and Pontypool; the situation of the latter place is very striking. There are here great tin works belonging to Mr Leigh* the High Sheriff. Arrived at Angel at Abergavenny at 6; had dinner and then rambled about the town.

**Tuesday 28 August** Off from Abergavenny at 9; skirted along the Skyryd. The road (for 24 miles) to Hereford is through a rich hilly district with a trout stream close. Hereford at 12; at the coach office found Gunning,* who escorted me to the Palace. The Bishop was examining the boys at the National school, but came to us in an hour.

Romilly stayed at Hereford till 3 September.

### NOTES

**8 August** Swabey was probably Maurice Charles Merttins, a boy at Westminster School, who went up to Oxford in 1839.[1]

The Great Western Railway had opened the line from Paddington (the old station, a short distance north-west of the 1854 terminus) to Maidenhead as recently as 4 June. Lady Charlotte Guest had beaten Romilly to it: she took a train on 20 July. 'It rocked the whole way like a steam vessel, and there were hundreds of men employed in patching up the line over which we were passing'. Ten days later she made the return journey to Paddington and found it much improved and very fast. She did not notice the impact when the train killed two horses. Broad-gauge track was laid on timbers lengthwise beneath the rails, rather than on transverse sleepers; cross-transoms at wide intervals kept the 'baulk road', as it was called, rigid. The design made for a hard ride, but simple conversion to standard gauge.[2]

The Apollo was a broad-gauge 2-2-2 engine with central eight-foot driving wheels (reduced to six feet two inches the following year). Romilly thought it absurdly named, perhaps because Apollo is associated with Greek ideals of male beauty. On the other hand, Homer depicts Apollo as a death-dealing god of distance: quite appropriate for a fire-driven locomotive.[3]

**9 August** The Bell in Southgate Street dates back to 1650. George Whitefield the Methodist (1714) and Cardinal Vaughan (1832) were born here. Another inn called the Bell traded in Barton Street at about this time. Grim, running away from school later this year, stopped at the Bell, which ate up his money too fast, so he moved to a small pub.[4]

Was the Concertroom the Guildhall? This dated from 1770, replacing a timber building of 1624; it was substantially altered in 1883.[5]

The mail passed conveniently close to Cilrhiw; the drive straddled the coach road near Princes Gate.

The wheelbarrow was no doubt for the luggage.

**10 August** For the Lloyd Watkinses and Boydell's *Shakespeare*, see note on 19 August 1837.

'bating': excepting.

The Six Clerk mentioned was Edward Vernon Utterson. Was it a coincidence that he married Sarah Elizabeth Brown?[6]

The name Browne, spelt as in the diary, occurs fairly often in the Laugharne parish registers, but the only candidate for the colonel seems to be John Frederick Browne of King Street, born in about 1768 and buried on 29 March 1844.

Miss Woodcock may have been the girl aged fifteen at the Grayhound, Laugharne, in the 1841 census; her Christian name is not clear, but ended in '-ina'. The only Woodcock in the Laugharne registers was buried on 31 May 1843: Amelia Stuart Woodcock of King Street. Her age and marital status are not given.

Mrs Shekell was in fact Ann Shickle, widow of John Hayle Shickle, late of Jamaica and an alderman of Laugharne (such titles happily survive in the township). She died on 27 October 1840 aged seventy-four.[7]

**12 August** Someone, probably Bertha Eaton, painted a little watercolour of the inside of Crinow church a few years after this, showing the rising seats built at the west end by Thomas Page of Droslyn Fach, Llanddewi Velfrey.[8]

David Jones was Rector of Crinow and Vicar of Llanddewi Velfrey from 1830 to 1873; he also held Castlemartin till he resigned it on 23 October 1838. Llanddewi has had only twelve Vicars since 1673. Jones's son, Charles, red whiskered and five foot seven and a half inches according to the Haverfordwest Jail records (he had assaulted John Lewis, squire of Henllan, with a whip), married Anna Eaton.[9]

The lessons referred to were from I Kings 18 and Acts 10, for the ninth Sunday after Trinity.

**13 August** The beautiful, well-wooded valley leads past Colby Lodge with its fine gardens, which the National Trust is restoring.

James Allen succeeded David Jones as Vicar of Castlemartin in 1839. He became Chancellor of St Davids Cathedral in 1871 and Dean seven years later, long past the present retiring age of seventy; he held the post for seventeen years, continuing Lewellin's great work of restoration, even paying himself for foreign marble to floor the nave.[10]

Bird Allen served as Rector of Burton from 1814, dying in office in 1831.[11]

**14 August** The Gonnes lived at Great Vaynor, 'a very elegant little abode' according to Anna Eaton, 'yet they are not elegant'.[12]

**15 August** Ridgeway is the Italianate house overlooking the main road just west of Canaston Bridge. It is now a residential home.

Admiral Sir Thomas Foley had been Nelson's flag captain at Copenhagen. To him Nelson had said, 'I really do not see the signal'.[13]

**17 August** Stackpole Court, demolished in 1962, had been rebuilt in 1734-54, with additions from 1821 by Sir Jeffry Wyatville and Henry Ashton. It had a hundred and fifty rooms. Until the Victorians spoilt it, it was a U-shaped house with two matching, curved flights of steps to a pedimented main entrance. The pair of cannon were trophies from the French invaders at Fishguard in 1797.[14]

William Allen had been Rector of Bosherston since 1831 and of St Bride's since 1825. He held both till his death in 1872.[15]

Romilly may have been familiar with Malkin's book, or even had it with him, for Malkin called it Sir Gawaine's chapel.[16]

The Devil's Cauldron is usually known now as the Devil's Punch Bowl, and Adam's Leap as Huntsman's Leap. Tradition says that the huntsman died of fright when he looked back at the chasm he had jumped.

**19 August** Seaton's 'beautifying' had included the inexcusable demolition of two sections of the medieval arcade and the erection of 'a projecting roof with Gothic finishing all round the building'. His work was undone by his successor, Richard Lewis, in 1860-2; the arcade was restored save for a matching pillar being substituted for a pier near the chancel step. Lewis also transformed the Rectory, though the room where the service was held, about seventeen feet square, is not much altered.[17]

William Seaton, after a colourful career as an English Nonconformist minister, had taken Anglican orders (and the sister of Sir John Owen of Orielton, M.P. for the Pembroke boroughs, to wife), arriving in Lampeter Velfrey in 1830 with little experience for so different a ministry. He almost emptied the church through his inability to preach in Welsh. Undaunted, he announced some Welsh sermons, and crowds flocked to snigger at his malapropisms.[18]

His sermon this Sunday was based on Hebrews 3, verse 8 or 15, or on Psalm 95, verse 8, which besides being read at morning prayer every day happened to be set for the nineteenth morning of the month.

The son Romilly mentions may have been Abdiel or William (see page 31, ref 34; page 98, ref 43).

Edward was doubtless Edward Romilly at Porthkerry.

**20 August** Dunford was Romilly's gyp (college servant); see note on 28 July 1840.[19]

**21 August** Romilly's brother Frank had married a French girl, Joséphine Cinte, and settled in Paris, where they had three children, Estéphanie, Sophie and Jacques. There are many references to Romilly writing a letter to Frank and enclosing £10.[20]

**22 August** 'ready to cry out': that is, in childbirth.

Sir Thomas Noon Talfourd (1795-1854) was a Reading brewer's son, who rose to become a judge and an M.P.: the man behind the idea of literary copyright. Dickens dedicated *Pickwick* to him in gratitude. *The Athenian Captive, a Tragedy*, came out in 1838.[21]

Napoleon called Laure Junot, Duchesse d'Abrantès, 'la petite peste'. Her *Histoires des Salons de Paris* appeared in 1836-8.[22]

'the Ton': people of fashion ('Ton' with a French pronunciation).

Tadeusz Andrzej Bonawentura Kosciuszko (1746-1817) was a Polish general and statesman, who distinguished himself fighting for American as well as Polish independence.[23]

Mme de Staël (Anne Louise Germaine Necker, Baronne de Staël-Holstein) (1766-1817), of Swiss parentage, a friend of Sismondi and James Mackintosh, became through her writings and salons a focus of Romantic, anti-Napoleonic ideas. 'She was a large, masculine-looking woman, rather coarse, and with a thoracic development worthy of a wet nurse'.[24]

**24 August** John Hensleigh Allen's son 'little John' (also known as 'long John') joined the Colonial Office and devoted himself, presumably in his spare time, to London's poor.[25]

**25 August** The beautiful view at Briton Ferry (painted by Thomas Hornor in 1819) contrasts with the arrogant motorways, high-speed trains and sprawling industrial development of today: a telling example of the changes between Romilly's world and ours.

Arthur was the only surviving son of Dr Malkin; his brother, Sir Benjamin, a judge in India, had died the year before.[26]

Mrs Jane Marcet (1769-1858), daughter of a wealthy Swiss merchant, Francis Haldimand, based in London, had married an eminent Geneva-born doctor, Alexander Marcet; he practised medicine in Britain and became—like their son, Francis—a Fellow of the Royal Society. Jane wrote best-selling books popularising the sciences: she ranged from chemistry to mineralogy, but was best on political economy. She also wrote many books for children. She used to attend Mrs Sismondi's soirées, 'but did not often add to their pleasure'; her loud voice ruined the conversation. She once called unexpectedly and said with her usual rudeness to another lady present, 'But who are you?', making Jessie's ears tingle.[27]

Thomas Chandler Haliburton (1796-1865), a Canadian judge and politician, wrote several tales about his character Sam Slick. The first appeared in 1835.[28]

**26 August** For Casberd, see note on 10 July 1830.

The Bishop of Llandaff was Edward Copleston, who held the see from 1828 to 1849. He did not speak Welsh, or really understand the peculiar problems of a bilingual and increasingly industrial diocese; a learned and kindly man in the wrong job.[29]

Paul Ashmore was Rector of Porthkerry from 1837. The following year, 1838, the Bishop of London (according to Romilly; he surely meant Llandaff) agreed to institute him to Barry as well, provoking Canon Sydney Smith of St Paul's, a famous wit, to remark, 'Well, I would not wish a bishop worse luck than to get into a nest of Romillys'. Ashmore resigned in 1865.[30]

**27 August** Capel Hanbury-Leigh of Pontypool Park (1776-1861) married twice, his second wife being Emma Elizabeth Rous of Cwrt-yr-Ala, Glamorgan; Romilly called at her home on 17 September 1831.[31]

**28 August** Henry Gunning was Senior Esquire Bedell of the University. His duty was to attend the Chancellor or Vice Chancellor bearing one of the University's silver maces.[32]

## SOURCES

1  Bury, 253. I am at a loss to explain the nickname. Was the boy's family from Swabia?

2  E.T. Macdermot (C.R. Clinker, rev), *History of the Great Western Railway* vol I, 1833-1863 (London, 1964) [hereafter Macdermot, *G.W.R.*], 23, 452; Earl of Bessborough (ed), *Lady Charlotte Guest: Extracts from Her Journal 1832-1852* (London, 1950), 73-4; P. Whitehouse and D.St J. Thomas (ed), *The Great Western Railway 150 Glorious Years* (Newton Abbot, 1984), 23, 38.

3  Macdermot, *G.W.R.*, 379, 382, 466.

4  *Enc. Brit.*, vol 10, 492; Robson's *Commercial Directory of London and the Western Counties* (London, 1840?), Gloucester section, 22; H.E. Litchfield, *Emma Darwin* vol II (Cambridge, 1904) [hereafter Litchfield, *Darwin*], 25.

5  R. Haslam, *Powys* (Harmondsworth and Cardiff, 1979), 299.

6  *D.N.B.*, LVIII, 73-4.

7  Mr Thomas Lloyd identified her; memorial in Laugharne church.

8  Lambeth Palace Library, Incorporated Church Building Society, 1st series, 2569, box C8. The painting is signed 'B.E.', and the work dated from 1839-40, when Page may have moved to Scappin farm (Droslyn Fach no longer exists). Mr Thomas Lloyd drew my attention to this picture.

9  *W.W.H.R.*, I, 269-70; Pembs R.O., PQ/AG/7/82. H.M. Vaughan, *The South Wales Squires* (London, 1926), 118-9, has an account of the assault (which was in 1850), but omits the material fact that the squire had caught Charles shooting on his estate. See also 'Owen Square', *Memories of above Half a Century* (London, no date, c1889), 120-1. The fullest account is in Pembs R.O., D/LEW/7/934.

10 *W.W.H.R.*, I, 269; IV, 286, 291; D.W. James, 'James Allen: Master of the Fabric', *J.P.H.S.*, no 3 (1989), 28-40, with photograph. The present Dean, the Very Rev J. Wyn Evans, pointed out to me how ancient Dean Allen was. Even in 1852 when he married he was described as aged, with the look 'somewhat of the stiffened Bachelor', though with 'one of those noble Souls that women are safe with': letter in Allen Papers.

11 *W.W.H.R.*, I, 256; see also note on 30 August 1854.

12 Pembs R.O., DX/4/35. I owe this quotation to Mrs Corinne Streets.

13 C. Oman, *Nelson* (London, 1950), 391.

14 F. Jones, 'The Old Families of Wales' in D. Moore (ed), *Wales in the Eighteenth Century* (Swansea, 1976), 43; T. Lloyd, *The Lost Houses of Wales* (London, 1989), 71, with photograph showing the cannon; Ward Lock & Co, *Guide to Cardiff and South Wales* (London, 1947), 165.

15 *W.W.H.R.*, I, 246; III, 274.

16 B.H. Malkin, *The Scenery, Antiquities, and Biography, of South Wales* (London, 1804, reprinted 1970), 528-9.

17 Lambeth Palace Library, Incorporated Church Building Society, file no 2224 (Lampeter Velfrey, 1837-9).

18 M.G.R. Morris, 'Bishop Richard Lewis: His Life Before Llandaff', *J.W.E.H.*, vol 4 (1987), 66.

19 Bury, 241.

20 Bury & Pickles, 243, 260 and refs.

21 S.A. Allibone, *A Critical Dictionary of English Literature and British and American Authors* (Philadelphia and London, 1900), 2330; S.J. Kunitz and H. Haycraft, *British Authors of the Nineteenth Century* (New York, 1936), 603; G. Gissing (rev), *Forster's Life of Dickens* (London, 1903), 68, with signed portrait of Talfourd opposite (I owe this source to Col Andrew Man).

22 *Enc. Brit.*, vol 13, 139-40.

23 *Enc. Brit.*, vol 13, 477-8 (with portrait). Romilly spelt his name 'Koschiousko' and then crossed out the 'h' and the second 'o'.

24 *Enc. Brit.*, vol 21, 73-4 (with portrait); C. Hibbert (ed), *Captain Gronow His Reminiscences of Regency and Victorian Life 1810-60* (London, 1991), 254.

25 Litchfield, *Darwin*, 62.

26 E. Walford, *The County Families of the United Kingdom* (London, 1880), 682; *D.W.B.*, 610.

27 *D.N.B.*, XXXVI, 122-3; A.O. Allen, *John Allen and His Friends* (London, no date, c1901?), 191; letter to Emma Allen, 10 August 1839, in Allen Papers. Romilly (Bury, 229) recorded another gaucherie by Mrs Marcet: dining at Lady Holland's with a Dr Holland, she attributed her hostess's health to the 'sudden appearance' of *Lord* Holland. Since he had been dead two years, the company expected to see a ghost. See also Bury & Pickles, 87.

28 *Enc. Brit.*, vol 10, 1133.

29 E.T. Davies, 'The Church in the Industrial Revolution' in D. Walker (ed), *A History of the Church in Wales* (Penarth, 1976), 127-31.

30 N.L.W., LL/P/20-1; LL/NR/5; LL/RES/4. Smith's remark quoted by Romilly, 8 November 1838; Copleston being also Dean of St Paul's (to eke out his meagre episcopal stipend) may have made him confuse the dioceses. On the question whether an incumbent could be appointed to a parish with Welsh speakers if he himself knew no Welsh but agreed to learn it, or had a Welsh-speaking curate, see R.L. Brown, 'Pastoral Problems and Legal Solutions in the Established Church in Wales' in N. Doe (ed), *Essays in Canon Law* (Cardiff, 1992), 7-24. The Pluralities Act, 1838, strengthened the hand of those wanting an incumbent who could minister in Welsh. The problem is still with us.

31 J.A. Bradney, *A History of Monmouthshire* part II, *The Hundred of Abergavenny* (London, 1906), 438-9; C.U.L., Add 6813.

32 Bury, 243; Bury & Pickles, 252 (these authorities differ on when he held office); F. Stubbings, *Bedders, Bulldogs and Bedells* (Cambridge, 1991), 21. The word 'bedell', usually stressed on the second syllable, derives from 'beadle'; at Oxford it is spelt 'bedel'.

# 9   PRESTEIGNE TO PEMBROKESHIRE

## 22 July—8 August 1840

This time Romilly, accompanied by Baugh Allen, entered Wales from Monmouthshire. It gave him a chance to see Clyro again, twenty years after that first unrecorded visit for his cousin's wedding, as well as Knill Court, which had been the family home of Sir Samuel Romilly's wife; he had not been there since their funeral in 1818, and in the meantime the house had been rebuilt. He went on to explore Brecon, and stopped at Llandeilo, where Baugh found he had friends.

They set off by train from London on 21 July, travelling second class on cushionless seats next to the engine. At Worcester they transferred to Baugh's open carriage, and made their way by stages to Pembrokeshire, where they found Baugh's sons and George Romilly, all in their late teens, awaiting them at Cilrhiw. Uncle Joseph tutored two of the boys in trigonometry, enjoyed a few excursions despite the heat, and eventually took the Bristol steamer from Tenby in perfect sailing weather.

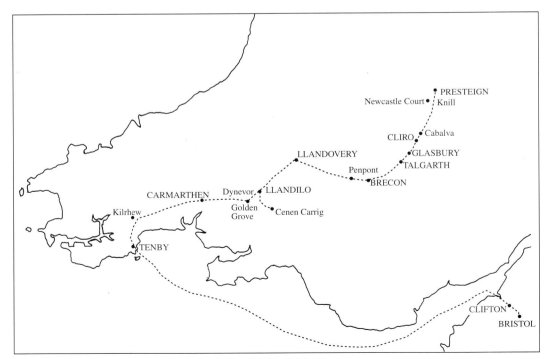

South Wales  (1840)

Pembrokeshire (1840)

We pick up the journey as the brothers-in-law cross the border into Wales.

**Wednesday 22 July** ... We reached Presteign (14 miles) about 6 and while our eggs and bacon were getting ready we went to the church, which has a good substantial tower. I was amused with the following epitaphs:

A ling'ring sickness did we seize,
That no physicians could we ease,
We sought for means, but all in vain
Till God did ease we of our pain.

Weep not for we our children dear,
We are not dead but sleeping here;
Our glass is run, our graves you see,
Therefore prepare to follow we.

Here lies the husband and the wife,
Now joined in death as once in life.
What happy Parents sh$^d$ we be
Should we in Heav'n our children see!

Affliction sore long time I bore:
Phys[icia]$^{ns}$ were in vain;
Till X [Christ] the L[ord] removed them all
And eas'd me of my pain.

We walked the 4 miles from Presteign and got to Newcastle Court* at 8½ before the carriage. Found Mr, Mrs, Miss and John Whittaker* at home. I was delighted with the position of the house on sloping ground, beautifully wooded. Walked about the grounds till dark and then tea and talk till bedtime. Found Mrs Whittaker wonderfully little altered; the 20 years since I had seen Penelope had given her rather a matronly look, and John is beginning to lose his hair. They both made themselves very agreeable. Mr and Mrs Whittaker received us with a hearty welcome. Mr Whittaker has had several paralytic strokes but they have affected his appearance very little, and he chiefly reminds one of increased infirmities by walking with a stick and being more quiet before dinner and very sleepy after. Mrs Whittaker holds herself in the same upright manner that she used formerly and supports conversation with the same talent. John is devoting himself to improvement of the poor.

**Thursday 23 July** Mr Whittaker drove Penelope, Baugh and me to call on the Frankland Lewises.* Mrs Frankland Lewis (the 2nd) newly married: her maiden name Ashton. I ought to have known her as it appears, but I don't at all remember meeting her at Cambridge in the days of old. She is about 40, very good looking and agreeable. I had a good deal of talk with Mr Frankland Lewis about my uncle's mémoirs. He took great interest in the Cambridge Agricultural Society, being himself a breeder of cattle. We then drove to Knill (now let by Sir J. Walsham* to Sir J. Walsh*). I found it melancholy going to a place which I had never visited except on the mournful occasion of the funeral of my uncle and Lady Romilly. The old house was pulled down and the present one built by Walsham a few years ago. Sir John Walsh was absent, so we went over the house. In one room is a beautiful miniature of Lady Romilly as a girl of 18 with her hair covering her forehead. It was painted by Engleheart* (I think). Mr Whittaker was out of spirits on seeing the church and talked of his son being laid there. Today (like all days since the beginning of my travels) was very cold and uncomfortable and sunless; no rain however while we were out. Before our drive this morning some friends of the Whittakers came to lunch: their names were Mr and Mrs McMurdo, she pretty and both agreeable. At dinner there was no company, but we made a party of 6 and had a good deal of interesting conversation about new schoolrooms and other matters of improvement of the condition of the poor, in which John Whittaker takes great interest. I like very much the tone of his mind, and his manners to his parents are manly and respectful.

**Friday 24 July** Left the Whittakers directly after breakfast (about 10½). Our route was intended to be through Kingston* and the Hay to Brecon, but we took a wrong turn and missed the Hay and came along a higher and more picturesque road, but villainous for horses from the new stone laid down for 3 miles. From the top of the hill (4 miles from the Hay) we had a beautiful view of the Wye. We passed Cabalva* and I was sorry to find that Mr Davies* is living with his cook, by whom he has 2 children; of course all respectable people have dropped his acquaintance. Passed also Cliro church,* where 20 years ago I married Mrs Kennedy.* Within a mile of Glasbury we passed a very handsome turreted house* belonging to a family now called de Winton,* but formerly Wilkins. A mile beyond Glasbury we baited our horses, they having performed 24 miles. This house (the 3 Cocks) is a very neat one and kept by very civil people, so we had some lunch though we were not hungry. We now walked on 2½ miles to Talgarth, where Baugh left me sitting on a stone and writing my journal, while he called on the clergyman of the place, one of his

Brecon Priory (now the Cathedral) in about 1845

unnumbered cousins (John Morgan*); he found him just going to dinner, but staid with him half an hour or so. We travelled along the banks of the Honddu (a tributary of the Usk, which it joins at Brecon) and in about 10 miles reached Brecon at 6 o'clock.

We put up at an excellent hotel, the Castle, and proceeded to view the curiosities of the town. The principal object of interest is the Priory church* and gardens. The church has been wonderfully brutified, but contains still some interesting remains of early English architecture. There is here a rude font of Saxon sculpture. There are several recumbent figures of men and women in stone. The chancel is separated by 5 windows after the Early English style; these are glazed to keep the place warm. We walked through the Priory gardens, which overhang the Honddu and make a charming promenade. The Priory-house* is the property of Lord Camden.* We perambulated the town, visiting the Barracks (where were the regiment which quelled the Newport insurrection of Frost*), the promenade on the Usk &c. We dined fashionably at near 9. Wrote* to Thirlwall* both at Kirby Underdale and in town to wish him joy of his appointment as Bishop of Bangor* to succeed Jenkinson; also to Gordon,* about the mandate degree.*

**Saturday 25 July** Left the Castle Inn at Brecon at 7½. Along the banks of the Usk to Penpont (5 miles), where we found Mr Penry Williams* (Sheriff of the county) in bed, but he and his wife got up and gave us breakfast and received us most cordially. His house* is a beautiful one with a fine colonnade, and the views in his grounds (which are on the Usk) are charming. He walked us through his gardens &c and exhibited his chapel* in the park, and where the wooden lions used to stand (the admiration of travellers in the days of old, but wisely condemned by Mr Williams to the flames). In the house is a very good portrait of Anna Boleyn, from whom Mr Williams is descended, and a capital Weenix* (cocks and hens, ducks and dog); he has also a curious coarse portrait of O. Cromwell, not comparable to that at Sidney lodge.* At ¼ to 12 we left these very friendly people (their children were absent), and proceeded along the banks of the Usk* to Llandovery. We stopped to examine the spot where the mail coach fell down more than 100 feet into the river without killing any body.* We baited for an hour at Llandovery and had some capital trout for luncheon. We staid in doors as the rain came down in torrents. We reached Llandilo (having travelled about 32 miles) at 6 and having ordered dinner at ¼ to 9 we sallied forth to visit Lord Dynevor's castle. The modern house* is not worth speaking of; but the ruins of the old castle (in themselves worthless) command an enchanting view of the windings of the Usk,* which reminded me of the view from Stirling Castle. These ruins are perched on very high ground in the midst of a noble wood.* We saw lying beneath us on the other side of the river Golden Grove (a modern house just built by Lord Cawdor,* to whom the Vaughans left the old seat of Lord Carberry, which he pulled down). We enjoyed the walks in this wood particularly, the evening fortunately having turned out fine and there being a beautiful sunset.

**Sunday 26 July** Miserable wet morning, rain coming down in torrents. Wrote to Grim and also to Margaret and Lucy. To the great church* (the only one), where Mr Pugh* (an Oxonian) did the whole duty; he preached from Matthew 5.20* on the righteousness of the scribes and Pharisees. I liked his sermon very much, and his manner of reading and preaching. He repeated the text in Welsh as well as English but did not preach in Welsh (his Welsh service being in the evening). While looking over the monuments after the service we fell in with him and were pleased with his conversation. At 4 o'clock we attended the English service at Lord Cawdor's little chapel* in Dynevor park. The clergyman is Mr Herbert Griffies Williams* (of St John's Cambridge); he preached from Psalm 119.60 on hasting to keep the commandments; his manner was simple and devout and the small congregation very attentive. The singing here and at the church remarkably good; there was no accompaniment at either place, the organ at the church being out of repair, and there being none in the chapel. Baugh discovered by a monument to his only boy (a baby) that the clergyman was a friend of his, so we stopped to speak to him. Mrs Griffies Williams* is a very pretty lady in delicate health; she had her 3 little girls with her (who are very pretty) and her governess (a plain but very accomplished Miss Beal,* who draws well and has written a tragedy). Mr and Mrs Williams received Baugh in the kindest and most pressing way possible and insisted upon our coming to sleep at their house, which we agreed to do.

Dined at our inn (the Cawdor Arms) at 6 and then walked to Golden Grove (built by Wyattville* of a dingy slate colored stone). I regretted the destruction of the old place, which for Jeremy Taylor's* sake I should like to have seen. The evening was fine and the view from the terrace good, though not so striking as that from Dynevor Castle. We got to Mr H.G. Williams to tea about 9 o'clock and passed a very agreeable evening discussing ghost stories, in which Mrs Williams and Miss Beal took great interest, and the former seemed to me to believe in ghosts and to be much frightened. She is a granddaughter of Lord Robert Seymour* (by his daughter Mrs Davies*); a very pretty sister of hers is married to Lord Charles Russell.* Mr Williams is a gentlemanlike man most attentive to his guests, and made us quite at home. His parsonage* is very well appointed and is an excellent house and every thing in the best style. He will become a baronet on his father's death. Lord Cawdor gave him his 2 chapels, one* in Golden Grove park, the other in Dynevor park.

**Monday 27 July** Breakfasted at 8 without our hostess. Directly after breakfast Mr Williams drove us in his landau to see a ruined castle 3 miles off, most picturesquely situated; it is called Cenen Carrig* (or the rock on the rivulet Cenen). It is on the summit of a very high (and on one side precipitous) rock and commands a very extensive view. It has no architectural beauty whatever, and gains its interest entirely by its position. A passage is cut through the solid rock to a little well, which is always full. We visited this with tapers in our hands. This castle belongs to Lord Cawdor. We dined with our kind host and hostess at 1 and started on our journey again at 2¼. Reached Carmarthen at 6 and went into the Courthouse for an hour while our horses were baiting and heard an absurd trial about *sitting up*.* The weather which had been fine till now turned to rain and the rain continued till we reached home* at ¼ to 10. Found the 3 lads waiting for us; tea and then bed. George Romilly and Edward Allen left Dulwich last Thursday and got to Clifton that night; on Friday they went by the steam boat to Tenby and arrived at 5 o'clock on Saturday morning very sick and very wet and miserable; George had remained on deck all night—he had a bad cold in consequence, but is getting better.

**Tuesday 28 July** Wrote to Gordon about getting a Deputy Registrary for me; also to Dunford.* Lessons in trigonometry with George Romilly and Edward Allen till 2. We dined at 3. Walk with Mr Allen in the evening. No sun today, but also no rain. Worked at trigonometry with George and Edward till 2.

**Wednesday 29 July** Trigonometry till 2 with George and Edward; then George Allen rode over to the Eatons to take leave as they quit the country tomorrow. Mr Allen drove George Romilly, Edward and me over to Cresselly where we found considerable excitement from a stack of hay being pulled down in consequence of its being nearly on 5 [sic—fire] from having been put up too green. Found here Robert Wedgwood* and his American wife, Mr and Mrs Sismondi, Mrs Surtees, Fanny and Emma; we lay down on the hay in a field and had a pleasant chat. We paid a visit to the hothouse to eat grapes. Dined at Kilrhew at 7. Letters from Margaret and Lucy. Dull day but no rain.

**Thursday 30 July** Baugh Allen left early in the morning (7) for Haverford West assizes. Heavy mist till 11. George Allen and George Romilly then drove over to Tenby, where George Romilly made some sketches.* Edward and I worked at trigonometry till 2. I then walked to Narbeth to post letters to Margaret and Lucy written by me and George. Dined at 6. George Allen all the evening putting up a hammock which is arrived. I began reading *The Prairie** but didn't much like it.

**Friday 31 July** The 2 Georges rode to Amroth and had a good gallop on the sands. Edward and I walked to Castle Meherran and had a view of the sea with our telescopes. Dined at 6. A fine day.

**Saturday 1 August** In speaking of Llandilo I should have mentioned that the bridge is at right angles to the road at the foot of a steep hill and the bridge used to be extremely low in its walls. Consequently it was a most dangerous place, and very lately 2 ladies were dashed to pieces from their horse running away and throwing them and their servant and the carriage into the river.* The parapet walls have now been raised to prevent such misfortunes. Grim drove me over to Tenby. The day was delightful; we bathed, and continued walking about St Catherine's and lounging on the sands till 4 o'clock. Called on John Allen (of Coram Street*); he and his mother and wife all out. Today George Romilly rode over to Ludchurch and made a drawing of it. Mr Allen returned today; we dined at 7.

**Sunday 2 August** Another fine day. To church at Lampeter [Velfrey]. This church was undergoing repair* when I was here 2 years ago. It is repaired in admirable stile, and is one of the neatest country churches I have seen a long while. The preacher was Mr Seaton* (the Rector's) son; his text was 2 Corinthians 5.21, 'He hath made him to sin &c': it was extempore and was high Calvinism.* The singing was abominable, being an untunable bellow. Letters from Thirlwall (to say the Archbishop of Canterbury will give him a degree* and that he does not mean to throw down the gauntlet to the Bishop of Exeter* [?]), and Margaret (giving a good account of Lucy). We dined at 5 and took a good walk afterwards; in the evening I read a lesson and family prayers.

**Monday 3 August** Lovely day. Baugh drove me over to Cresselly where I saw all the family, viz Mr Allen, Miss Isabel, Seymour and Harry, Mr and Mrs Sismondi, Mrs Surtees, Fanny and Emma, R. Mackintosh* and wife,* Col Wedgwood and Miss Darwin.* George Romilly took a ride with Grim to Whitland. Dinner at 7.

**Tuesday 4 August** Fine hot weather. Studies as usual with the boys till 2. Too hot to walk in the morning. Dined at 5. Afterwards walked with Baugh over 52 acres of land adjoining his which he thinks of buying for £700. I finished Cooper's *Prairie* and found the most interesting character Mahtorea (the Sioux's) young deserted wife (the 'skipping fawn'). There is a ridiculous character of a naturalist riding on an 'asinus', a prosing insufferable old trapper (who acts interpreter with the Indians), an animated Pawnee chieftain (who first appears coiled up like a snake, is afterwards found hid under a buffalo hide in a burning prairie, and achieves prodigies of valour), a vulgar beehunter, and the family of Bush the squatter. Bush's dragon wife is well drawn, and there is rather a touching scene of her sorrow on her eldest boy's being murdered by her brother Abiram (this Abiram is made to hang himself by the squatter). All the Indian dialogue I found insufferable, and the kidnapping part of the plot most absurd.

**Wednesday 5 August** Set off at 7 in the morning to go to Haverfordwest Races. Mr Allen drove me and my 3 nephews in the phaeton. We breakfasted at Haverfordwest and at 1 went on to the race course. The day was baking hot. Got introduced to Lord and Lady Cawdor* (who told me of a walk in the woods at Golden Grove still called the Bishop's* Walk), and Mrs Ackland* (born Tyler) (who told me good tidings of the Chapter of St Davids having given Meares* the little living of Uzmaston, worth £120 per annum). Dined at the Mariners at Haverfordwest and drove home in the cool of the evening. Found agreeable letters from Margaret and Lucy and also one from Meares telling me of his preferment.

**Thursday 6 August** Wrote to Margaret and Lucy and Meares. Vastly hot. Walked to Narbeth with my letters and was obliged to sit down under the hedges. Grim walked over to Amroth to bathe and knocked himself up. Dinner at 7.

**Friday 7 August** Left Kilrhew at 7; Baugh drove me and George Romilly and Edward. Edward very poorly indeed, sick and out of order. We breakfasted at Cresselly, where they put poor Edward to bed and gave him slops. After a couple of hours' conversation with Mr Allen and Sismondi &c we set off again on our travels, leaving poor Grim behind. We paid a visit to the James Allens of Freestone (Mary Allen is going to marry her cousin Charles Allen* next Tuesday) and then went to Pembroke. We went over the beautiful old castle with a jolly old dame who was my cicerone when I was there before. She showed us a hole 30 feet deep down which she says she fell and found the stones very rough. This castle was the birthplace of Henry 7. Then to the dockyard at Pater. They are building several 80 gun ships; we went into the skeleton of one (the *Centurion*). We went into the model room and had the plans and drawings of ships explained by a very intelligent man. We afterwards went aboard a 26 gun frigate (*Iris*) launched a fortnight ago, and were delighted with seeing all over it under the guidance of the boatswain. Dined at the hotel at Hobbs Point at 7 and walked in the evening. The view from our window was beautiful and the sea was as calm as a lake and the sunset lovely. George made a sketch for Mr Allen; by the way, he has made a great many others for him, partly original and partly views at Kilrhew and Tenby.

**Saturday 8 August** Left the Royal Hotel at Hobbs Point at 7; a delicious day. Got to Tenby (10 miles) at 9½. We bathed, all 3 of us (viz Baugh, George and I), and then breakfasted at the White Lion. Afterwards we called on Mrs Bird Allen, and saw her and 3 of her sons (John* (of King's College), James and Charles (who is going to marry his cousin Mary on Tuesday)), and Mrs John Allen. We had an early dinner with her and embarked at 1½ aboard the *Star*\* steamer (Capt Rees). John Allen (of King's College) and Mr Seaton (whom we heard preach last Sunday) were among the passengers. Most luxurious day: bright sunshine and a gentle breeze, which scarcely ruffled the water. Every body aboard perfectly well. Reached Clifton at 1½ and went to the Gloucester Hotel; found it rather difficult jumping from the paddlebox of our steamer on to the next at landing, the moon being set and the glimmering of light most imperfect. ...

Next Sunday Romilly went to the Cathedral, where the Dean of Bristol preached; later to St Mary Redcliffe, where the Curate, Mr Irving, preached painfully loudly. 'In spite of all this a person in the same pew with us was so fast asleep that we had some difficulty in waking him when the sermon was over'. On 10 August Romilly went on to Bath, Salisbury and Southampton.

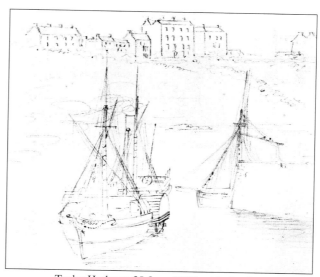

Tenby Harbour, 30 June 1838, with the *Star*

## NOTES

**22 July** Newcastle Court, near Evenjobb, a late Georgian house of seven bays (since gothicised), was the home of John Whittaker (c1773-1843). He came of a Westminster family, went to New College, Oxford, and served as a captain in the 3rd Light Dragoons.[1]

**23 July** Thomas Frankland Lewis (1780-1855), 'formal, verbose, and dull', had resigned the chairmanship of the Poor Law Commission the year before in favour of his son George (later Chancellor of the Exchequer and Home Secretary). In 1843 he chaired the commission on the Rebecca riots, and received a baronetcy three years later. Mary Anne Ashton was his second wife (1839). Their home, Harpton Court, had interiors by John Nash, who probably designed the austere, pedimented south front. Most of the house was pulled down in 1956.[2]

Sir John James Walsham Bt (1805-1874) of Knill Court, nephew by marriage of Sir Samuel Romilly, had evidently let his house to Sir John Benn Walsh (1798-1881), who had been returned unopposed as M.P. for Radnorshire on 10 June.[3]

George Engleheart (1752?-1829) was a prolific painter of miniatures. The portrait would have been executed in about 1791; as his fee-book survives, it should be possible to check the attribution.[4]

**24 July** 'Kingston' should be 'Kington'.

Cabalva House is of timber with later additions, some neo-classical.[5]

According to a memorial in Clyro church, William Davies of Cabalva was widowed on 4 March 1836, so that mitigated his offence (see note on 21 August 1854).

Clyro church, where Kilvert served as Curate (1865-72), was rebuilt, except for the tower, in 1853 (see note on 26 August 1854). It is extraordinary to think that this parish on the English border lay in a diocese with its Cathedral as far away as St David's.[6]

Mrs Kennedy was Sophie, daughter of Sir Samuel Romilly and only sister to Sir John and to Edward Romilly of Porthkerry. She had married Thomas Francis Kennedy in 1820, Joseph officiating at the service. As he was ordained only on 11 June that year and not priested till 1821, he did so in deacon's orders. This was uncanonical because of the nuptial blessing, but it often happened.[7]

Walter Wilkins made a fortune in India, changed his name to de Winton and commissioned Robert Lugar to rebuild the family home, Maesllwch Castle (1829-50). Lugar unstintingly reproduced the plan he had used at Glanusk Park, Penmyarth, but varied the style: the outside followed that of Cyfarthfa, while the inside ranged from Norman to Regency. The main block was demolished in 1951.[8]

James (not John) Morgan was Vicar of Talgarth, and had been since 1832.[9]

Brecon Priory is now the Cathedral. The font is thought to be twelfth century. ('Saxon' in Romilly's day was often applied to what we would term Norman or Romanesque.)

The Priory-house became the Deanery but is so no longer.

The Marquess Camden (1759-1840) was elected Chancellor of Cambridge University in 1834, having held several government posts, including that of Lord Lieutenant of Ireland; the 1798 rebellion was the result. He died on 8 October.[10]

John Frost (1784-1877), a former Mayor of Newport, was one of the leaders of the Chartist rebellion there on 4 November 1839. It was put down with the help of the 45th Foot (better known as the Sherwood Foresters). Twenty-two died. Chartism was a working-class movement for Parliamentary reform; of its six aims, all but one (annual Parliaments) have been achieved.[11]

The 'penny post' had become available since 6 May, when the famous black adhesive stamps could be used for post weighing less than half an ounce. What was revolutionary was that postage was pre-paid, at the same rate regardless of distance.[12]

Connop Thirlwall (1797-1875) had been dismissed as Assistant Tutor at Trinity because he had published a pamphlet supporting the admission of Nonconformists to University degrees and denouncing compulsory attendance at the College chapel; he remarked that the difference between compulsory religion and no religion at all was too subtle for his grasp. He took the living of Kirby Underdale in Yorkshire. On the death of John Banks Jenkinson, 7 July 1840, he was appointed Bishop of St Davids (not Bangor, as Romilly wrote), and elected on 4 August. (In those days before Disestablishment, the Crown sent the Chapter permission to elect, enclosing the name of the only candidate; failure to choose him laid them open to life imprisonment and loss of all their goods.) Archdeacon Richard Davies of Brecon had petitioned the Queen on 21 July, asking for a Welsh-speaking Welshman and the appointment of Bruce Knight, Chancellor of Llandaff. The diocese found Thirlwall a diligent pastor, formidable, generous and immensely learned; moreover he encouraged the use of the Welsh language and even learnt it himself, though not every native Welsh speaker could understand him.[13]

Gordon was probably Anthony Gordon, an exhibitioner at Trinity, who returned to the College as Chaplain in 1838.[14]

A mandate degree was one granted by the Crown to someone not strictly admissible, on petition from the University.[15]

**25 July** Penry Williams was apparently Sheriff in 1848.[16]

Penpont dates from about 1670, but was much altered in about 1810. G.G. Scott rebuilt the eighteenth-century chapel in 1864-5; the tower was always circular.[17]

There were two Dutch painters called Jan Weenix: father (born in 1621) and son (1640-1719). Both painted subjects like this.[18]

Oliver Cromwell was a Fellow Commoner at Sidney Sussex College. Romilly was referring to the Master's Lodge, and to the 'celebrated portrait-drawing of Cromwell, of which the fame is actually greater than the iconographic importance'.[19]

Romilly did not notice that the Usk turns off at Trecastle; thereafter he was following the Gwydderig, until at Llandeilo it meets the Tywi.

The mail coach accident, caused by drunken driving, occurred on 19 December 1835. The coach fell 121 feet, rolling over three times, but an ash tree prevented it from falling further into the Gwydderig. A pillar was erected nearby in 1841 with a cautionary account of the accident.[20]

Dynevor (Dinefwr in Welsh) was one of the great royal centres of Wales, the capital of Deheubarth, the seat of Rhodri Mawr in the ninth century and of Rhys ap Gruffydd in the twelfth. The castle is perhaps a little older than Rhys. It is said to have been occupied till a fire eighty years before Romilly's visit. The modern house (Newton House) was built in the 1660s, given domed corner towers in the 18th century, and remodelled with Venetian gothick detail and restyled towers in 1856-8.[21]

The Tywi, not the Usk, winds past Dynevor.

The park was landscaped by 'Capability' Brown, and has long been the home of white oxen. The War Office apparently had them painted brown in the Second World War lest they lead the Luftwaffe to more important targets like Swansea; they promptly fought one another.[22]

John Frederick Campbell (1790-1860), 2nd Baron and since 1827 1st Earl Cawdor, owned the greatest estate in west Wales, some 70,000 acres. About 40,000 had been left to his father (the Lord Cawdor mentioned by Romilly on 24 August 1837) by John Vaughan of Golden Grove, descendant by a roundabout route of the Earls of Carbery.[23]

**26 July** The last service in Llandeilo's old church, double aisled like the present one, was on 20 February 1848. The rebuilt church (by G.G. Scott; the tower is original) was opened on 10 October 1850. It cost £3,723 13s 10d.[24]

J.W. Pugh was the Vicar of Llandeilo.[25]

Romilly in fact gave his text as chapter 6, but he meant 5.

The chapel in Dynevor park was the former parish church of Llandyfeisant, dedicated to St Teilo's nephew Tyfai (Llan+Tyfai+Sant). Wedged into a steep hillside, it had a small south aisle with two plain, very low arches opening into the nave. These were replaced at the restoration of 1875.[26]

David Herbert Thackeray Griffies Williams (c1806-1877), fifth son of Sir George Griffies Williams Bt of Llwynwormwood Park (whose mother was Anne Thackeray), had married Anne Frances Gertrude Davies of Penlan and held a number of preferments, including Nevern (1834-40) and Llandyfeisant (1834-77). In fact, when Sir George died in 1843 the baronetcy went to his son Erasmus, later Chancellor of St Davids Cathedral, where he tried to pull rank as a baronet, but the Dean (Lewellin) resisted. Herbert Vaughan called Erasmus pompous and litigious.[27]

Anne Beale (1816-1900) published *The Vale of the Towey; or, Sketches in South Wales* in 1844, and later works.[28]

Sir Jeffry Wyatville had died the previous February. Nephew of James Wyatt, the designer of Fonthill, he is best remembered for his extensive and costly alterations to Windsor Castle; the Round Tower owes its top to him. One's estimate of the artistic loss in the recent fire at Windsor will depend on how one rates him as an architect. His own view is suggested by his asking George IV to let him change his name to the grander 'Wyatville' because some of the Wyatts were mere builders.[29]

Jeremy Taylor (1613-1667), author of *Holy Living* and *Holy Dying*, was chaplain to Lord Carbery here from 1645 to 1658. The Golden Grove he knew was lower down.[30]

Lord Robert Seymour, a son of the 1st Marquess of Hertford, had bought the Taliaris estate near Llandeilo, with its refaced seventeenth-century mansion. His daughter Elizabeth married William Griffith Davies (Mrs Williams was their daughter), and Elizabeth's sister Gertrude married Baugh Allen's elder brother but died in 1825.[31]

Lord Charles was a half-brother of Lord John Russell, later Prime Minister. His sister Lady Georgiana married Romilly's cousin Charles (Sir Samuel's son) in 1842.[32]

Griffies Williams's parsonage was Llwynhelyg, Llandeilo. Anne Beale wrote the preface of her book here in 1844.[33]

The Golden Grove chapel is Llanfihangel Aberbythych parish church, built by Sir John Vaughan in 1617, repaired in 1763 but described as new in 1917.[34]

**27 July** Carreg Cennen Castle has a highly picturesque and dramatic site, perched on the edge of a 300-foot cliff. The passage, partly man-made, is about 150 feet long. Thomas Jenkins explored it three years before Romilly, and found 'a fine spring of clean water near the further extremity'; this water, noted Robert Parker (here in 1804), was considered 'a Specifick for weak Eyes'.[35]

The case Romilly heard at the assizes was for breach of promise. An innkeeper's daughter from Llanegwad worked at a farm in the neighbourhood. The farmer's son paid addresses to her and sat up with her all one night, when both her sister and her mother overheard him promise to marry her (or so they claimed). Later the lad seduced her and she became *enceinte*. His father paid a shilling a week to support the child, and the girl ended up in the workhouse. She claimed damages of £500 (a huge sum then), but was awarded only £15[36] 'home': Cilrhiw.

**28 July** Poor Dunford, Romilly's servant at Trinity, had broken his leg in May—for the third time. He became lightheaded, and had to be put in a strait waistcoat for two days. Drink was his downfall.[37]

**29 July** Robert Wedgwood (1806-1880), youngest child of John and Jane (Baugh's sister) and brother of Col Tom Wedgwood, received the living of Dumbleton, Gloucestershire, in 1850, having been offered the next presentation by his wealthy cousin Edward Holland, the patron, as long ago as 1827-8.[38]

**30 July** George Romilly had decided artistic talent. He took 'a good likeness of Baugh's baby', Charles Hensleigh Allen, in 1843; but, despite a long stay in Paris, he failed to earn a living from his brush.[39]

James Fenimore Cooper (1789-1851), U.S. novelist, published *The Prairie* in 1827, a year after *The Last of the Mohicans*.[40]

**1 August** The accident happened at 1 p.m. on 8 March. Both Mrs Williams, a surgeon's wife, and the horse died on the spot; Miss Williams, the daughter, an hour and a half later at the Crown. The boy driving the phaeton (which was dashed to pieces) was taken up senseless. They had fallen about thirty-five feet. The bridge was very narrow, and not on the site of the present one. A painting by M.A. Rooker (1743-1801) shows a seven-arched stone bridge with the central span ruined and filled with a flimsy wooden structure.[41]

'Coram Street': his London address. Was this the John Allen referred to a week later (see note on 8 August)?

**2 August** The repairs (see note on 19 August 1838) included moving the pulpit and reading desk, previously against the wall halfway down the south aisle, to a more conventional position. Some parishioners showed their regard for Seaton by firing his hayricks on the glebe the night before the church was reopened.[42]

The preacher was probably the Rector's son William. His text was II Corinthians 5, verse 21, where St Paul writes of the sinless Christ's identification with human sin. Calvin held that mankind is totally corrupt, and that God has willed some to be saved and others to be damned. Christ died only for the elect. Such teaching is not without its difficulties.[43]

New bishops who were graduates of Cambridge or Oxford were given doctorates of divinity by their University. Canterbury took over with Lambeth doctorates (recipients wore the robes of the Archbishop's own University) when that system was largely abandoned in 1923-4, until Michael Ramsey stopped automatic awards to bishops in 1961.[44]

The Bishop of Exeter was Henry Phillpotts (1778-1869), High Church Tory and enemy of reform, a 'born controversialist and a matchless debater', who spent huge sums on disciplinary lawsuits. His wife was niece of Harriet Allen's unlamented husband, Matthew Surtees.[45]

**3 August** Robert Mackintosh (1806-1864) was the 'lethargic and somewhat effete' son of Sir James by his second wife, Catherine Allen. He had prudently married a rich American from Boston, Mary Appleton. Her sister, Frances, married Henry Wadsworth Longfellow, and left this candid pen-portrait of Robert: 'quite a good face, an awkward figure, however, laughs spasmodically, is constantly absent when present, & jerks out his words like a badly working pump'.[46]

Miss Darwin was one of the daughters of Robert and Susanna (née Wedgwood): probably Susan, or her younger sister, Catherine, who married late. Charles Darwin the naturalist was her brother.

**5 August** Lord Cawdor (see note on 25 July) had married Lady Elizabeth Thynne, daughter of the 2nd Marquess of Bath.[47]

Jeremy Taylor became Bishop of Down and Connor in 1660.[48]

For Mrs Ackland, see note on 11 July 1830, and for Meares, see note on 11 August 1837.

**7 August** Charles Allen (1808-1884), Bird's fifth son, had his nose kicked off by a horse and fastened back crooked; it was eventually reset without anaesthetic. He joined the East India Company and became an adviser to the Viceroy.[49]

The *Centurion*, named after Anson's flagship in his voyage round the world, was launched on 2 May 1844, and the *Iris* on 14 July 1840. Thomas Jenkins of Llandeilo went aboard the *Centurion* in 1860, when the Channel Fleet was lying off Milford; by then she had been converted to steam. *Iris* (907 tons) became a cable vessel.[50]

**8 August** John Allen (1810-1886), the youngest of six brothers, had been horribly bullied at Westminster School. Some boys roasted him before a fire, like Tom Brown, and forced him to look at pictures which shocked him so much that he refused to look at them again, so they made him toast bread with his bare hands. He ran away, begging for food and shelter as he walked home to Burton. Ordained to the chaplaincy of King's College, London, he married Harriet Higgins and became Archdeacon of Salop.[51]

The *Star* (150 tons, built in 1835 and commanded by William Rees) sailed from Bristol on Wednesdays for Milford and Haverfordwest. Another Bristol General Steam Navigation Company vessel, the *Phoenix*, called at Carmarthen.[52]

## SOURCES

1 R. Haslam, *Powys* (Harmondsworth and Cardiff, 1979) [hereafter Haslam, *Powys*], 232; Foster, 1545.

2 *D.W.B.*, 553, 562; *D.N.B.*, XXXIII, 198; Haslam, *Powys*, 261-2; T. Lloyd, *The Lost Houses of Wales* (London, 1989) [hereafter Lloyd, *Lost Houses*], 46. Romilly discussed Petrarch and German poetry with Miss Ashton in 1832, finding her clever, 'about 30 and looks well at night': Bury, 22.

3 Burke's *Peerage* (1970 ed), 2745; *D.N.B.*, LIX, 216; Bury & Pickles, 192. Walsh was created Lord Ormathwaite in 1868.

4 J.J. Foster (E.M. Foster, ed), *A Dictionary of Painters of Miniatures (1525-1850)* (London, 1926), 104; *D.N.B.*, XVII, 375; *Enc. Brit.*, vol 8, 443-4, which says he was born 26 October 1750. K.K. Yung (comp) (M. Pettman, ed), *National Portrait Gallery Complete Illustrated Catalogue 1856-1979* (London, 1981), 721, says 1752.

5 Haslam, *Powys*, 226.

6 Haslam, *Powys*, 226.

7 *D.N.B.*, XLIX, 191.

8 Haslam, *Powys*, 234-5; Lloyd, *Lost Houses*, 45.

9 *Clergy List* (1864), 233. Canon William Price supplied this.

10 *Enc. Brit.*, vol 4, 695; Bury, 63, 239.

11 *Enc. Brit.*, vol 9, 962; C.J.O. Evans, *Monmouthshire* (Cardiff, 1953), 134-8. J.A. Bradney (M. Gray, ed), *A History of Monmouthshire* vol 5, *The Hundred of Newport* (Cardiff and Aberystwyth, 1993), 41-5, has another and often contradictory account of the riot. 5,000 are said to have marched into Newport.

12 *Enc. Brit.*, vol 18, 307.

13 G.M. Trevelyan, *Trinity College* (Cambridge, 1946), 94-5; J.C. Thirlwall, *Connop Thirlwall Historian and Theologian* (London, 1936), 76 (quoting Romilly); *O.D.C.C.*, 1348; *W.W.H.R.*, IV, 281; Carmarthen Reference Library, *The Carmarthen Journal* [hereafter *Journal*], 24 July 1840. Romilly deplored Thirlwall's

dismissal: Bury, 57-9. He took his place in the select Cambridge dining club (still existing) known as the Family; he found the food excellent, but the 'spitting boxes most filthy': Bury, 64. Harriet Allen's husband, Matthew Surtees, had been Rector of Kirby Underdale: Burke, 1815. It was Thirlwall who, quoting Plutarch, told his barber he wanted his hair cut 'in silence'; and, when a new gardener asked three times how he wanted a border laid out, he said, 'You are the gardener, I believe, and I am the Bishop': G. Huntington, *Random Recollections of Some Noted Bishops, Divines and Worthies of the 'Old Church' of Manchester* (London, 1893) [hereafter Huntington, *Recollections*], 93-4.

14 In 1846 he was 'not in his right mind': Bury & Pickles, 186.

15 I owe this explanation to Dr Pickles.

16 T. Nicholas, *Annals and Antiquities of the Counties and County Families of Wales* (London, 1872), 107; but Nicholas is not to be relied on.

17 Haslam, *Powys*, 367; J.B. Hilling, *The Historic Architecture of Wales* (Cardiff, 1976) [hereafter Hilling, *Architecture*], 110, 171.

18 P. and L. Murray, *A Dictionary of Art and Artists* (Harmondsworth, 1959), 343.

19 J. Steegman (B. Little, rev), *Cambridge* (London, 1954), 25.

20 H. Williams, *Stage Coaches in Wales* (Barry, 1977), 11-3

21 Hilling, *Architecture*, 67; Ward Lock & Co, *Guide to Cardiff and South Wales* (London, 1947) [hereafter Ward Lock, *Guide*], 135; Lloyd, *Lost Houses*, 54; information from Fr John Barnes. The National Trust has recently restored Newton House.

22 L. Hughes, 'Two Estates in Wales' in *The National Trust Magazine*, no 52, autumn 1987, 24, 26 (can this story be true?).

23 Burke's *Peerage* (1970 ed), 508; D. Williams, *The Rebecca Riots* (Cardiff, 1955), 4-6; F. Jones, 'The Old Families of Wales' in D. Moore (ed), *Wales in the Eighteenth Century* (Swansea, 1976), 40.

24 D.C. Jenkins (ed), *The Diary of Thomas Jenkins of Llandeilo 1826-1870* (Bala, 1976) [hereafter Jenkins, *Diary*], 65, 80; R.C.A.H.M., 91; W. Davies, *Llandeilo-Vawr and its Neighbourhood* (Llandeilo, 1858, reprinted as part of *Llandeilo*, Carmarthen, 1993) [hereafter Davies, *Llandeilo*], 12, where the opening is given as 1848 (I am grateful to Miss Helen Palmer for checking this; Thomas Jenkins was at the service in 1850). A plan (c1845) is in Carmarthen Record Office, Cawdor MSS, 1/229: see N. Yates, 'Church Buildings of the Protestant Establishments in Wales and Scotland: Some Points of Comparison', *J.W.E.H.*, vol 9 (1992), 10, 14.

25 Jenkins, *Diary*, 200.

26 Mr and Mrs S.C. Hall, *The Book of South Wales, The Wye, and the Coast* (London, 1861, reprinted East Ardsley, 1977), 365; S. Baring-Gould and J. Fisher, *The Lives of the British Saints* vol IV (London, 1913), 289-90; J.E. Lloyd (ed), *A History of Carmarthenshire* vol I (Cardiff, 1935), 110; R.C.A.H.M., 110; J.F. Jones, 'Nineteenth Century Church Restorations in St Davids Diocese' part XXIII, *St Davids Diocesan Gazette*, no 171, July 1971 [hereafter Jones, 'Restorations'], 10-3; I.G. Jones and D. Williams, *The Religious Census of 1851 A Calendar of the Returns Relating to Wales* vol I (Cardiff, 1976) [hereafter Jones, *Census*], 316.

27 Venn, VI, 486; *W.W.H.R.*, III, 219; IV, 294; Jones, 'Restorations', 11; E.M.N. (née Lewellin), *Pleasant Memories of Eminent Churchmen* (Carmarthen, no date), 42; H.M. Vaughan, *The South Wales Squires* (London, 1926), 122.

28 *D.W.B.*, 29. M. Stephens (ed), *The Oxford Companion to the Literature of Wales* (Oxford, 1986), 34, gives the title as *The Vale of Towey* (1844), republished (1849) as *Traits and Stories of the Welsh Peasantry*. I have quoted the title of the copy in St Davids Cathedral Library. See also Davies, *Llandeilo*, 45-51.

29 C. Hibbert, *The Court at Windsor* (Harmondsworth, 1966), 212-3; *D.N.B.*, LXIII, 191. The King is supposed to have replied, 'Ville or mutton, call yourself what you like'.

30 *O.D.C.C.*, 1325.

31 Burke's *Peerage* (1970 ed), 1317; E. Inglis-Jones, 'A Pembrokeshire County Family in the Eighteenth Century', *N.L.W.J.*, vol XVII no 2 (1971), 157-8; Hilling, *Architecture*, 116, 126, 135.

32 *Enc. Brit.*, vol 19, 771; Bury & Pickles, xiii, 243.

33 Jones, *Census*, 320; Jones, 'Restorations', 11.

34  Jones, *Census*, 320; R.C.A.H.M., 125.

35  Ward Lock, *Guide*, 136; Jenkins, *Diary*, 16; R. Gard (ed), *The Observant Traveller* (London, 1989), 92.

36  *Journal*, 31 July 1840.

37  Bury, 193-4; Bury & Pickles, 46-8, 100, 118.

38  B. and H. Wedgwood, *The Wedgwood Circle 1730-1897* (Ontario, 1980) [hereafter Wedgwood, *Wedgwood Circle*], 224, 385; deed of institution, 23 July 1850, and letter from Robert to Edward Holland, January 1828, in Allen Papers. Edward (c1806-1875), a Trinity man, was a leading agriculturalist; his sporting brother George Henry married Charlotte, eldest daughter of Lord Gifford and Harriet née Drewe (Robert Wedgwood's first cousin) in 1844: information from Mr Roland Thorne and Venn, vol III, 414-5.

39  Bury & Pickles, 47, 50, 54, 228, 232. Baugh's wife annoyed George by adding 'beautifying touches of her own to the portrait'.

40  *Enc. Brit.*, vol 6, 444-5.

41  Jenkins, *Diary*, 25; painting by Rooker in N.L.W. According to Davies, *Llandeilo*, 52, the bridge 'has four narrow stone-arches; the centre is built of wood, and comprises more than two-thirds of the whole structure'. Evidently it had become even more dilapidated by 1858.

42  Lambeth Palace Library, Incorporated Church Building Society, file no 2224 (Lampeter Velfrey, 1837-9); *Journal*, 24 August 1838.

43  M.G.R. Morris, 'Bishop Richard Lewis: His Life Before Llandaff', *J.W.E.H.*, vol 4 (1987), 66-7, 73. The Rector's youngest son, Abdiel, became his Curate, but he was not ordained till 1843: N.L.W., SD/O/914. William *fils*, the eldest, was Curate and Lecturer at St Thomas's, Thomas Street, Bristol, in 1840, and also Lecturer at St Mary-le-Port; hence his passage with Romilly from Tenby to Bristol on 8 August.

44  O. Chadwick, *Michael Ramsey* (Oxford, 1991), 405. Welsh diocesan bishops are now chosen by an Electoral College, itself elected by and from the clergy and laity.

45  *D.N.B.*, XLV, 222-5. Romilly wrote 'the B. of E'—I think. At first I read it as 'the B. of G', taking it to mean the Bishop of Gloucester, James Henry Monk, whose see was united with that of Bristol in 1836 (see note on 6 September 1854); but on 27 September 1839 Romilly abbreviated his title as 'B. of Gl.' (Bury, 179). For the link with Surtees and Allen, see Burke, 1815.

46  Wedgwood, *Wedgwood Circle*, 248-9, quoting E. Wagenknecht, *Mrs Longfellow: Selected Letters and Journals of Fanny Appleton Longfellow* (New York, 1956), 143.

47  Burke's *Peerage* (1970 ed), 508.

48  *O.D.C.C.*, 1325.

49  Family tree, 1904, in Allen Papers; R.M. Grier, *John Allen, Vicar of Prees and Archdeacon of Salop* (London, 1889) [hereafter Grier, *Allen*], 11-2.

50  S. Peters, *The History of Pembroke Dock* (London, 1905), appendix I; Jenkins, *Diary*, 125; further information from Miss J.M. Wraight of the National Maritime Museum.

51  J.S. Allen, *Olim Meminisse Iuvabit*, and family tree in Allen Papers; Grier, *Allen*, 20-1; A.O. Allen, *John Allen and His Friends* (London, no date, c1901?), *passim*; Huntington, *Recollections*, 184 (pp 180-97 recall Archdeacon Allen).

52  R.F. Walker, 'Tenby Guides and Tenby Visitors, c1800-1987', *J.P.H.S.*, no 2 (1986-7), 51; Robson's *Commercial Directory of London and the Western Counties* (London, 1840?), Bristol section, 117; *Journal*, 7 August 1840 (the *Star*'s departure from Tenby on 8 August at half past one was as advertised in the local press). Both vessels are listed in G. Farr, *Shipbuilding in the Port of Bristol* (London, 1977), 41.

# 10  A SUNSHINE HOLIDAY

## 21 August—8 September 1854

In baking summer heat, Romilly came back to south Wales, and enjoyed meeting a new generation —

> young and old come out to play
> On a sunshine holiday.

This final visit in some ways resembled the one before it. He entered Wales through Radnorshire, went to Brecon and (albeit by a different route) crossed into Pembrokeshire, where he followed his usual programme of excursions and family calls. But circumstances had changed. Baugh lay nine years in his grave. His sons were now both married, with children of their own. Romilly himself was nearly sixty-two—though the diary betrays no let-up in his activities, and no hint of ageing beyond some trouble with his legs, which may have portended the illness that eventually killed him.

He left Cambridge for London on 18 August in the company of a Miss Lestourgeon, wild with delight at the prospect of seeing the Crystal Palace, and a Mr John Croker, who was going to town to buy a bath chair for his wife. Romilly whiled away a few hours inspecting progress on the towers of the new Houses of Parliament and strolling through St James's Park to enjoy the pictures at the British Gallery in Pall Mall. (Ten years earlier he had seen the newly-acquired 'Arnolfini Marriage' in the National Gallery and dismissed it as 'a small hideous picture of a man and woman by Van Eyck'!)[1] After dinner at the Athenaeum he retired to Charing Cross, but he was plagued by irritation in his legs and sleep was hard to come by.

The 9.40 express from Paddington carried him second class next morning 124 miles to Hopebrook, ten miles beyond Gloucester. Since the train got in at about half past one, it had averaged over thirty-two miles an hour. From Hopebrook he took a coach to Hereford. The Cathedral was being restored 'in a magnificent style', and only the nave was available for services. Romilly went twice next day, which was Sunday; he noted that the women all sat on the south side and the men on the north. Bishop Hampden preached at 'moderate length' (thirty-five minutes). At the parish service in the afternoon 'the drowsy Rector prayed for Queen Adelaide', dead since 1849, and the Curate delivered a 'dry sermon that could do no good to any one'.

Some unimportant passages have been omitted from the account of Romilly's tour up to his arrival at Brecon. We join him at Cabalva, about a mile and a half beyond Whitney bridge, to which he had travelled as an inside passenger on the mail coach from Hereford.

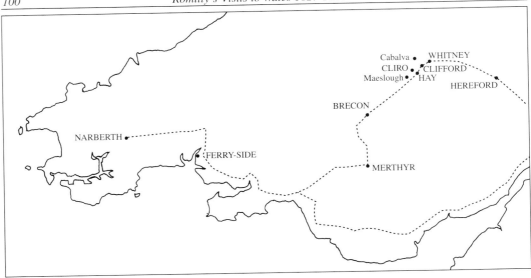

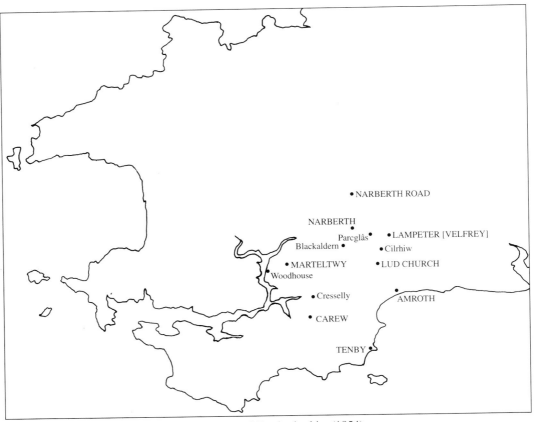

South Wales and Pembrokeshire (1854)

**Monday 21 August** ... I here found John's carriage waiting for me. At Cabalva* I received a most kind welcome. I found John* perfectly well and Lady Romilly very much better than she has been. All the children* (except Willy) are at home, viz Edward (who looks most frail and delicate), Annie, who is plump and prosperous with very pleasing features, Henry (a very gay joyous lad), Mary (a genteel-looking young lady), Sophie (a sharp clever little thing, very affectionate), little Lucy (very pretty) and the baby Arthur (now 4 year old with very light lovely curling hair); he also is very pretty. The governess is Miss Kingston, non più giovane ni bella.* We breakfasted directly after my arrival. I seemed quite familiar with the beautiful view from the drawing-room window though it is now 34 years since I was here to marry Sophie* in 1820 at Cliro church. After breakfast John and I (cigars in mouth) walked about the grounds and saw the good points of view. I then went to my own room (which is at the front of the house and has no view) and read *The Lamplighter** till luncheon at 1.

At 3 I went out with Lady Romilly and Sophie in the carriage. We made a very pretty circuit over Whitney bridge passing the ruins of Clifford Castle through 'Hay' and then crossed the Wye again coming through Cliro. Lady R. is very timid about the bridges and gets out to walk over them. Little Sophie had had 1s given her by Mamma and told me in confidence that she feared it would not be enough to buy a present for Mary; so I made her a paper purse and put 1/6 into it, and she with her accumulated treasure bought a pretty little blue bottle at my suggestion. Lady R. wanted a large-print bible with references; so we went to a "Christian Knowledge" dépôt* and I treated her with a good octavo one at the moderate cost of 5s/5d and 3 other devotional books for 2s/9d. I bought for myself Hele's *Devotions** (cost 2s/)—a book much admired by Lady R. ...

In my walk with John I learned a good deal about the heiress of the estate of Cabalva. Miss Davies* (Isabella I think) is now about 12—her brother died last year. The estate is worth £1000 a year. Mr Davies (who was very fond of money) screwed it up to £1500 a year; but John lowered the rents to £1000 and allowed (while he was guardian) Mrs Davies £100 a year, which is still kept up by the Court of Chancery. The allowance left her by Mr D. was £14 (or £18) a year as long as she conducted herself well. She has always done so and has married a very respectable farmer in Worcestershire, he having been informed of her past life. She has borne this farmer 3 children. Miss Davies lives entirely with Mrs Malthus. John told her that she might see Miss D. whenever she pleased but that she must pay her own travelling expenses—this wise determination of John's has prevented her visiting Isabella! I learned from Lady R. that Jack Vane has given up the preachership at the Rolls,* and that her brother-in-law Henry Malthus* has succeeded him. ... [At] lunch (the children's dinner) French is talked. ...

**Tuesday 22 August** ... I was sorry to hear that Dr Roget* has a polypus again forming in his nose—he underwent an operation for one more than 20 years ago. ... In the evening Lady R. read loud to the children who were not gone to bed; her subject was 'the habits of vultures and other birds of prey'; I thought a good deal of what she read revolting and nasty, but I kept my thoughts to myself.

**Wednesday 23 August** ... I went in the carriage with Annie, Mary and Henry to see the fine view from Mr de Winton's* park; he lives in a magnificent modern castellated house at a village called Maeslough* (5 miles from Cabalva). ...

**Thursday 24 August** ... Miss Kingston, Annie and I went in the carriage through Cliro (where we met Mr Venables* on horseback and received instructions concerning our route) and the Hay to Clifford new church. It is only 2 or 3 years old. It is fitted up in the most elaborate perfection of High-Church ecclesiastical architecture: all the windows are painted glass—there is an organ with fantastically painted pipes, a lectern, a credence by the communion table, &c, &c. The only defect in my eyes was the darkness when one was inside. There is a pretty belfry in the Italian style with 2 visible bells. The church is Gothic. It is built and endowed by a very wealthy man of the name of Pennoyre: he is a clergyman but is unable to do duty being paralysed. His wife is nearly blind. They are childless, and his aged mother (also grievously afflicted) lives with them. They of course see no company. He does great good with his riches. We then went to old Clifford church, where there are large marble monuments of the Pennoyre family with sculptured figures. We went to this old church for the sake of the view from its churchyard; the view however rather disappointed me, for it was obscured by several ancient yew trees. The spelling in the church yard was not good: "Mari*er*" and "Wi*d*dow" are specimens. We came back over Whitney bridge. The excursion was most agreeable. We didn't get home till more than ¼ past 6. The evening being fine we looked at Jupiter and 2 of his satellites through the telescope. Plaid 4 rubbers with Lady R. and lost 2/-. The dinner party the customary 5.

**Friday 25 August** (Charming day) Agreeable letter from Grim—George and wife and children are still with him. Grim gives information concerning my route. John however suggests a different line through the Hay, Brecon and Merthyr, and sent over to Hay to get all the details about coaches &c. ... John gave me a very interesting account of Alexander Dumas' *Monte Christo.** [Romilly summarises the plot] After lunch John and Annie, Mary, Edward and I started with 2 ponies to ascend the steep ascent of Cliro Hill: it is about 4 miles to the high ground which we reached (7 or 800 feet above Cabalva). John walked the whole way; the rest rode on the ride and tie system.* The view from the top was very fine. We laid down among the gorse for ½ an hour; it was in beautiful flower, but John says it blossoms more or less all the year, and that it was said to be like kissing—always in season. He asked me what quadrupeds got up from their hind legs first and which from their fore. I knew nothing about it. Cows (I think he said) and sheep rose from their hind legs first, and horses from their fore. He asked me what quadruped had no front teeth in the upper jaw. Of course I didn't know. He said it was the cow. He looked in a book of natural history in the evening but could not find this fact mentioned. Lady R. amused me by the name of a tit bit on the back of a fowl, called by the French 'Le sot l'y laisse';* to my surprise it is found in the French cookery books as she showed me. It took us 2 hours to get to the top of Cliro Hill. On our descent we visited Cliro chapel:* it is one of the most miserable barn-like sacred buildings I ever saw. We here saw the farmer (Mr Wall*). A sad accident befel him lately: one of his horses in the farmyard was scared by a flash of lightning and dashed against him—he broke his arm and dislocated his shoulder. We didn't get home till near 6½. In the evening plaid whist with Lady R. against John and Miss Kingston: won 7/-.

**Saturday 26 August** (Lovely day) John told an amusing anecdote of the gourmandise of Sir George Warrender.* He was dining by himself on a haunch of venison and after eating prodigiously said to his butler, 'That will make a hash for tomorrow'—'Yes, Sir G., if you leave off now' ... I wrote also to Grim saying I hoped to be with him on Tuesday and to appear at Narberth Road at 5.30. Cigar walk with John. After lunch I went with Miss Kingston, Annie and Mary to 'the Hay'; we pulled up at Cliro and ordered a flitch of bacon from Mrs Preece. I was amused by this Dunmow* emblem of happy matrimonial life: this is the 21st year of John's marriage. We had a long chat with Mr Venables, whom we saw in his churchyard with an architect examining the old tower*—the restoring it will cost £150 and Mr V. has collected £100. ...

**Sunday 27 August** 11th after Trinity (beautiful day). [John walked to church. Lady Romilly and Sophie did not venture out, but Romilly and nine others, with two maids in the rumble, went by carriage.] Mr Venables did the duty at Cliro and preached (fairly) from 1 Thessalonians 5.6.* The singing here is remarkably good; it is unaccompanied by any instrument. It is presided over by Mrs Venables. The church is very pretty inside. There is a very odd arrangement for the clerk. There is a lectern half-way between the reading desk and the pulpit (which are opposite to each other) and the clerk sits on a stool in the chancel by this lectern with his back to the communion table. He is a queer animal. During the first lesson he got up and in his clattering shoes stumpt about the chancel, arranging the books at the communion table. Mr Venables turned round and gave a hard look at him—but the clerk was callous to all reproving looks.

After lunch Annie, Mary and I (escorted by John) went to Whitney church. John declined going in because he has no respect to the clergyman (Mr Dew*) on account of dishonorable shuffling conduct at a parliamentary election. This is a neat little church and the singing (unaccompanied by instruments) decidedly good—though inferior to that at Cliro. They sang the evening hymn very nicely. The text 2 Kings 5, 'but he was a leper'. It was an interesting short sermon on the life of Naaman. Mr Dew rather offended Annie by reproving his flock for not having attended the sacrament in the morning. She thought it would have been much better to have spoken to them in private.

John had a cow's mouth opened for us and we had ocular demonstration of there being no front teeth in the upper jaw. We had a specimen of the want of all delicacy in country folks. The man who looks after the cows said to John and Lady R., 'that cow's milk will fail if she don't have the bull'. Caroline* and I walked off (the children fortunately were not by). She said naivement to me, 'I think he might have made that observation when I was not present'.

**Monday 28 August** (baking hot) ... John and I walked to the Hay. ... We paid a visit to Mr and Mrs Venables; they were at home. Mrs Venables* claims being a cousin of John's by the mother's side; it is far off, 2nd cousin twice removed!! She produced a miniature of her mother and says she is reckoned very like her. We could not see the resemblance:

she is decidedly ugly, and her mother handsome. ... At night we had out the telescope and saw all 4 of Jupiter's satellites.* Miss Kingston from the dark walk took me in by her imitation of the hooting of an owl....

I begged a lock of Prince Arthur's hair, which was given me. This excited the jealousy of Sophie and little Lucy (who is her father's pet though not nearly so clever as Sophie, and though she has lost a great deal of her prettiness, he used to think her the prettiest child he had ever seen: she has very handsome large eyes). So I had also a lock of each of their hair. Henry proposed my having one of his, but I told him I didn't keep the hair of boys of his age. He insisted on giving me a paper of acidulated drops, which I accepted. I begged of Lady R. to let me keep a scarlet napkin-holder which she made for my napkin; she consented. Today was one of her bright days and she thought she had made a decided step in improvement.

**Tuesday 29 August** (very beautiful day) Breakfasted at 7½; every body (except Edward) came to see me off. 'The Prince' [Arthur] asked if I had got his lock of hair—he had been rather unwilling to part with it. Off in the carriage. I am afraid I led the footman (Joseph) into temptation: I gave him 2/6 to give the page (whom I had not lit upon). Some mishap befel the train and I had to wait for the mail at Whitney bridge more than ½ hour. Mr Venables (who was riding by) stopt and talked with me for 10 minutes. I of course went outside the mail. The 18 miles drive to Brecon was delightful. Wrote to Grim to say my arrival might be looked for tomorrow at 5.30 just 24 hours after the proposed time.

Reached Brecon a little after 12. This town is beautifully situated on the confluence of the Honddu with the Usk; it is surrounded by picturesque mountains. I ordered dinner at 3.30 and then went to a barber's to have my hair cut. There are several little bridges in the town, and these together with the striking church of St Mary and the County Hall* &c &c and the neat streets make it a remarkably pretty place. My 1st walk was one called 'the Captain's':* it is a sort of boulevard running down from the County Hall to the Usk and is nothing remarkable. (By the direction of an urchin) I trespassed through some private gardens to get back into the town. I went under the guidance of my hairdresser (son of the parish clerk) to see the old Collegiate church.* This Chapter has been dissolved since 1839. It is now used as a parish church—the parishioners of St David's attend here. The ['unsightly' crossed out] ruins of St David's are still standing (about 200 yards off). The church (all but the tower) fell down bodily not long ago.* This Chapter church contains some monuments with marble figures. There are two long inscriptions on the tombs of Bishops Lucy* and Bull.* It is only the chancel of the old church which now stands. The Early English windows are not bad. The stall work with its most rude and grotesque carving under the seats is preserved; the names of the prebends are written on the stalls.

After dinner I went to see the Priory church: this is a noble building, as large as a cathedral.* It is very striking in the interior. The Early English windows in the chancel are very fine. Under the advice of my cicerone (a young girl) I have trespassed again. I went into the grounds adjoining the church. A stately dame flew at the girl. I told her that

Brecon in 1849, looking down the Honddu

I was a stranger, that I hoped I was not trespassing and that if she would give me leave I would walk round. I told her also that I knew the present Marquess (for this turned out to be the Marquess Camden's* place called 'the Priory') and had known his father before him. She gave me leave, but not very graciously—probably because I did not ask to see the house. I presume she was housekeeper. I then spent two hours in 'the Priory walks': they skirt the Honddu for a very considerable distance and are really beautiful; their shade was most grateful this burning hot day. I ended my day's pleasuring by walking along the banks of the Usk. I saw a brilliant sunset, such as Claude alone could have painted. After tea I strolled out again in the starlight and smoked a cigar. I wrote to Lady Romilly an account of my day's achievements.

**Wednesday 30 August** (delicious day—intensely hot) Left the Castle at Brecon by the 3-horse omnibus at 9. The inside of the omnibus was deserted; we were 6 outsiders. One of them, a Christ Church clergyman (Charles Griffith*), was going to visit Bishop Thirlwall; so I gave him my card to deliver. In going out of Brecon one sees the handsome house (Pennoyre*) of Col Watkins the Lord Lieutenant of the county. The whole of the scenery from Brecon to Merthyr (18 miles) through the mountains is very beautiful. A great deal of damage has been done to the road by inundations these 2 last years from the mountain-torrents, which carried away several of the bridges; one of these is still not repaired and we had to make a short détour through a field. In entering Merthyr one passes the fine house* and grounds (with water and swans) of Mr Crawshay. Mr Griffith pointed out to me the heights overhanging the road, from which the insurgents in the Merthyr riots* rolled down stones on the soldiers. There being an hour to spare at Merthyr I spent it in looking at the National schools, market &c &c.

Parc Glas, Crinow, in 1996

At 1.50 I left Merthyr for Narberth Road by the rail.* Mr Griffith and I travelled by 2nd class. I read a good bit of *The Lamplighter*; the latter part of the book is common-place. I was agreeably surprised at Ferry-side (19 miles from Narberth and opposite the very picturesque ruin of Lansteffan Castle) to see Grim's face at the carriage-window; he got into my carriage and we travelled together the rest of the journey. His cousins Seymour* and Harry* were also in the same train but they were in a 1st class carriage. At Narberth Road I shook hands with Seymour and Harry (who went to Cresselly) and got into Grim's trap. He drove the 4 miles to Parcglâs in good style and we reached his house at 6.30. He had 2 Cambridge friends to dinner at 7, John Lewis* (of Henllan) and his guest (Mr Shadwell—son of Sir Lancelot*). There was a great contrast between these 2 men: Mr Lewis was a merry jocund laughing bachelor, the other (an equally young man) an uncomfortable gloomy-looking married man. We were a party of 5 at dinner and it was very pleasant. In the evening we had [a] fire. Bertha sang 3 songs; we men plaid 6 penny whist. We plaid 4 rubbers and I (who plaid with both the guests) carried off 11/6 of my host's money. I saw only 2 of Grim's children today, viz Bertha and little Lucy. They are not in the least shy; so one gets on famously with them. They are very merry and as fat as butter. Bed at 11.30.

**Thursday 31 August** (same magnificent weather) (nice breeze) Breakfast at 9. Made the acquaintance of Grim's other 2 children, viz Caroline and Edward; they also seem very healthy and flourishing. Bertha received me very kindly and does the honors of her house very nicely and most amiably. Two of George's children made their appearance with Grim's 4, making a large display of the rising generation. After breakfast wrote to George T. Romilly (£10). Read some of *The Lamplighter* under the shadow of the trees on the terrace, occasionally interrupted by a romp with the children. This terrace commands a good view of the Carmarthen hills. At 12 George and Dora and two more of their children arrived from Tenby; the 5th is with his aunt Mrs Peel.*

Went with George and Grim to Narberth. It was marketday, so the little town was on the qui-vive. Grim and I accompanied George to the Townhall; George sat on the bench with 2 other magistrates (Dr Thomas*—a great liar—and Mr Buckler,* an intelligent Irish clergyman) to license publicans. On these licensing occasions the magistrates are provided with a green bottle of sherry and a bag of biscuits; I profited by the latter part of their refreshments. We then went to the Reading Room (of which George is president). Narberth is a mile from Parcglâs.

After lunch George and Grim, Dora, the 2 Berthas and I walked over to Cilrhiw—2 miles; a pleasant walk, especially the part through the woods of Cilrhiw. Since I was there (14 or 15 years ago) a conservatory (with a productive vine in it) has been added at one end and a wing at the other. The last tenant (an obnoxious bad one) left at midsummer; the house is not yet let and is in the act of being repaired. On our return home we looked in upon Mrs Morgan (the wife of a substantial farmer) and saw her dairy and her cheese-room and her beautiful black cows (20 of them); every thing most neat and clean. She showed us one object to which she attached much interest and which was carefully wrapt up in paper and treasured up in a drawer—a bit of bone that had come out of one of her fingers! Dinner at 6: a party of 5, viz the Adelphi* and their sister-wives and myself. We had a fire after dinner. Very short prayers at 9 o'clock; afterwards 4 rubbers of whist, Grim and I against George and Dora. We won 11 points. George and I plaid 6 pennies, Dora and Grim pence.

**Friday 1 September** (sunny—fine air) After breakfast Grim went out shooting, but never saw a bird. I walked in the dark walk and read Thackeray's lecture* on Swift: I was much struck by the talent of it. He has a proper feeling of esteem and admiration but is (I think) too harsh and even cruel about poor Vanessa.* George drove Dora, Bertha and me over to Cresselly. We found Seymour and Harry both at home (they not having gone out shooting). Lady Catherine* and 3 (of the 4 children*) also made their appearance. We had an excellent lunch here with delicious grapes. Miss Allen (Kitty—age 10) is a favorite of Grim's, for having asked him for what blemish it was that her Papa sold him a horse. After lunch we went to see Seymour's cornricks and his horses; he has burnt his fingers in farming and is going to sell all his farming implements &c. We afterwards drove to Cilrhiw to inspect the repairs &c. Dined at 6½, a party of 5. Prayers in evening at 9 (as usual). I afterwards played 2 rubbers with Dora against George and Bertha; won them both 4/6.

**Saturday 2 September** (sun and air) Letters from Sophie* and George T. Romilly in answer to mine.* Grim and I walked over to Lampeter [Velfrey] and went into the church and the school* (both of which are in very good condition): the school is quite new and I was much pleased with it. In the church is a plain tablet to Baugh Allen commemorating nothing* but that he died in October 1845 in his 71st year; there is a similar inscription on the tomb in the church-yard. Mr Lewis (brother of Lewis of Henllan who dined at Parcglâs on Wednesday) succeeded old Mr Seaton as the Rector. We are to dine with Mr Lewis next Wednesday.

At 4 o'clock we left Parcglâs for Cresselly. George drove over his baby (Dora Blanche*) and nurse and the manservant Jenkins. Grim drove Bertha and Dora and me in his trap drawn by 2 ponies. He made an agreeable variety from yesterday's route by taking me through a wood of the Baron de Rutzen.* We dined at 7; we were a party of 8, viz Seymour Allen and Lady Catharine, Harry Allen and our 5 selves. Of course I took in Lady Catharine. She talked to me a good deal about the Wale family.* I know not how many years ago it is since she and her mother (then Lady Catharine Fellows) visited Cambridge; if I remember right they dined with me. Her mother (who had that dreadful impediment in her speech) became Lady Portsmouth for a short time; she survived her husband only a few months. Lady Catharine Allen is now in mourning for her. She is a clever spirited woman—unfortunately out of health at present. She draws very well and has taken good likenesses of her husband and children. She is a very bold rider and a good judge of horses.

Seymour Allen greatly astonished me by quoting 3 lines of Homer in the original. Harry made himself very agreeable (as he always does). He amused us with some stories of Thesiger's* wit. On one occasion he took up Baron Pollock's* hat for his own and said, 'Where is my Castor? This is Pollux'. On another, Thesiger asked a man who omitted the *h*'s what he had been doing; the man answered, 'Making ay'. Thesiger was immediately down upon him. 'While you were making a letter you had better have made an H'. Harry told us also of a joke of Alderson* about a hole in the keel of a ship. 'Nobody could have seen it—except you, Mr Fish'—a poor innocent man who was in court but had nothing to do with the trial. After tea Lady Catherine played the piano. Bertha and Harry and Grim sang; Grim's choice were nigger songs. Bed at 11.

**Sunday 3 September** 12th after Trinity (baking hot). Lady Catharine and Bertha and Harry and Lady Catherine's two little boys didn't go to morning church, and eventually went to no church. It had been intended to go to the evening service at Yerbeston, but Grim (who was very lately Curate of Yerbeston*) showed that we should not be able to dine before 9, so the project was abandoned.* Grim rode over to Lud Church to do duty there. Seymour drove Dora and little Kitty and me in his dog-cart to Carew (where are the fine remains of a castle) and George walked. Mr Phelps* (an Oxonian) did the duty and preached a good sermon (of 25 minutes) on the Lord's Prayer.

In the churchyard we saw Tom Allen of Freestone and wife (born Acland); they invited us to lunch and we accepted. Tom's father and mother (Mr and Mrs James Allen) are alive and live in the house but they are never seen. His mother is paralytic and retains her faculties entirely; his poor father is imbecile and recollects nothing for 2 minutes together. He perpetually says that Tom an't married, though his wife and 2 children live in the house. Tom's children (a boy and pretty curly-haired girl) were not brought down to my regret; but I caught a glimpse of them at the nursery window. Tom Allen is an odd man: he is a London lawyer and has his wife living in Pembrokeshire, only running down occasionally and passing the long vacation with her.

After lunch Seymour Allen drove Harry, Grim and me through his woods; this drive was cool and very pleasant. Afterwards all the household (except the baby and the French governess—neither of whom did I see) walked about the shadiest parts of the grounds and drove out the cattle which had trespassed into the plantations. The governess (as I learned afterwards) made her appearance at lunch, but Bertha told me that she was afraid to talk to her. Harry and little Kitty (an animated child—very fond of her dog Spicy) climbed into a tree! The rest of the party (except myself, who went home with one of the boys and then read *Laconics** in my own room) sat underneath till dressing time. Same party of 8 at dinner at 7½. About 10 o'clock the servants assembled and (at Lady Catharine's request) I read Bishop Blomfield's* prayers. I afterwards read loud to the company (for the servants were dismissed) a sermon of Porteus's* selected by Lady Catharine, viz that on the text, 'How long halt ye between 2 opinions?'* Bed at 11¼.

**Monday 4 September** (intensely hot) We left Cresselly about 10½: I (as before) was of Grim, Dora and Bertha's division; George took home baby &c. He afterwards went to the Narberth Union* where he and his brother guardians (of whom Seymour is chairman) did a kind act which thoroughly met with my approbation: they agreed to send all the children of the Union tomorrow in a waggon to Amroth to spend the day there. Grim drove us 7 miles to Tenby. Our 1st visit was to his aunts Fanny* and Emma*; they live at a very pretty house ½ mile* from Tenby but commanding a fine view of the sea. We were very hospitably received and staid lunch. Grim and I then bathed; I found the water truly delicious and staid in ½ hour; it was high tide. We then called on Mrs Eaton and her elder unmarried sister (Miss Alicia Wilton or Wilmot*—I don't know which). Here they kindly insisted on our eating grouse pie. I then went with Grim to call on Baugh's widow.* We found her at home, very fair, fat and good humoured. Her two boys* (one of whom was christened in Dulwich chapel by the names of Clement Romilly) (I am his godfather) were at school, but we saw the governess (a conversible well-mannered happy-looking lady) and the little girl (named Jessy) age 9. I found her a very frank hearty child, who readily became friends with me and showed me her shells and other treasures and her miniature. We then went with Mrs Eaton and Dora and Bertha to call on Mrs Marsh* (authoress of *2 old men's tales*); she was gone to Cresselly but we saw her daughter, Rose, and had some pleasant conversation. We staid in Tenby till past 5, and as the mountainous 11 miles didn't admit of rapid driving we didn't get home till 7.15. In the evening plaid 4 rubbers with Dora against George and Grim and won 1/-, which I gave to John Romilly* to help him in buying a pump.

**Tuesday 5 September** (prodigiously hot) Letter from Sir John in answer to mine to Caroline; she alas! was not well enough to write herself. I wrote to him in reply. Grim went out with Mr Lewis (Rector of Lampeter [Velfrey]) to Fairy Bank* (how poetical!) shooting—they bagged one bird between them. Morning call from a neighbouring clergyman (Mr James*) and wife, both of them goodhumoured and loquacious. George drove Grim and his [George's] son John Romilly and me over to Amroth: this place is beautifully situated in the middle of Tenby bay. George and Grim were lazy; but I bathed and found the water delightful, it being high tide. I bruised one of my feet considerably on the shingle and made it bleed. We didn't dine till past 7. Tea at 8; prayers at 9. We then had some whist. The 1st rubber I begged to sit out and instruct Dora how to play her cards. I afterwards plaid 3 rubbers with George against Bertha and Grim. I plaid love with Bertha and won 11 points. Today I read Thackeray's lecture on Steele* and found it very brilliant.

**Wednesday 6 September** (intensely hot) Wrote to Harriet* announcing my return on Saturday next. Read Thackeray's lecture on Prior,* Gay* and Pope. Grim and I walked to Narberth (where George and other magistrates sate all day upon assessed-taxes appeals). At Narberth Grim hired a jaunting-car* and we were driven to Marteltwy*—a distance of 5 miles—and visited the school* and schoolmaster's house which he built. It is a very commodious school and tidy to look at. 45 children (in 3 classes) out of the 88 were present. One class was spelling l-o-v-e—love: which the monitor and the class pronounced *loave*. We accompanied the master into his house. He professes dislike of the children's noise and is anxious to become a clerk. We had a peep in at the windows of the church, a neat double-bodied building without tower or spire, its single bell visible in the belfrey. There is some coloured glass. We had not time to go on two miles further to Woodhouse* (where Grim resided for nearly 2 years). The view of Narberth on this Marteltwy road is striking.

Near Narberth we quitted the car and came back by a pretty walk through Grim's property of Blackaldern. Just as we reached the turn to Parcglâs we met George, Dora and Bertha on their way to the Rectory of Lampeter [Velfrey]. We (in undue time) reached our destination, travelling the 2 miles by the other dog-cart; we must have been more than ½ hour after our time. I was glad to find the party already seated. There were 13 of us, viz our host and hostess (Mr and Mrs* Lewis), his brother (Mr Lewis* of Henllan—the goodtempered man who dined with Grim last Wednesday), his ½ brother (an invalid Major Lewis), Mrs Lewis's ½ sister Miss Lord,* the Hon Mrs Yelverton* and daughter, a vulgar Mr Sayers* and our 5 selves. It was a comical circumstance that the 3 candidates* for Lampeter at the death of Mr Seaton were at this dinner, viz the successful Mr Lewis, Mr Sayers and Grim. Mr Sayers is a coarse loud-laughing man, who was a pupil of Jack Brass* and is as vulgar as his Tutor. He spoke much and vehemently in disparagement of Bishop Monk.* He is no relation of my former pupil. Miss Lord sang 'The Swallow'* (words of Tennyson) and other ditties (one of them German). The large unattractive Mrs Yelverton also sang—so too did Bertha (very nicely though reluctantly). Home at ¼ past 11.

**Thursday 7 September** (hotter than ever) After breakfast I betook myself (with a volume of Thackeray's early tales *The Plush Papers* &c) to Crinow churchyard. There is in this churchyard a monument to George Allen's 2nd son: his name was George. He died of atrophy 9th September 1850 and was then 2 years old. There is on the stone 'Blessed are the pure in heart for &c'. When I had been in the churchyard a couple of hours I was found by Grim, who procured the keys* of the church and exhibited to me this nutshell of a place of worship.

There was a considerable party expected from Tenby to lunch; the only person who did come was Mrs Eaton. Dora and Bertha made this lunch their dinner (without telling us of such intention); so George and Grim and I dined at 7¼ without any ladies, Mrs Eaton returning at that time to Tenby. There was a very pictureque teadrinking in the open air at 5, at which Mrs Eaton, Dora, Bertha, 7 children (including Wilfred,* whom they call Fred and who today returned from his aunt Mary (Mrs Peel))—Grim and I looked on and I called out for the 2 babes (Edward Lancelot Baugh* and Dora Blanche) to be exhibited at the nursery window, which was accordingly done. I thought Wilfred a pretty boy. George's other children are John Romilly, Kate (properly Mary Catharine—a god daughter of Kate Roget*) and Dora Blanche. Kate is very peevish and looks delicate and sickly. Dora is a lilliputian child. Grim's girls are far finer, fatter and prettier than George's; their respective names are Bertha, Lucy and Caroline (the last 2 are lovely children). Bertha today took her baby (Edward) to see the doctor at Narberth about his teeth, which he is cutting with much pain. George was engaged all day in affiliation cases at Narberth.

After lunch Grim, Dora and the 2 Berthas and I walked in the baking heat to Blackaldern farm. The house is a very commodious good one, built by Grim. We found the tenant at home; his name is Gwynne.* He is a well-mannered gentlemanly slim young man who has risen in the world by his good conduct. He began life as a cabin-boy and rose to be captain. His wife* (who brought him money) and their only child* (a nice little girl) were at home. I saw also their governess (Miss Whishaw), who had been procured by Dora and recommended by Kate Roget. I told her that I must shake hands with her for the sake of her name, which was a very interesting one to me. I asked her if she was any relation of Sir Samuel Romilly's great friend John Whishaw; she immediately pronounced herself his grand-daughter. I of course did not tell her that John Whishaw was never married!

I was amused today in finding Mrs Houghton's* name carved on one of the trees in the favorite beech walk.* Having presented little Bertha with a washed shilling in a paper purse of my own manufacture, I have had to fabricate several purses and to wash divers shillings and sixpences. After tea I asked Grim to read loud Longfellow's poem of 'the building of the ship'.* Grim read it far too quick; it was obvious that nobody but myself admired it. Grim and I plaid 4 rubbers against George and Dora and lost 8/6 at 6d points.

**Friday 8 September** (charming day—not too hot) I discovered by mere accident that Grim has morning prayers about hour before breakfast. We breakfasted this morning at 8; and at ¼ to 9 Grim and Bertha most kindly drove me over to Narberth Road station. Bertha amiably gave me a bag of biscuits, I having stoutly refused sandwiches. Romilly (as he is called) earned 1/- this morning by working out for me the number of seconds in

7½ hours [footnote: The time was rather more than 8 hours]—the time of performing the 264 miles from Narberth Road station to Paddington. Grim amused himself at the Narberth Road station by weighing Bertha, himself and me. She is under 8 stone; to my surprise I weighed more than Grim—he made my weight 10 stone 13 lbs,* a stone heavier than I thought myself. I bought Dumas' *Monte Christo* in a horrid English translation and read it all the way to town with much interest. At Swindon I had a cup of coffee and a sponge cake by way of lunch. Reached Paddington at 6.30. I put up at the Golden Cross and instead of dinner had a couple of eggs with my tea. I then went to the Athenaeum (which is in a state of confusion for repairs and alterations and does not furnish eatables). I went into the library (the only available room) and wrote up my life and read *Monte Christo* till bed time. I met with no incident in my journey; my companions read a little and slept much. Paid 39/9 for my 2nd class ticket.

The following day in London Romilly went to inspect the new Houses of Parliament, begun in 1840 after the great fire, and 'found the towers a good deal advanced'. In fact the clock came into service only in June 1859.

## NOTES

**21 August** Cabalva: see note on 24 July 1840.

Sir John Romilly (1802-1874), second son of Sir Samuel, had been Master of the Rolls since 1851. He was created Lord Romilly in 1865. William (1835-1891), the son Joseph missed, succeeded to the barony, and was Clerk of Enrolments in Chancery. Edward, three years younger, may have looked delicate, but he lived till 1886. So did Henry, born in 1845. Arthur died in 1884; like Edward he was a barrister. Anne, Mary and Lucy Henrietta all outlived them: they died in 1913, 1921 and 1923 respectively. Sophie was the only girl that did not marry.[2]

'non più giovane ni bella': no longer young or beautiful.[3]

Sophie: Sir John's sister—see note on 24 July 1840.

*The Lamplighter* was a romance published in 1854 by Maria Susanna Cummins (1827-1866) of Massachusetts. It tells of a lamplighter, Trueman Flint, who befriended a Boston orphan girl. Forty thousand copies were issued in the first eight weeks. Critics have pronounced Miss Cummins a tedious stylist, too much given to moralising, but with a genuine gift for creating characters. Romilly read his copy all the way to London, except when his eyes were blinded with tears.[4]

The Christian Knowledge depot was evidently a branch of the S.P.C.K., which, like other Church societies and publishers, had local depots for the sale of religious books.[5]

Richard Hele, 'master of the school belonging to the Church of Sarum' (Salisbury), published *Select Offices of Private Devotion* in 1717. A new and improved edition came out in 1831.[6]

A memorial in Clyro church records that William and Sophia Davies of Cabalva had an only child, Elizabeth Sophia, who died in Paris in 1822 aged nineteen. So who were Miss Davies (born about 1842, the year William died) and her late brother? Sophia had died in 1836. Were these William's children by his cook (see 24 July 1840)? If so, he seems to have married her.

The Rolls chapel, so called because the rolls of the Court of Chancery were once kept there, dated back to the thirteenth century but was largely reconstructed by Inigo Jones. Joseph Butler, later Bishop of Durham, preached some famous sermons here. The Chancery Lane section of the Public Record Office is built over the site.[7]

Henry Malthus may have been the son of the political economist and demographer Thomas Robert Malthus (1766-1834), who claimed that population increases naturally faster than production. That Henry (c1806-1882) was certainly ordained; and it may be no coincidence that one of his father's books contained a memoir by W. Otter, since Otter was Lady Romilly's maiden name.[8]

**22 August** Dr Roget: author of the *Thesaurus*, first published in 1852.

**23 August** Mr de Winton and Maeslough (Maesllwch): see note on 24 July 1840.

**24 August** Richard Lister Venables, Vicar of Clyro, was a rich man, much occupied in administrative work as a justice of the peace in Radnorshire. Francis Kilvert served as his Curate from 1865 to 1872; Venables often appears in his diary.[9]

**25 August** Alexandre Dumas finished *The Count of Monte Cristo* in 1844. His output—some 277 volumes—was prodigious, though less so than he claimed (1,200). It is odd that Romilly misspells his name and that of his book.[10]

The ride and tie system, in this instance, meant that two of the party rode on ahead, dismounted, tethered their ponies and began walking; the other two caught up on foot and took their turn in the saddle. The view from Clyro Hill is panoramic—on a clear day, which I was lucky to have, it is breathtaking.

'Le sot l'y laisse' ('the fool leaves it there') is a delicate morsel below the parson's nose.[11]

Clyro chapel is across a field at Betws—*betws* means a bedehouse or chapelry. Kilvert served it one February day wearing two waistcoats, two coats and a mackintosh; his beard froze to his clothes, and there was ice floating in the font at the christening. Largely rebuilt in 1878-9, the chapel is not as uninteresting as Romilly implies. The remains of a fourteenth or fifteenth century rood screen—a double beam with pierced tracery—are still in place. The bowl of the font is even older.[12]

Mr Wall at Chapel farm was Churchwarden when Kilvert left Clyro in 1872, and presented him with a silver cup. He seems to have been a man of substance, for he sent his girls Eliza and Lucretia to school in Bristol.[13]

**26 August** Sir George Warrender (1782-1849), 4th baronet, a Lord Commissioner of the Admiralty, loved food; he was known as Sir George Provender.[14]

The Dunmow flitch dates back to the thirteenth century (some say earlier), when Robert Fitzwalter, leader of the barons who obtained Magna Carta, offered a flitch or side of bacon to the man who had not repented of his marriage for a year and a day. Piers Plowman and Chaucer mention it, and eight rewards are documented between 1445 and 1773. Claimants had to kneel on two sharp stones at the door of Little Dunmow church (in Essex). The ceremony was revived in the nineteenth century—indeed *The Flitch of Bacon, or The Custom of Dunmow* by W. Harrison Ainsworth was published in this same year, 1854.[15]

Clyro church tower, at the west end, is all that remains of the building Romilly officiated at in 1820 and passed in 1840 (the top dates from 1894). The rest, nave, chancel and north aisle, had been rebuilt by Thomas Nicholson in 1853, so recently that it is strange Romilly did not mention it. Perhaps Mr Venables intended a drastic restoration to the tower as well, but never carried it out.[16]

**27 August** I Thessalonians 5, verse 6: 'Therefore let us not sleep as do others, but let us watch and be sober'.

Henry Dew (1819-1901) was Rector of Whitney from 1843 till his death. His wife and William Wordsworth's were close relatives. Kilvert often mentions the family.[17]

Caroline: Lady Romilly.

**28 August** Mrs Venables was sister-in-law of Capt Cowper Coles (1819-1870), the man who first developed a warship with armoured, revolving turrets. Unfortunately one of the earliest such ships, the *Captain*, proved to have a freeboard even lower than Coles had calculated. A squall caught her one night off Finisterre with her sails set, and she capsized and sank with the loss of nearly five hundred men, including Coles, who left a wife and nine children.[18]

Jupiter's satellites that can easily be seen through a small telescope are, in descending order of size, Ganymede, Callisto, Io and Europa. Ganymede, at 3,720 miles through bigger than Mercury, is the largest moon we know of. At least sixteen Jovian satellites have been found, as well as a ring system.[19]

**29 August** Brecon County Hall is now the Museum: a fine Greek revival building by T.H. Wyatt and David Brandon (1839-43).[20]

The Captain's Walk is apparently so called because it was used by French officers held here on parole during the Napoleonic Wars.[21]

The Collegiate church had belonged to the College of Prebends, originally in Abergwili, and moved here by Bishop William Barlow of St Davids in 1541 to occupy the dissolved Dominican Friary. At the same time a small school was started. It had mixed fortunes until refounded in 1853, since when Christ College has become a flourishing public school. The choir of the Friary church of St Nicholas is now the school chapel. St David's parish church collapsed in 1852, so no doubt the parishioners were using it temporarily. The prebends were suppressed (apart from life interests) under an Act of Parliament of 1840, and the prebendaries finally lost control of the school in 1853. Their crudely-carved stalls were later thrown out; some have been recovered and put in the ante-chapel.[22]

William Lucy (1591-1677) and George Bull (1634-1710) were among Bishop Barlow's successors. Bull was a respected High Church theologian, but from Lucy 'may be dated all ye calamities of St Davids'; he it was who stopped the Archdeacons from holding their visitations.[23]

Romilly was prophetic: in 1923 the Priory became the Cathedral of the new diocese of Swansea and Brecon.

For the Marquess Camden, see note on 24 July 1840.

**30 August** Charles Griffith (c1805-1886) of Brecon was Vicar of Talach-ddu from 1832 or 1833 until 1882. He held the prebend of Trefloden in St Davids Cathedral from 1832 till his death; previously it had been held by Bird Allen. The stall is next to that of the Sovereign, who is, uniquely, a member of the St Davids Chapter (see note on 24 August 1837).[24]

Pennoyre was designed in 1846 by Anthony Salvin, a pupil of Nash, for Col Lloyd Vaughan Watkins. The house alone cost £30,000. Kilvert saw it deserted and unfurnished in 1870: 'a pretentious house and the tower and great glass dome of the observatory give it a grand look, but ... there were only 25 bedrooms'; and the marble pillars proved to be painted deal.[25]

Robert Lugar designed Cyfarthfa Castle in 1825 for William Crawshay the ironmaster. With its machicolated towers, it has something of the air of Windsor Castle, which was being remodelled by Wyatville at about the same time. Cyfarthfa has 365 windows and seventy-two rooms, for which Crawshay ordered a quarter of a mile of the best carpet.[26]

The Merthyr rising took place in June 1831. At least twenty workers were killed and seventy wounded (only eleven died at 'Peterloo' in 1819). It took several days and some 800 troops to restore order. One miner, Richard Lewis (Dic Penderyn), was hanged, probably unjustly.[27]

Romilly took the broad-gauge Vale of Neath line from Merthyr, connecting at Neath with the South Wales Railway. Narberth Road (now known as Clunderwen) was the nearest station to Narberth on the main line, as distinct from the Pembroke and Tenby branch line, which came through Narberth, or very near it, but not till 1866.[28]

Seymour (1814-1861) and Henry (1815-1908) were the eldest sons of John Hensleigh Allen of Cresselly. Henry, who was at Rugby under Thomas Arnold, became a king's counsel and an M.P.[29]

For John Lewis, see note on 6 September.

Sir Lancelot Shadwell (1779-1850) was Vice Chancellor of England. He bathed every day through the winter, and is said to have granted an injunction while swimming in the Thames. He had twelve sons.[30]

**31 August** Mrs Peel: Dora and Bertha's elder sister Mary.

Dr Thomas was probably the Lampeter Velfrey surgeon and magistrate Thomas Reece Thomas. He died in 1883 at the age of ninety-one. His son married the niece of Lord Roberts V.C.[31]

Mr Buckler must have been Richard Buckby, Rector of Begelly, who was born in Armagh. He married into another branch of the Allen family, descended from William Allen of Gelliswick (died 1744), brother of John Bartlett Allen's grandfather. So Mrs Buckby was Baugh Allen's third cousin.[32]

Adelphi, or rather Adelphoi, is the Greek for brothers. Romilly meant George and Edward (Grim); their wives were sisters.

**1 September** William Makepeace Thackeray (1811-1863) was a Trinity undergraduate, who toyed with law and painting before settling down to writing. *Vanity Fair* (1847-8) is his best-known work. In 1851 he gave six lectures at Willis's Rooms in London on English humorists of the eighteenth century, and published them two years later.[33]

Vanessa was Esther Vanhomrigh (1690-1723), who felt great passion for Jonathan Swift and followed him to Dublin in 1714, the year after he became Dean of St Patrick's Cathedral. He wrote a poem about her, but seems not to have returned her feelings.[34]

Lady Catherine (Romilly sometimes spelt it 'Catharine') Fellowes (1821-1900), daughter of the 4th Earl of Portsmouth, married Seymour Allen and bore him eight children. Her mother according to Romilly (10 July 1839) was 'totally deaf: she produces a kind of scarcely articulate sound, which is most painful to hear'. Kitty was Gertrude Catherine (1847-1894), whose only sister had died in 1853. She married Sir Owen Scourfield of The Moat. The sons Romilly met were Henry (1847-1928), Frederick (1849-1941) and Francis (1853-1932). Of their brothers, the eldest died in childhood; the two youngest, John and Newton, were not born till 1855 and 1857. John bought Parc Glas and lived there from 1936. He left a short memoir entitled *Olim Meminisse Iuvabit* (Virgil: 'One day it will be a pleasure to remember'). In it he recalled Lady Catherine giving the children's Christmas dinner to the servants and making them eat theirs in exchange.[35]

**2 September** Sophie may have been Sir John Romilly's daughter, with whom Joseph had just been staying, or Sir John's sister Mrs Kennedy, or perhaps the younger daughter of Joseph's brother Frank (George's first cousin therefore). Mrs Edward Romilly was Sophia.

Joseph seems to have written only to George—on 31 August, so the post was efficient.

Lewis had had the small Church school in the village street rebuilt in a mildly ecclesiastical style. Bishop Thirlwall opened it on 18 April. The local Congregationalists, who had already been stung into opening their own school in the chapel vestry, promptly built a new school and chapel much closer to the village. Tradition has it that Lewis refused to go past them, preferring the short cut still known as Bishop's Lane (Lewis left Lampeter Velfrey to be Bishop of Llandaff in 1883). He had been Rural Dean of Lower Carmarthen since 1852, when he came to the parish; in 1875 he became Archdeacon of St Davids, though Lampeter Velfrey was and still is in the Archdeaconry of Carmarthen.[36]

Baugh's monument in Lampeter Velfrey church says he was one of the Six Clerks. It is a pity that Romilly did not attend the funeral.

Dora Blanche seems to have died in infancy. She is not mentioned in any other source yet found.

Baron de Rutzen (1795-1874) was the owner of Slebech through his wife, granddaughter of another Rector (and native) of Lampeter Velfrey, Edward Philipps. Romilly related (18 October 1844) how 'Baugh's aversion' the Baron tried to get the University to allow his son the privilege, accorded to the nobility, of wearing a hat instead of a square or academical cap. He took it in high dudgeon when told that a foreign nobleman's son was not entitled to it.[37]

The Wale family was probably that of Sir Charles Wale (1763-1845) of Little Shelford near Cambridge. He had twelve children.[38]

Frederic Thesiger (1794-1878) had been Attorney General; in 1858 he became Lord Chancellor, taking the title Lord Chelmsford.[39]

Jonathan Frederick Pollock (1783-1870), a saddler's son, was twice Attorney General, and rose to be Chief Baron of the Exchequer, a judicial office, in 1844. Both Thesiger and Pollock were Trinity men.[40]

Sir Edward Hall Alderson (1787-1857), a Baron of the Exchequer (like Pollock, a judge and not a peer), was a humane and witty man, who wrote playful verses. He married Georgina, daughter of Mrs Caroline Drewe, Baugh's sister.[41]

**3 September** Romilly noted four years earlier that Grim was leaving Shrewsbury for joint curacies near Cresselly called Yerbeston and 'Marlton Towy' (Martletwy; Romilly seems to have heard a pronunciation nearer the origin of 'twy'—see note on 6 September). Here he was to build a parsonage and school. He meant to do great things in reforming the local colliers and the fishermen of Milford Haven.[42]

The gentry's attitude to churchgoing shows that human nature does not change! An equally blatant excuse was made by J.T. Beynon of Trewern, Llanddewi Velfrey, on Sunday 29 January 1837: 'At Home the Horses much too tired to go to Church'. Beynon expected his servants to walk.[43]

John Phelps was Vicar of Carew from 1845 to 1877.[44]

*Laconics, or the best words of the best authors*, compiled by John Timbs in 1826 (eighth edition, 1843), may have been the work Romilly was reading. An alternative was *Laconics: or new maxims of state and conversation relating to the affairs and manners of the present times* (an inaptly long subtitle), first published in 1701 and mostly from the pen of Thomas Brown (1663-1704). Brown avoided being sent down from Christ Church, Oxford, by the Dean, John Fell, for dissolute behaviour by (so it is said) translating for him one of Martial's epigrams off the cuff, deftly—and cheekily—changing the name of the victim: 'Non amo te, Sabidi, nec possum dicere quare: Hoc tantum possum dicere, non amo te' being rendered, 'I do not love thee, Dr Fell, The reason why I cannot tell; But this I know, and know full well, I do not love thee, Dr Fell'. That surely compounded his offence.[45]

Charles James Blomfield (1786-1857) was Bishop of London from 1828 till forced by paralysis to resign in 1856: Greek scholar, former Fellow of Trinity, church builder (his son and grandson were well-known architects) and a zealous reformer of Church finances and abuses. Beilby Porteus (1731-1808), of American descent, was also Bishop of London. The sermon was on I Kings 18, verse 21.[46]

**4 September** The Narberth Union was the workhouse, built in 1838 beside the Templeton road. Now known as Allensbank, it has been much altered.

Fanny (Frances) (1781-1875) and Emma (1780-1864) were the youngest and only-surviving children of John Bartlett Allen of Cresselly by his first wife, Elizabeth Hensleigh of Panteg, Llanddewi Velfrey (where the three eldest girls were born). Fanny was very pretty, vivacious, clever, rather sharp and a fan of Napoleon: 'one of the intellectual women who were the advance guard of the feminist movement'. Emma was the only plain sister. Neither married.[47]

The sisters' last home was in Heywood Lane, to which they moved in 1850. In those days it was indeed half a mile from Tenby.[48]

Mrs Eaton's maiden name was Wilmot.

Baugh's widow, Georgiana, died in 1859.

Clement Allen went to Repton School. His godfather noted (12 August 1859, when the boy was fifteen), 'he is in the upper 5th; he seems to have good abilities—he has a high notion of himself'. Clement was there under the school's 'second founder', S.A. Pears, who inherited forty-eight pupils in 1854 and resigned as Headmaster twenty years later leaving 260 in seven boarding houses. Clement married a Wedgwood, the daughter of Robert, Rector of Dumbleton.[49]

His elder brother, Charles Hensleigh Allen, died on 5 April 1855, just short of his thirteenth birthday. He wrote home to his 'dearest Mama' (Georgiana) a fortnight before, asking for money to cover his fares and 'grub', and whether his sister had really begun to learn Italian. 'I read my Bible yesterday and the day before yesterday was a day of humiliation'. Some pupils had mumps—was that why he died?[50]

Mrs Anne Marsh (1791-1874) first published *Two Old Men's Tales* in 1834. Her many novels were well thought of by contemporary critics; others have found them smug. She also wrote two books on the Huguenots, so it is a pity Romilly missed her. Rose was one of her seven children.[51]

John Romilly Allen (1847-1907) was George's eldest son. He became an archaeologist and antiquarian, and suffered from a 'certain hastiness of temper'. Romilly christened him.[52]

**5 September** Fairy Bank, where Grim and the Rector made their unspectacular bag, was a farm almost midway on a line between Blackaldern and Allensbank, standing amid fields which in 1840 had belonged to Thomas Eaton, Bertha and Dora's uncle. He had died in 1852.[53]

James William James (1789-1865) lived with his wife Elizabeth in Robeston House, Robeston Wathen, although he had presented himself to the distant benefices of Puncheston and Llanychaer in 1825 and remained Rector till his death. Earlier this year he had been badly hurt in a phaeton accident.[54]

Sir Richard Steele (1672-1729) founded *The Tatler* and (with Addison) *The Spectator*. His second wife came from Llangynnwr, and he spent his last years there and in nearby Carmarthen, where he is buried.[55]

**6 September** Harriet, as Romilly's will put it, was his 'faithful & most attentive & kind servant Harriett Sandfield', to whom he left money, his clothes, linen, glass and crockery at his Cambridge house and the coal in the cellar there.[56]

Matthew Prior (1664-1721) was a poet and diplomat. Romilly would have been familiar with Kneller's striking portrait of him at Trinity.[57]

John Gay (1685-1732) wrote *The Beggar's Opera*.[58]

A jaunting-car was an open two-wheeled vehicle of Irish origin, drawn by one horse, with room for four or six passengers seated back to back down the middle—not a secure perch if the driver cornered quickly. Romilly had sampled one in Ireland.[59]

Martletwy (now pronounced Martle-twai, with stress on the last syllable) may derive from Merthyr Tyfai, the shrine or burial place of St Tyfai, whom we met at Llandyfeisant on 26 July 1840.[60]

The school at Martletwy was designed by T.E. Owen of Portsmouth.[61]

Grim had been given very short notice to quit Woodhouse the year before. He sold his least valuable furniture, and stayed in Narberth before settling at Parc Glas.[62]

Mrs Georgiana King Lewis (1817-1895) was the daughter of John Lewis, a captain in the East India Company. His widow married Eyre Coote Lord of Swainswick, Somerset—hence the half-sister.[63]

John Lewis of Henllan, in Llanddewi Velfrey, the father of John and Richard (the Rector), married twice and had a second family.

Mrs Yelverton was born Elizabeth Lucy Morgan. In 1825 she had married the Hon William Henry Yelverton, younger son of the 2nd Viscount Avonmore. The Yelvertons lived at Whitland Abbey, a mansion near the ruins of the medieval monastery.[64]

Sayers may have been Andrew Sayers (c1800-1874), who held two livings in Gloucestershire; but he was an Oxford man.[65]

Tom Allen of Freestone had asked Romilly to help Samuel Meares succeed the ailing Seaton at Lampeter Velfrey. Romilly agreed, provided that Grim was not a candidate.[66]

John Brass was a former Fellow of Trinity and Vicar of Stotfold in Bedfordshire. He used to carry a flask of brandy in his pocket.[67]

John Henry Monk (1784-1856) had been seventh wrangler at Cambridge, Fellow and Tutor of Trinity and Regius Professor of Greek, before becoming Bishop of Gloucester in 1830 (since 1836, of Gloucester and Bristol).[68]

Alfred Tennyson (1809-1892), Poet Laureate for the past four years, had himself been an undergraduate at Trinity. His poem begins, 'O Swallow, Swallow, flying, flying South'.[69]

**7 September** Thackeray's *The Yellowplush Papers* were first published serially in 1837-8, and together in 1852.[70]

Even in those days the church was kept locked.

Wilfred (Fred) Allen (1849-1922) narrowly escaped drowning in a sailing accident on Milford Haven in 1875. He became a county court judge. It will come as no surprise that his wife was a Wedgwood.[71]

Edward Lancelot Baugh Allen (1853-1920), like his great-uncle and father before him, held the living of Porthkerry. He arrived there driving the same pair of horses which had first drawn him from Pembrokeshire to his previous parish in Cumberland twenty years before.[72]

Kate Roget, daughter of Dr Roget of *Thesaurus* fame, was Romilly's first cousin once removed.

William Gwynne was born in about 1818. His wife, Emma, came from Poplar. Their daughter, Clara, was baptised on 1 February 1848, and married John Edmund Corbett of Tenby in 1871.[73]

Mrs Houghton seems to have been an old lady Romilly knew. On 1 February 1844 he noted in his diary, 'A cod fish from Mrs Houghton'.[74]

The beech walk was the scene of a touching farewell in 1838, recorded by Anna Eaton in her diary: 'yes he came the creature—I was by myself and got over the worst at once—we walked together in the Llandewy fields and I liked him very much—I think 'twas a strong struggle between my worldliness and natural love for a blythe ingenuous spirit—but my choice is made—

we stopped at the end of the beech walk, "stay a minute" he said "that I may take a last farewell here"—I shuddered, for I thought of the passionate adieu of *another* on that very spot—I was saved this trial for Mamma made her appearance—and soon after that he went—I was very sorry and I am afraid he saw my tears—for he said—"in two years you will see me back again Mrs Eaton" Oh these doubts are very tormenting—I almost felt relieved when he was quite gone—'[75]

Henry Wadsworth Longfellow (1807-1882), the American poet, published 'The Building of the Ship' in 1849, in a collection entitled *The Seaside and the Fireside*. He married into the family of Baugh Allen's sister Lady Mackintosh—to her son's sister-in-law (see note on 3 August 1840).[76]

**8 September** I was once told off at school for abbreviating 'pounds' (the weight) as 'lbs', because I was learning Latin and should have known that the plural of 'libra' is 'librae', not 'libras'. (If I had been quicker and cheekier I would have pointed out that 'libras' is the accusative plural.) Such pedantry seems not to have bothered Romilly.

## SOURCES

1 Bury & Pickles, 98-9. I had assumed that Romilly meant 'National' by 'British' Gallery, but Jane Austen referred to the British Gallery in 1811, before the National existed even in its previous home: P. Hughes-Hallett, *My Dear Cassandra: The Letters of Jane Austen* (London, 1990), 84, where the letter is illustrated with a print of the British Museum. Dr Pickles tells me that the British Gallery was John Boydell's former Gallery in Pall Mall, reopened in 1806.

2 *D.N.B.*, XLIX, 191; Burke's *Peerage* (1970 ed), 2287. For some reason Burke does not mention Sophie by name.

3 Miss Jayne Ringrose kindly checked my transcription of this Italian phrase, and Mr Geoffrey Eatough confirmed my translation; apparently Romilly's 'ni' should have been 'nè'. He wrote 'piu' for 'più'.

4 J.D.Hart, *The Oxford Companion to American Literature* (New York and Oxford, 1983) [hereafter Hart, *American Literature*], 179; S.A. Allibone, *A Critical Dictionary of English Literature and British and American Authors* (Philadelphia and London, 1900) [hereafter Allibone, *Authors*], 459; S.J. Kunitz and H. Haycraft, *American Authors 1600-1900* (New York, 1938), 194-5. I had first thought Romilly had been reading Dickens's story of the same title (1841), about a crazy old astrologer searching for the philosopher's stone. Canon William Price pointed me to Miss Cummins; the diary entry for 18 August, which I had overlooked, proved him right.

5 T. Johnson (ed), *The Parish Guide* (London, 1887), 67.

6 Allibone, *Authors*, 817.

7 *O.D.C.C.*, 1173.

8 *D.N.B.* XXXVI, 3; *Enc. Brit.*, vol 14, 717-8. Lady Romilly's father was Bishop William Otter of Chichester, who founded the Theological College there in 1839: Bury, 251.

9 W. Plomer (ed), *Kilvert's Diary* (London, 1978) [hereafter Plomer, *Kilvert*], 5; B. Colloms, *Victorian Country Parsons* (London, 1977), 173.

10 *Enc. Brit.*, vol 7, 747-9.

11 My Parisian friend Mlle Emmanuelle Chalbos (now Mme Cornet) threw light on this titbit.

12 Plomer, *Kilvert*, 8; R. Haslam, *Powys* (Harmondsworth and Cardiff, 1979) [hereafter Haslam, *Powys*], 221. My brother Peter told me of the etymological link between *betws* and bedehouse; *betws* has also been defined as a secluded place—also apt, as I had great difficulty finding it.

13 Plomer, *Kilvert*, 131-2, 195, 216.

14 Burke's *Peerage* (1970 ed), 391; C. Hibbert (ed), *Captain Gronow His Reminiscences of Regency and Victorian Life 1810-60* (London, 1991), 90.

15 *Enc. Brit.*, vol 7, 764; I.H. Evans (ed) *Brewer's Dictionary of Phrase and Fable* (London, 1981), 365-6.

16 Haslam, *Powys*, 226.

17 Plomer, *Kilvert*, 6.

18 Account of news of disaster reaching Clyro in Plomer, *Kilvert*, 74-5; P. Kemp (ed), *The Oxford Companion to Ships and the Sea* (Oxford, 1988), 138, 179; *Enc. Brit.*, vol 3, 292.

19 J.K. Beatty and A. Chaikin (ed), *The New Solar System* (Cambridge, 1990), 158-60, 171-88, 290-1.

20 Haslam, *Powys*, 298.

21 Ward Lock & Co, *Guide to Cardiff and South Wales* (London, 1947) [hereafter Ward Lock, *Guide*], 36-7.

22 E.G. Parry, *Christ College Brecon 1541-1991 An Illustrated History* (Brecon, 1991), 6-14; G. Williams, *Welsh Reformation Essays* (Cardiff, 1967), 121; O.W. Jones, 'The Welsh Church in the Nineteenth Century' in D. Walker (ed), *A History of the Church in Wales* (Penarth, 1976), 148; E. Yardley (F. Green, ed) *Menevia Sacra* (London, 1927) [hereafter Yardley, *Menevia*], 406-10; Ward Lock, *Guide*, 42; A.H. Thompson, 'The Welsh Medieval Dioceses', *J.H.S.C.W.*, vol I no 2 (1947), 108-10. If Thompson is right in saying that the College of Prebends has never been formally dissolved, the Bishop of St Davids is *ex officio* Dean of Brecon—or at least of Christ College.

23 L.W. Barnard, 'Bishop George Bull of St David's: Scholar and Defender of the Faith', *J.W.E.H.*, vol 9 (1992), 37-51; Yardley, *Menevia*, 112; *D.N.B.*, XXXIV, 251-2.

24 Foster, 566; *W.W.H.R.*, V, 200, 202.

25 Haslam, *Powys*, 281-2; Plomer, *Kilvert* (1938 ed), 215.

26 J.B. Hilling. *The Historic Architecture of Wales* (Cardiff, 1976), 178.

27 G.A. Williams, *The Merthyr Rising* (London, 1978), *passim*; E. Davies, *Merthyr Iron and Merthyr Riots 1750-1860* (Harlow, 1987), 21; C. Wilkins, *The History of Merthyr Tydfil* (Merthyr Tydfil, 1867), 295-305; J. Davies, *A History of Wales* (London, 1994), 366-7.

28 D.S.M. Barrie, *A Regional History of the Railways of Great Britain* vol XII *South Wales* (Newton Abbot, 1980), 39, 163, 197; M.G.R. Morris (ed), *The Story of Narberth* (Narberth, 1990), 35.

29 Family tree and reminiscences of John Seymour Allen, *Olim Meminisse Iuvabit*, in Allen Papers.

30 *D.N.B.*, LI, 339-40.

31 Information from a family scrapbook lent to me by Mrs George Brownrigg. The 1851 census described Thomas, ambiguously, as a surgeon out of practice.

32 W.R. Morgan, *A Pembrokeshire Countryman Looks Back* (Crymych, 1988), 160; *W.W.H.R.*, I, 243; Allen family tree.

33 *D.N.B.*, LVI, 99, 104; *Enc. Brit.*, vol 21, 923.

34 *Enc. Brit.*, vol 21, 516; M. Magnusson (ed), *Chambers Biographical Dictionary* (Edinburgh, 1990), 1423.

35 Information from the Allen family; Bury, 174.

36 M.G.R. Morris, 'Bishop Richard Lewis: His Life Before Llandaff', *J.W.E.H.*, vol 4 (1987) [hereafter Morris, 'Lewis'], 71-3, 75, 86-7, 90.

37 Bury & Pickles, 113.

38 *D.N.B.*, LIX, 28-9; Bury & Pickles, 264.

39 *Enc. Brit.*, vol 5, 374-5.

40 *Enc. Brit.*, vol 18, 180.

41 *D.N.B.*, I, 242-3; B. and H. Wedgwood, *The Wedgwood Circle 1730-1897* (Ontario, 1980), 375, where 'later Lord Alderson' and 'Georgiana Drewe' are errors.

42 Information from Mrs Bury, quoting Romilly, 20 and 22 September 1850.

43 Diaries of John Thomas Beynon, vol 2, lent to me by Mrs Fenner Clayton, Laugharne. The entries are generally brief and dwell overmuch on the slaughter of wild life (he was a real hunting, shooting, fishing squire), but there are valuable nuggets.

44 *W.W.H.R.*, I, 264.

45 G. Watson (ed), *The New Cambridge Bibliography of English Literature* vol 2, 1660-1800 (Cambridge, 1971), col 1044-5; *Enc. Brit.* (15th ed, 1990), vol 2, 560; *The Oxford Dictionary of Quotations* (3rd ed) (Oxford, 1979), 95, 331 (I have given the more usual version of the translation).

46 *O.D.C.C.*, 178, 1092; O. Chadwick, *The Victorian Church* part I (London, 1966), 133-4. Blomfield's son Sir Arthur designed Selwyn College, Cambridge; Arthur's nephew Sir Reginald rebuilt Nash's elegant Quadrant in Regent Street, apparently because the original colonnades harboured prostitutes.

47 H.E. Litchfield, *Emma Darwin* (Cambridge, 1904) [hereafter Litchfield, *Darwin*], vol I, 8, 9; C. Woodham-Smith, *Florence Nightingale* (London, 1952), 19.

48 Litchfield, *Darwin*, vol II, 133.

49 C.U.L., Add 6839; A. Macdonald, *A Short History of Repton* (London, 1929), 166-96; B. Thomas (ed) *Repton 1557-1957* (London, 1957), 23-60; Burke (1906 ed), 19. Dr Pears's granddaughter married another Headmaster of Repton, Geoffrey Fisher, successor there to William Temple and teacher of Michael Ramsey—three successive Archbishops of Canterbury. Rachel Allen has left a delightful description of Clement's wedding, at which she was one of the eight bridesmaids, dressed in white muslin and mob caps with tilleul (lime-green) bows and sashes: Pembs R.O., HDX/132/2 (August 1877).

50 Letter in Allen Papers.

51 Allibone, *Authors*, 1224; S.J. Kunitz and H. Haycraft, *British Authors of the Nineteenth Century* (New York, 1936), 109.

52 *D.W.B.*, 5; Bury & Pickles, 219.

53 Pembs R.O., D/LJ/2051 and Ordnance Survey 25-inch map of Narberth, 1889.

54 Pembs R.O., HPR/37/4; Robeston Wathen census, 1851; *W.W.H.R.*, II, 267; III, 250-1; *Haverfordwest and Milford Haven Telegraph*, 12 April 1854.

55 *Enc. Brit.*, vol 21, 193; C.L. Treharne, *The History of Llangunnor Church* (Llangynnwr, 1989), 138-41.

56 Details of Romilly's will supplied by Dr Pickles through Mr Thomas Lloyd.

57 *Enc. Brit.*, vol 18, 554 H.

58 *Enc. Brit.*, vol 10, 40.

59 *Enc. Brit.*, vol 4, 963; S. Walrond, *Looking at Carriages* (London, 1980), 124-6; C.U.L., Add 6808 (28 September 1827).

60 B.G. Charles, *The Place-Names of Pembrokeshire* (Aberystwyth, 1992), 521-2.

61 Pembs R.O., TSE/1/14 (August 1852).

62 Information from Mrs Bury, quoting Romilly, 2 April 1853; but the 1851 census of Crinow shows Grim and his family living at Parc Glas.

63 Morris, 'Lewis', 63; for a description of Mrs Lewis's dinner party and menu for Bishop Thirlwall in 1854, see page 72 (quoting Pembs R.O., D/LEW/8/1079). She did her guests proud.

64 T. Nicholas, *Annals and Antiquities of the Counties and County Families of Wales* (London, 1872), 307; Debrett's *Peerage* (1844 ed), 47; J. Buckley, *Genealogies of the Carmarthenshire Sheriffs from 1760 to 1913* (Carmarthen, 1913), 45.

65 Foster, 1260. 'Mr Sayers was to have joined the party but sent an excuse': letter to Col Wedgwood from his brother, October 1860, in Allen Papers.

66 18 January 1850; extract from Romilly sent me by Mrs Bury.

67 Bury, 21, 238.

68 *D.N.B.*, XXXVIII, 174-6.

69 F.T. Palgrave, *The Golden Treasury of the best Songs and Lyrical Poems in the English language* (London, 1941), 364; *Enc. Brit.*, vol 21, 853-4.

70 *Enc. Brit.*, vol 21, 923.

71 Reminiscences of John Seymour Allen, *Olim Meminisse Iuvabit*, in Allen Papers.

72 *Olim Meminisse Iuvabit*.

73 1851 census; Lampeter Velfrey parish registers.

74 Bury & Pickles, 94.

75 Pembs R.O., DX/4/35. Anna's admirer was, I think, Joseph Twyning (1813-1851), younger son of Capt William Twyning who once rented Cilrhiw.

76 Hart, *American Literature*, 443.

# ENVOI

## SUNSET IN THE EAST

For the ten years of life that remained to him, Romilly gave up visiting Wales altogether. He retired as Registrary in 1861, having held the office for almost thirty years. It had been a godsend to him. Without it he might have frittered away his academic career with little more than convivial parties and light reading, spiced with College politics.[1] He was not among the intellectual giants, like his friend Adam Sedgwick or Connop Thirlwall, breaking new ground or amassing vast erudition. The Registrary's job gave him a purpose, which he discharged conscientiously, perhaps even with distinction. It also put him in touch with a much wider circle. The University is still in his debt for the way he cared for its records. The broadened horizons made his diaries more interesting and valuable.

He wrote them up almost to the end. 6 August 1864 found him at Great Yarmouth on a fine, windy day. He had slept pretty well, enjoyed a very agreeable early morning dip, and sat on the jetty for a couple of hours watching a man of war, the *Vengeance*, setting sail, and reading a book (Mrs Bayly's *Ragged Homes and the way to mend them*[2]). He called on some newcomers to Yarmouth: two widowed sisters, Mrs Rackham and Mrs Beames, with their children, a very young-looking Mr Rackham (in fact thirty-three) employed in some register office, and a young Miss Beames.

Joseph Romilly

Perhaps that evening he felt unwell, for he failed to record the rest of the day. All that remains is a brief pencilled note, later inked over, stating that on Sunday 7 August 1864 'Mr Romilly died suddenly about 5 PM', with the initials 'G.B.A.', presumably those of his nephew George Baugh Allen.[3] His body was brought back to Cambridge and laid to rest on the outskirts of the town, at Christ Church, Barnwell.[4]

## SOURCES

1   Mrs Bury pointed out to me how becoming Registrary saved Romilly from idleness.

2   Mrs Mary Bayly published *Ragged Homes, and how to mend them* (apparently the correct title) in 1862, the second of seven works, mostly of a similar nature, which came out between 1861 and 1888: J.F. Kirk, *A Supplement to Allibone's Critical Dictionary of English Literature and British and American Authors* vol I (Philadelphia, 1900), 112.

3   C.U.L., Add 6842. George inherited the diaries: Bury & Pickles, 141.

4   Bury, ix. Many of the family, including Joseph's parents and grandparents and his brothers Samuel and Cuthbert, lie in the family vault at Paddington: list in the diary, 30 March 1862, C.U.L., Add 6841. Joseph's will (7 March 1864; George Allen was his executor) ordered a plain funeral and burial at the place where he died; if at Cambridge, as he hoped, with 'the women' in the vault at Barnwell.

# INDEX

*Names are indexed both under Romilly's spelling, with the current version in square brackets, and also under the latter where a separate entry may be helpful. Romilly's reading and other books etc are collected under 'books'; characters and places mentioned therein are not indexed, nor, with a few exceptions, are sources. Names of ships and boats are collected under 'ships'. Page numbers in italic type refer to Romilly's own words.*

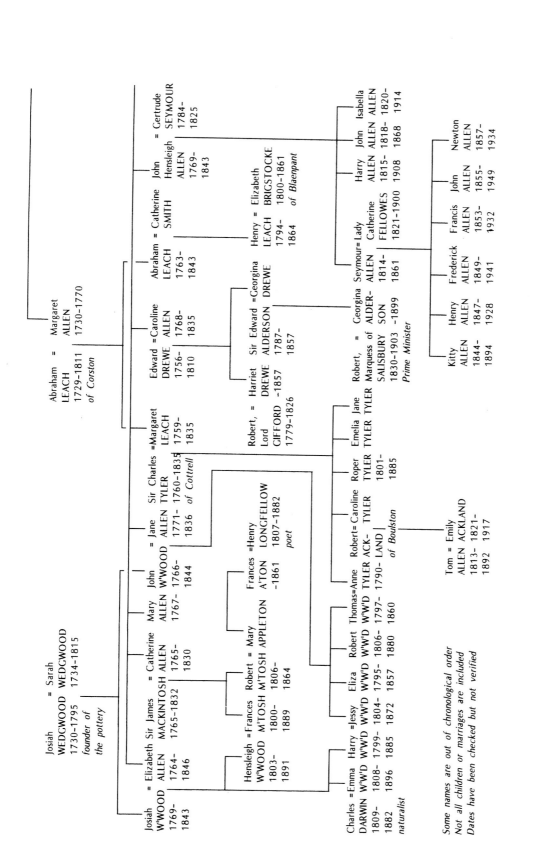

Josiah
WEDGWOOD = Sarah
WEDGWOOD
1730-1795
founder of
the pottery
1734-1815

Abraham = Margaret
LEACH ALLEN
1729-1811 1730-1770
of Corston

John
Hensleigh = Gertrude
ALLEN SEYMOUR
1769- 1784-
1843 1825

Abraham = Catherine
LEACH SMITH
1763-
1843

Henry = Elizabeth
LEACH BRIGSTOCKE
1794- 1800-1861
1864 of Blaenpant

Harry John Isabella
ALLEN ALLEN ALLEN
1815- 1818- 1820-
1908 1868 1914

Edward = Caroline
DREWE ALLEN
1756- 1768-
1810 1835

Sir Edward = Georgina
ALDERSON DREWE
1787- 1857
1857

Seymour = Lady
Catherine
ALLEN FELLOWES
1814- 1821-1900
1861

Kitty Henry Frederick Francis John Newton
ALLEN ALLEN ALLEN ALLEN ALLEN ALLEN
1844- 1847- 1849- 1853- 1855- 1857-
1894 1928 1941 1932 1949 1934

Margaret = Sir Charles
LEACH TYLER
1759- 1760-1835
1835 of Cottrell

Jane
ALLEN
1771-
1836

Robert, = Harriet
Lord DREWE
GIFFORD -1857
1779-1826

Robert, = Georgina
Marquess of ALDER-
SALISBURY SON
1830-1903 -1899
Prime Minister

Emelia Jane
TYLER TYLER

Roper
TYLER
1801-
1885

Mary John
ALLEN W'WOOD
1767- 1766-
1844

Frances = Henry
A'TON LONGFELLOW
-1861 1807-1882
poet

Catherine
ALLEN
1765-
1830

Robert = Mary
M'TOSH APPLETON
1806- 1806-
1864

Robert Thomas = Anne
W'W'D TYLER ACK-
1806- 1797- LAND
1880 1860 of Boulston

Robert = Caroline
W'W'D TYLER
1790-

Tom = Emily
ALLEN ACKLAND
1813- 1821-
1892 1917

Elizabeth Sir James
ALLEN MACKINTOSH
1764- 1765-1832
1846

Hensleigh = Frances
W'WOOD M'TOSH
1803- 1800-
1891 1889

Eliza
W'W'D
1795-
1857

Harry = Jessy
W'W'D W'W'D
1799- 1804-
1885 1872

Emma
W'W'D
1808-
1896

Charles = Emma
DARWIN W'W'D
1809- 1808-
1882 1896
naturalist

*Some names are out of chronological order*
*Not all children or marriages are included*
*Dates have been checked but not verified*

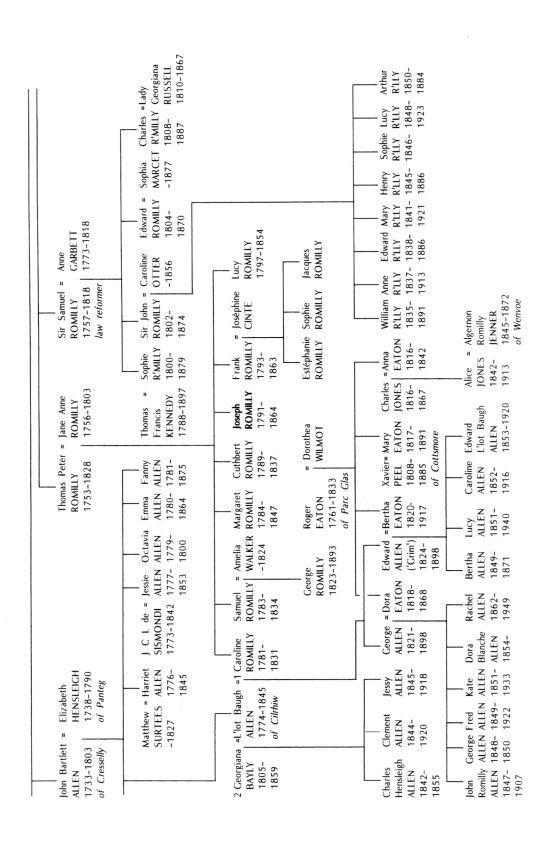

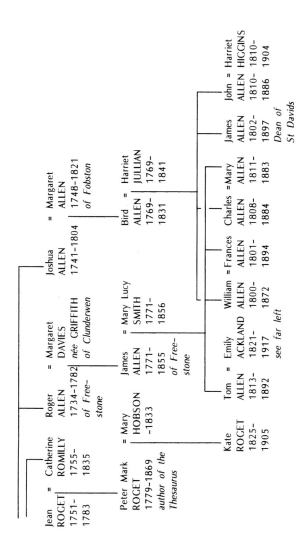